The World of Croquet

JOHN McCULLOUGH

and

STEPHEN MULLINER

The Crowood Press

First published in 1987 by
The Crowood Press
Ramsbury, Marlborough,
Wiltshire SN8 2HE

British Library Cataloguing in Publication Data

McCullough, John
   The world of croquet.
   1. Croquet
   I. Title   II. Mulliner, Stephen
   796.35'4   GV931

   ISBN 0 946284 59 8

Dedicated to those who introduced us to croquet.

Picture Credits

Figs 4, 25, 27, 56, 127, 167, 169, 175, 177, 198, 199, 202, 203, 204,
205, 209 and 213 by Peter Alvey; Figs 60, 188 and 207 by Jeff
Bowden; Fig 5 by Brian Donnan (courtesy of the Cheltenham &
Gloucester Building Society); Figs 6, 26, 136 and 137 by Granada
Television; Fig 8 courtesy of Hampshire County Museum
Service; Fig 10 by Masaru Ikeda; Fig 196 by Peter McCormack
(courtesy of the Royal Bank of Scotland); Figs 80, 125, 189 and 206
by Raymond McManus, Sportsfile Ltd; Fig 193 by Jean Louis
Mernier; Fig 191 by Martin Murray; Fig 210 by John Prince; Fig 1
by Derek Rowe (Photos) Ltd (courtesy of Bombay Gin); Fig 59 by
John Walters.

In this book the pronouns 'he', 'his' and 'him' have been used
inclusively, and are intended to refer to both men and women.

Typeset by Chippendale Type, Otley, West Yorkshire
Printed in Great Britain

Contents

Acknowledgements

So many people have helped to make this publication possible that we do not have the space to acknowledge their contributions in detail. Four people, however, deserve special mention.

Firstly we would like to thank Peter Alvey, both for his photographs and for his advice relating to the photographic content of the book.

Secondly we would like to thank Nigel Aspinall, John Prince and Neil Spooner, without whose help Chapter 20 could not have been written. All three also provided us with useful information for other parts of the book.

We are grateful to all the photographers and sponsors who have allowed their photographs to be used and, in addition, the following people who helped us obtain these photographs or offered photographs that we were unable to use: Enrique F. De Bobadilla, Roger Bray, Phil Cordingley, Norman Eatough, David Foulser, Lisle Guernsey, Donald Gugan, Carole Knox, Bernard Neal, Richard Pearman and Geoff Roy.

Many of those listed above also provided information for the text or helped in other ways, as did the following, whose help we greatly appreciate: Mark Avery, Niclas Behre, Jerry Brown, Nan Coetzee, Andrew Crawford, Arnold Curtis, Simon Garrett, Joy Guernsey, Ian Gillespie, John Grimshaw, Ashley Heenan, Joe Hogan, Peter Howell, Mrs. D. C. Hobbs, Andrew Hope, Chris Hudson, Colin Irwin, Christopher Jaques, Thor Kaijser, Jukka Kujansuu, Margaret Langley, Bill Langstroth, George Latham, Brian MacMillan, John Mc-Callum, Fumio Morooka, Roger Murfitt, David O'Connor, David Openshaw, Jack Osborn, Valerie Payne, William Prichard, Terence Read, Fred Rogerson, Jose Sanz-Tonnelier, Pat Shine, Eric Solomon, John Solomon, Pauleen Vickery, Carl von Schmieder, Johan Vunderink, John Walters and Ian Howard Wright.

We would also like to thank the Croquet Associations of Australia, England, Indonesia, Ireland, Japan, New Zealand, Scotland, South Africa, USA and Wales.

Finally we must thank Sarah, who kept us well fed throughout, and the 'dawn chorus' who reminded us from time to time that life existed outside the loft!

Foreword

I was delighted when John McCullough and Stephen Mulliner asked me to write a foreword to their new book. The publication of any new book about croquet is an event in itself for our small but vigorously growing sport. However, *The World of Croquet* seems destined to occupy a special place in the literature of the game , with the commendable breadth of its approach and the enormous enthusiasm of the authors.

A problem that confronts every sports author is deciding what level of competence he should assume in his readership. This is particularly true in the case of a minor sport because there is usually a dearth of supplementary literature. The authors have cheerfully avoided the difficulty by providing something for everybody, whether complete strangers to the game, garden enthusiasts, club novices or tournament experts.

Joint authorship is not always an easy route to literary success but John and Stephen have combined their talents in a particularly effective way. John McCullough is a leading tournament player who gained his Great Britain 'cap' in 1986. He is also Chairman of the Coaching Committee of the Council and was largely responsible for the recent establishment of the National Coaching Scheme. He is a teacher (and former policeman) by profession, and his attention to detail and clear insight of the problems faced by a novice have made him a very gifted coach. The Basic Croquet section is a really excellent instruction course for the beginner, while the broad sweep of the International Croquet section has a positively journalistic zest.

Stephen Mulliner took up croquet only ten years ago but soon forged his way to the top. He represented Great Britain in 1982 and 1986 and has won the President's Cup three times, the Men's Championship twice and the Doubles Championship four times in the last six years. Always ready to share his knowledge, Stephen is well known as one of the most thoughtful as well as one of the most competitive of today's leading players and the Advanced Croquet section is a detailed and lucid account of his view of modern expert tactics. Perhaps the most interesting novelty is Chapter 18, which represents the first detailed treatment of the place of sports psychology in croquet.

Croquet is steadily becoming a more international game. The United States has joined Australia and New Zealand as one of the major croquet nations and the Croquet Association has recently initiated the formation of the World Croquet Federation in order to accelerate the global development of the sport. Not the least of the virtues of this book is that it is designed to be of interest and use to croquet players everywhere.

It has been said that the most difficult thing about croquet is discovering it! The biggest sceptics usually become the keenest exponents and complain that it took them so long to start. Croquet is quite simply a really good game for all ages and both sexes to play and a visit to your nearest croquet club will ensure a friendly welcome and an immediate opportunity to try your hand. I sincerely hope that many of the non-players who pick up this book will give the most intellectual outdoor game a try. It could be a source of the most tremendous satisfaction and enjoyment for the rest of your life.

Andrew Hope,
Chairman, Council of the Croquet Association

Introduction

A game of croquet can be the final of the Croquet Association's Open Championship or a back garden frolic using flimsy equipment and local rules that bear a distant relationship to a game played in the last century. Although the amount of tournament croquet has steadily increased over the last twenty years, the greater part of all croquet played worldwide is still of the informal variety and the overriding purpose of this book is to provide a bridge between the two. Not so long ago

serious croquet players looked upon garden croquet with more than a little disdain and the few books written about the game assumed that the reader had already committed himself to the true faith. Attitudes have changed in recent years and Association Croquet's growing self-confidence has permitted its enthusiasts to see garden players as potential recruits rather than the objects of derision.

Accordingly, *The World of Croquet* is aimed at a wide range of potential readers. If you have never played, you will find that the game has more substance and is more widely played than you probably imagine, and that the history of croquet is an interesting story of individuals and social change over the last 130 years. Perhaps you are a home enthusiast who would like a better idea of how to play croquet as it should be played. Here you will find guidance on how to get the most out of garden croquet, including how to set the court correctly, what equipment to use and a description of the proper laws of Association Croquet, Golf Croquet and other variants.

The Basic Croquet section is directed mainly at the ambitious novice who wishes to improve to the level of playing breaks without bisques and entering tournaments with a reasonable chance of success. The Advanced Croquet section is for the player who has aspirations to play A-class and championship croquet. The last book to address these players was published in 1966. Many tactical developments have occurred since then, together with increased awareness of the relevance of psychology to peak achievement in sport, including croquet.

This book was written in 1986, the year in which teams from New Zealand and Australia travelled to Britain to compete for the

KEY	
—	Hoop
•	Peg
●	Ball (original position)
○	Ball (new position)
⊜	Ball (alternative position)
⟶	Path of ball
R	Red
Y	Yellow
Bk	Black
Bu	Blue
R_1, Y_1 **etc.**	New positions of R and Y
R_0, Y_0, **etc.**	Original positions of R and Y
R_2, Y_2, **etc.**	Later positions of R and Y
C	Ball to be croqueted
O	Object ball
S	Striker's ball
T	Target ball
C_1, S_1, **etc.**	New positions of C and S
C_0, S_0, **etc.**	Original positions of C and S

MacRobertson Shield, the Ashes of croquet, and in the British Open Championship. The section on International Croquet describes the modern international scene and gives a detailed account of the 1986 MacRobertson Shield contest, including biographies of three of the leading players.

CROQUET PAST
AND PRESENT

1 The Modern Game

Most of us have some idea that croquet is a game played outdoors on a lawn, using mallets, hoops and balls. It is only in the last few years that responsible media coverage and a successful development campaign have made it fairly common knowledge that croquet has a serious side. It is played competitively throughout the summer, by men and women of all ages, in clubs in most parts of Britain and New Zealand, and almost all the year round in Australia and the USA. International matches have been played regularly between Great Britain, Australia and New Zealand since 1925 and the inaugural Test Match between Great Britain and the USA took place in 1985. In fact, the international growth of croquet is much greater than this. In July 1986 the representatives of nine countries agreed that a World Croquet Federation should be established.

Fig 1   The modern game: 1986 Bombay Gin President's Cup players at Hurlingham.
Left to right, Nigel Aspinall, Keith Aiton, John Walters, Stephen Mulliner, Phil Cordingley, Jerry Guest, David Foulser, John McCullough.

Croquet is really a generic name for a number of different games with the common theme of mallets, hoops and balls. The list is headed by Association Croquet and Six-wicket American Croquet. Other croquet games include Short Croquet, which is a version of Association Croquet designed to appeal to beginners and to television audiences, Nine-wicket American Croquet, Golf Croquet, Two-ball Croquet, King-ball Croquet, Pirates and a variety of less formal games. Association Croquet is the principal competitive game throughout the croquet-playing world, with the exception of North America where it takes second place to Six-wicket American Croquet, and is thus the game we concentrate on in this book.

In Great Britain and Ireland, the sport's original governing body was the Croquet Association (known as the 'CA'). Following the formation of the Scottish Croquet Association in 1973, the Croquet Association of Ireland in 1985 and the Welsh Croquet

Association in 1986, the CA directly administers croquet only in England but has wider international responsibilities that give it an unofficial position akin to that of the MCC in cricket.

Domestically, the CA publicises croquet, organises an annual calendar of over eighty different tournaments and championships, publishes the official *Laws of Association Croquet and Golf Croquet and the Regulations for Tournaments*, appoints official Referees, Handicappers and Tournament Managers, publishes a magazine called *Croquet* every two months, organises coaching courses and services the needs of over 140 member clubs and their 4,000 players in many other ways. In 1985 the CA appointed its first national development officer as part of the implementation of a three-year development plan in co-operation with the Sports Council.

Internationally, the CA has historically played a leading role in the development of the laws of Association Croquet and the

Fig 2   A sport for all ages: Stephen Lewis in play at Hurlingham.

Fig 3   John Jeffrey coaching at the Loughborough Summer School.

Fig 4   A sport for both sexes: Liz Taylor-Webb at Bowdon.

various changes that have occurred in those laws over the years, although the Australian and New Zealand Croquet Councils are consulted before changes are made and, indeed, are often responsible for proposing improvements as new developments occur in the game.

Publicity is essential for the successful development of any sport. The CA has been assiduous in cultivating more effective links with the media and, since 1980, with commercial sponsors (*see* Figs 1, 5 and 6). The interest of companies such as Pimms, Mateus, the Royal Bank of Scotland, Debenham Tewson & Chinnocks, Frank Cooper, Anchor Foods, Westwood Engineering and Bombay Gin, together with a variety of local sponsors, has been of great benefit to croquet and the CA through the income, publicity and expert advice that these sponsors have offered. In May 1986, Granada Television filmed the first made-for-television croquet tournament and

Fig 5　Local sponsorship helps: Chris Steele, Marketing Manager of the Cheltenham and Gloucester Building Society, presenting the Federation Shield to South-west League winners, Bristol Croquet Club. Left to right, Roger Jenkins, John McCullough, Donald Gugan, Ray Ransom.

broadcast it in their home area with an encouraging degree of success.

Croquet is one of the most active minor sports in Britain and in the other principal croquet countries. The CA's tournament calendar provides competitive play for people of all ages, standards and circumstances. Thirty years ago, weekend tournaments were almost as rare as tournament players under the age of forty. Now the great majority of the top fifty players are young men between fifteen and forty, and the trend is still downwards. The establishment of Schools' and University Championships is turning out to be one of the CA's most successful ventures and seems set to provide a steady stream of fresh young talent. Even more encouraging is the emergence at long last of some girls with the potential to become first-class players and so to re-

establish the sexual equality that existed in the game at the top level fifty years ago.

The standard calendar tournament used to start on a Monday and finish on a Saturday, and there was a recognisable clique of retired or leisured individuals who played the croquet circuit, going from tournament to tournament. Just as the players have changed, so have the events and the week-long tournaments are now joined by an ever increasing number of weekend tournaments designed to appeal to players with jobs and families to consider. The season runs from April to October and is punctuated by three principal events, the Men's and Women's Championships in June, the Open Championship in July and the President's Cup in September. Success in these demanding events is just as hard to come by as in any other sport. Croquet is still an amateur

Fig 6   Televised Short Croquet: Nigel Aspinall at the Royal Bank Nations Trophy.

Fig 7   A far cry from Crinolines: 1986 Ladies' Field Champion, Debbie Cornelius.

game and it is a tribute to its extraordinary fascination that few who are bitten by the bug ever give it up.

The tremendous appeal of Association Croquet is best understood by practical experience of the unique challenge the game offers. A shorthand explanation is that it combines the best features of snooker, bowls and golf. Snooker professionals and expert croquet players can compile breaks of many consecutive strokes while the opponent has to sit patiently, unable to intervene. The touch needed to place a ball accurately forty yards (36m) away is common to bowls and croquet. The accuracy of a golfer driving two hundred yards (180m) straight down the fairway, or holing a twenty-foot (6m) putt, is mirrored by the croquet player hitting a roquet thirty yards (27m) away or gently running a hoop at a sharp angle. All these games require physical skill, tactical acumen and mental resilience to cope with competitive pressure. Although the physical skill required in croquet is not excessive, its tactical and psychological demands are considerable. Perhaps the secret of croquet's fascination is that it offers a more complete balance between these three factors than any other sport.

The best players are able to experience the satisfaction of competing at national and international level without becoming full-time or part-time professionals. It is quite possible to maintain a high standard of performance at croquet without interfering with family life and a regular job. Now that the aristocratic days of croquet are half a century in the past, croquet players come from all walks of life and they are a sociable and welcoming group of people. If you want to take up a sport that is demanding, satisfying, played in agreeable company and often in very pleasant surroundings, give croquet a try. The only risk is that you too will say 'I wish I had discovered this game five years ago'.

2 The Development of Croquet

BRIEF HISTORY

No one knows for certain when croquet was invented or from what other activity, if any, it was derived. People had been amusing themselves by hitting balls and other objects with a variety of implements long before the word croquet was ever assigned to a game, and one may speculate whether golf, the Dutch game of kolven, or the extinct English game of pall mall played any part in the origins of croquet. There is some evidence that croquet, or a very similar game, was played in Ireland in or about 1830, and that croquet reached England by about 1851. However, we do know that letters about croquet appeared in *The Field* in 1858 and the firm of Jaques & Son published a price list for croquet equipment which referred to the award of prize medals in 1862. It is worth recording that the firm has remained under family ownership ever since and, under the name John Jaques & Son Ltd, is still the leading manufacturer of croquet equipment in Britain.

Croquet rapidly grew in popularity during the 1860s among the county set and croquet

Fig 8   Crinoline.croquet in 1865: the Curtis family playing at their home in Alton, Hampshire.

parties became popular. The game also attracted a number of individuals who understood its competitive appeal, and a tournament was held at Evesham, Worcestershire in 1867 which has since been rather dubiously honoured with the title of the first Open Championship. The enthusiasm of these early founders appears to have been matched by their eccentricity and the All-England Croquet Club, formed in 1868, had to survive some extraordinary squabbling and the temporary formation of two rival organisations before it became established.

Croquet flourished until the rise of lawn tennis, marked in 1877 by the change of the name of the AECC to the All-England Croquet and Lawn Tennis Club, and in 1882 by the effective expulsion of croquet from the AEC & LTC for the heinous sin of having become a non-profit making activity. This uncharitable move was marked by the deletion of the reference to croquet in the club's title, and a spiteful order that the croquet records be destroyed. Fortunately, a groundsman had more sense than the committee and hid them until happier times returned.

The game effectively hibernated until 1892 when a trickle of tournament play reappeared. By 1896 the revival was well under way and, in order to give croquet players an identity independent of the perfidious AELTC, the United All-England Croquet Association was founded. The name was shortened to the Croquet Association in 1900. By 1899 the AELTC had again changed its spots and its name to the All-England Lawn Tennis and Croquet Club, the title Wimbledon officially retains today, although croquet plays only a very minor part in the club's activities.

After this somewhat turbulent establishment, croquet settled down to prosper in the Edwardian era as a game almost exclusively for those with time and money to spare. In 1914 the CA could claim over 2,300 individual members and 170 registered clubs. Croquet was played at over 120 tournaments during the season and at a multitude of country houses.

This golden age of croquet was ended abruptly by the First World War, and although activity restarted promptly enough in 1919, the damage suffered by croquet was significant. Individual membership of the CA was reduced to 1,400 and a number of clubs that had closed during the war never reopened.

The inter-war years were a time of gradual change. The CA recovered from some of the damage it had suffered and the game underwent many of the changes needed to bridge the gap between the old sequence game and the modern form of Association Croquet, such as the establishment of the either-ball game, the introduction of the single-peg Willis setting and the lifting principle. The most significant development, however, occurred when a self-made Australian confectionary millionaire, Sir MacPherson Robertson, became attracted to croquet and presented a trophy for international competition. The first Test Match was held in England in 1925 between England and Australia and stimulated an enthusiasm for excellence in croquet that has never been lost. An invitation to represent their country is still the highest ambition of all players of ability.

The players also changed. Croquet lost something of its aristocratic flavour, although it was still very much a gentleman's game. It was also a game for the ladies and one at which they were often just as good as the men. Miss D. D. Steel established herself as probably the finest lady player there has ever been and was undoubtedly more than capable of beating any man in open competition at the time. She won the Champion Cup for the fourth time in 1933 and, having won it outright by so doing, quite properly ignored hints that she should re-present it. This necessitated the presentation of a new perpetual trophy, the President's Cup, a somewhat massive octagonal silver trophy which requires considerable strength of mind to win and at least as much strength in the arms to hold. As strength of mind was Miss Steel's forte, it came as no surprise when she won again in 1934.

The game had by now achieved an equilibrium, albeit one that was marred by a slow but steady loss of members from the inter-war peak of 1,700 to 1,350 in 1939. However, any concerns there might have been for the future of the game were rendered pointless by the outbreak of the Second World War.

The period from 1945 to 1960 was not an optimistic time for British croquet. The membership of the CA was ageing steadily and young players were only coming forward in ones and twos. Apart from the emergence of a triumvirate consisting of John Solomon, Humphrey Hicks and Patrick Cotter, three croquet colossi whose best years virtually coincided, there is little of note to report. So complete was their dominance of English croquet that one of these three won the President's Cup in every year from 1947 to 1964 and the Open Championship in every year but four from 1947 to 1968.

In 1962 came the wind of change. A group of undergraduates competed in a tournament at Roehampton and there began a trickle of new faces into the game that has accelerated steadily ever since. The emergence in the late 1960s of Nigel Aspinall and Keith Wylie, as players of enormous promise and rapid achievement while still in their early twenties, indicated that the revival was soundly based on the appeal of the game's intrinsic competitive merits to young minds.

CROQUET WORLD-WIDE

Croquet came to England when Britain still had an empire and by the 1860s had reached India, Australia, New Zealand and, perhaps a little surprisingly, the USA. Roger Bray, a leading croquet historian, believes that contemporary novels which described croquet, such as *Little Women* by Louisa M. Alcott, played a significant part in extending knowledge of the game. Although Indian croquet never became much more than an evening amusement for the military and professional classes, events in the other countries took a more constructive turn and laid the foundations for the game's modern pre-eminence.

New Zealand

Croquet was brought to New Zealand by the early settlers in the years following 1850 as the garden party recreation becoming popular in England at that time. By 1864, a croquet lawn was among the facilities provided in Kohler's Promenade Gardens in Christchurch, South Island, and the game was probably played on an organised basis at the United Club in Christchurch in 1866. References to croquet can be found in New Zealand literature from 1870, including the classic *Station Life in New Zealand* by Lady Barker.

The first croquet club was formed in 1879 as part of the Ponsony Lawn Tennis Club in Auckland, North Island. Croquet clubs soon appeared elsewhere and many were established by civic bodies as a service to local communities. The need for greater organisation gradually arose, and the Canterbury Association, the first regional association, was formed in 1910. This association held its first tournament in 1911, and in 1913 the first New Zealand Open Championship was held in conjunction with the Canterbury Tournament. It was won by Keith Izard, a somewhat spectacular young man who had enjoyed considerable success in English croquet. The next major development occurred in 1920 when the New Zealand Croquet Council (the NZCC) was established under the presidency of E. J. Ross, a Christchurch player.

Once the NZCC had been established, regional associations were soon formed to cover the rest of the country. Croquet in New Zealand grew steadily and, untroubled by the effects of war, easily overtook the Croquet Association in England in membership. Croquet players were predominantly women until quite recently, although several men have been involved with the administration of the game and one, Arthur Ross, the son of the first president of the NZCC, became one of the finest players New Zealand has ever produced.

Ross won the New Zealand Open Championship eleven times and the British Open Championship in 1954. His career coincided with that of Mrs Clem Watkins, New Zealand's most successful woman player. She won the Championship five times, was runner-up on four occasions and won the Women's Championship seven times. Arthur Ross also founded a stylistic dynasty. He coached Ashley Heenan, his son-in-law, to international standard, and Heenan in turn introduced the young John Prince to the game in 1960. Prince has carried on the tradition, and the example of his smooth centre style combined with an acute tactical brain has inspired many of New Zealand's modern players.

The history of croquet in New Zealand as a game played mainly by women is linked to an extent to the game of bowls. Many croquet clubs were associated with bowls clubs because women were excluded from these chauvinistic institutions, and were therefore compelled to turn to croquet for their recreation. The advent of women's bowls in

Fig 9   John Prince – a classic style.

the 1950s had an alarming effect on croquet club memberships, and these have only stabilised in the last fifteen years. The most encouraging development has been the emergence of a generation of young men and women players of great talent with the result that New Zealand has captured the Mac-Robertson Shield twice since 1974. Ashley Heenan recently became president of the NZCC, and there is considerable optimism that under his guidance New Zealand croquet will capitalise on its recent international successes and continue to broaden its appeal to all sections and ages.

Australia

Croquet arrived in Australia in the same way as it did in New Zealand, namely in the baggage of the English settlers in the 1850s. Before long, a croquet court was a feature of the garden of every large country house. The Kyneton Croquet Club was formed in Victoria in 1866 and was the first of many clubs to be formed in country districts under the encouragement of the shire councils and the local churches. The game spread somewhat later to the towns. The Geelong Croquet Club was founded in a district of Melbourne in 1900 and tournaments are known to have been held by 1904. Organisation of the game rapidly proceeded upon state lines, and the Tasmanian Croquet Association was founded in 1908. It was followed by the formation of the Victorian Croquet Association in 1914, the South Australia Croquet Association in 1916, the New South Wales Croquet Players' Association in 1918, the Queensland Croquet Association in 1922 and the Western Australia Croquet Association in 1928.

The modern taste for international croquet competition owes much to Australian croquet. In March 1919, the Victorian Croquet Association invited the CA to send a team to Australia, but owing to the very recent end of the war, nothing could be done. The Australians were not discouraged and, in 1925, a team of enthusiastic men arrived in England to play several test matches. As a result of this endeavour, MacPherson Robertson, an Australian confectionary millionaire, donated a trophy for international competition and so initiated the official test matches between England (now Great Britain) and Australia and, since 1930, New Zealand, for the MacRobertson Shield.

The vast size of the Australian continent and the consequent difficulty of travel in the early years hampered the formation of a federal croquet authority. No inter-state body existed until the Australian Croquet Council (the ACC) was formed in 1949 under the influence of Colonel A. E. Saalfeld, a recent English expatriate who had become fascinated by the game while stationed at Cairo during the war. He was assisted by other prominent players including Mrs James Wall, Miss Agnes Morrison and Major Robert Tingey, another Englishman who was also a noted instructor.

The ACC occupies a singular position as a governing body in the croquet world. Each state body is responsible for the administration of the game within its jurisdiction and the relationships between these bodies and the ACC have not been without difficulty over the years. The most unfortunate result of these internal dissensions occurred in 1979 when a comparatively weak team was despatched to New Zealand to contest the MacRobertson Shield. Owing to personality clashes and inter-state bargaining, the team selected was a pale shadow of Australia's true strength and was predictably demolished. However, a valuable lesson was learned and the teams picked for the 1982 and 1986 test matches were based on merit and performed most impressively.

The first National and Inter-state Championships were held under the auspices of the ACC in 1950 and, together with the English Silver Medal tournament, which is competed for by the Gold Medallist from each of the States, constitute the principal events in the Australian Croquet Carnival. This is the highlight of the croquet year and is hosted by each state in turn. The Carnival lasts for about three weeks and represents the main opportunity for players from all parts of Australia to meet.

Until 1914, the majority of Australian croquet players were men. An interesting consequence of the outbreak of the First World War was that croquet in Australia then became a game played and administered principally by women. This was compounded by the increasing popularity of bowls, and bowls clubs with membership open only to men and bars open, on Sundays. The women responded by turning many croquet clubs into institutions where men were either excluded completely or tolerated only as players. The situation is much more relaxed nowadays. Although nine-tenths of Australian croquet players are still women, with many in the middle-aged and senior categories, there has been a clear resurgence of youth in the last twenty years. The majority of the best players are young men, and their appetite for enterprising play and international competition is gradually raising the standard of croquet throughout Australia. It is more significant still that younger men and women are now playing their part in the administration of the game, with wide support from club members across the continent. The future of Australian croquet has never looked brighter.

United States of America

It is not widely known that croquet swept America at the same time as it came to prominence in England and for reasons principally attributable to the nature of the game. The Newport Croquet Club was in existence in Rhode Island in 1865 and the National American Croquet Association was founded in 1882. However, the rise of lawn tennis and opposition from the Boston clergy on the grounds that croquet promoted licentiousness on the lawns led to a surprisingly rapid collapse in interest among the smart set, and croquet was effectively relegated to the backyard for most of the next ninety years.

Croquet resurfaced in the 1920s as part of the well-publicised recreations of the literary and stage set, fell away in the 1950s and re-emerged in the 1960s when the Westhampton Mallet Club from Long Island challenged a team from the Hurlingham Club in London. The Americans visited London in 1966 and were soundly beaten. In 1967 the Londoners visited Long Island and, captained by John Solomon who was by then regarded by many as the greatest player in the history of the game, had something of a shock when they encountered the nine hoops, two winning posts and two-inch (5cm) grass then typical of American backyard croquet.

The English team adjusted rapidly enough to these unfamiliar conditions and demonstrated to their hosts something of the gulf that existed between modern English croquet and the American version which used a hoop setting abandoned in Britain in 1872, and a sequence law discarded in 1920. The Americans travelled to Hurlingham again in 1968 and were beaten 8–0. The stroke-making skills of the English players on a flat, closely mown English lawn were still far superior to anything the Americans were used to and the result of the match was never in doubt.

The 1968 American team included Jack Osborn, who over the next nine years masterminded the considerable task of founding a new national croquet body with a unified set of laws for two separate standard games. Six-wicket American Croquet is an American-style form of croquet using the English court setting. Nine-wicket American Croquet was designed to retain the interest of the American backyard player using the nine hoop and two peg setting that had been in use for over eighty years. The United States Croquet Association (the USCA) was formed in 1977 with Jack Osborn as its first president.

This is not a complete account of American croquet. There exist other versions of which the best known is roque. The name is derived by omitting the first and last letters from the word 'croquet' and reflects the refusal of certain American players to accept the English ban on rubber-faced mallets at the turn of the century. The game is typically played on a court surrounded by a low wall, off which the balls can be bounced, using a nine-wicket court setting.

There is considerable interest in Association Croquet in the USA. The laws of Association Croquet encourage boldness in shooting and rushing and more adventurous tactics among the best players. Clubs on the West Coast and in Arizona have shown most enthusiasm for the Association game and, armed with the greater stroke-making skills this encourages, have dominated the USCA National Championships in recent years. It is perhaps rather typical of American dynamism that the first international Association Croquet tournament should take place in California rather than somewhere in the Commonwealth. In August 1986, Brice C. Jones, the proprietor of the Sonoma-Cutrer Vineyards, constructed two first-class courts at his winery and, assisted by the sponsorship of Continental Airlines, invited twenty-two players from Great Britain, Australia, New Zealand and the United States to compete in a singles championship. Although Stephen Mulliner of Great Britain narrowly defeated Neil Spooner of Australia in the final, the American contingent demonstrated that they were rapidly becoming expert at Association Croquet, and there can be little doubt it will flourish in the USA in the future.

In 1986, the CA encouraged the USCA to apply to take part in the next MacRobertson Shield contest in New Zealand in 1990. However, admission of a new participant requires the unanimous approval of the currently competing countries and doubts were expressed as to whether the USA was yet ready to take part. Although it is to be hoped that such doubts will soon be resolved, it is unfortunate that the opportunity to confirm the USA as the fourth great Association Croquet nation was not grasped.

Japan

After the Second World War, a game called Gate-ball became very popular among senior citizens and today has over three million players. It involves two teams of five and a great deal of frenetic activity, but shares the common features of croquet games, namely the use of mallets, hoops and balls, and, indeed, uses a croquet stroke played with a foot on one ball. Professor Masaru Ikeda, a teacher of sport sociology at the National Institute of Fitness and Sports in Kanoya, investigated the origin of Gate-ball and discovered that it was derived from backyard croquet using the nine hoop, two peg setting. He became interested in the development of croquet and visited England and the USA in 1982 to see how the parent game was played.

The Croquet Association of Japan (the CAJ)

Fig 10   One of the CA and USCA coaches in Tokyo.

was formed by Ikeda in July 1983 and in November of that year coaches from the CA and the USCA visited Japan to demonstrate Association and Six-wicket American Croquet. The CAJ decided to adopt Association Croquet and held the first Japanese Open Championship in 1984. The first croquet book in Japanese was published in the same year. Judging from the performance of Japanese golfers, it may not be too long before a Japanese player makes his mark in international competition.

Other Countries

Apart from the countries mentioned above, croquet clubs have existed for many years in most parts of the former British Empire, such as the Bahamas, Bermuda, Canada, Egypt, Kenya, Singapore and South Africa. Clubs have also been formed recently in countries such as Mexico, Spain and Switzerland. We know that croquet has been played informally in almost every country where it is possible to maintain a lawn. Tolstoy had a croquet court in his garden in Moscow, and the game is still played in the Soviet Union on a number of private lawns.

It would be wrong to end this chapter without referring the reader eager for greater detail of the development of the game, and an insight into the personalities involved, to *The History of Croquet* by D. M. C. Prichard (Cassell, 1981). This is an entertaining and learned account of a subject for which the author was supremely qualified. The fact that it is widely regarded as a literary masterpiece is a fitting memorial to David Prichard who died in 1986.

BASIC CROQUET

3 Getting Started

THE CROQUET COURT

(Fig 11)

Have a look at Fig 11, which shows the main features of a full-sized croquet court or lawn. It measures 35yds (32.0m) long by 28yds (25.6m) wide, which is about the same size as two lawn tennis doubles courts side by side. Notice that the boundaries are named after the points of the compass. This is quite arbitrary and bears no relation to the actual orientation of the court, but is very useful for describing the game. The south boundary is defined as the short boundary nearest hoop 1. Notice that there are six hoops and a central winning post or *peg*. Each corner hoop is placed 7yds (6.4m) from its adjacent boundaries and the centre hoops are placed 7yds (6.4m) north and south of the peg. The hoops are numbered as shown and this represents the order in which they have to be scored, namely, 1, 2, 3, 4, 5, 6, 1-back, 2-back, 3-back, 4-back, penultimate (or 'penult') and rover. Each hoop is run twice, once in each direction, and thus has two numbers, one for the outward circuit and one for the return circuit..

The boundaries are marked with a chalk line or with string which, if well secured, is distinctly preferable as it is much more precise. However, the yard-line and the baulk-lines, which are marked on Fig 11, are not marked on the court. The yard-line is an imaginary line, running, as its name suggests, exactly one yard (90cm) inside the boundary. It exists because, subject to certain important exceptions, whenever a ball is sent off the court it has to be replaced a set distance inside the boundary. That distance is one yard and is measured using the player's mallet. It may sound rather approximate but it works very well in practice. The baulk-lines, A-baulk and B-baulk, are simply special parts of the yard-line from which a ball can be played into the game. Some clubs mark the mid-court ends of the two baulks for convenience.

The corners are numbered as shown, after the appropriate hoop on the outward circuit. The point where the boundaries meet is usually marked by a small flag or post and corner pegs, standing about three inches

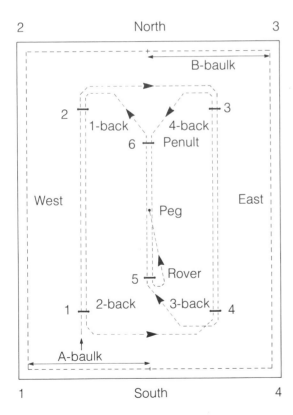

Fig 11

(7.5cm) high, mark the points one yard (90cm) from the corner flag along each boundary. They are useful when replacing a ball that has left the court in, or close to, the corner.

Smaller Courts

There is no need to play croquet at home on a full-sized court, which is just as well for most of us. If you have an area of lawn at least 15yds by 12yds (13.5m by 10.8m), you simply need to set up the hoops and peg by scaling down the distances, while maintaining the length/width ratio at 5:4. If your lawn is smaller than this, you might try the 5 hoop setting shown in Fig 12. Do not feel that croquet on a small court is not worth while. You will find it easier to play breaks, and will enjoy the game more as a result.

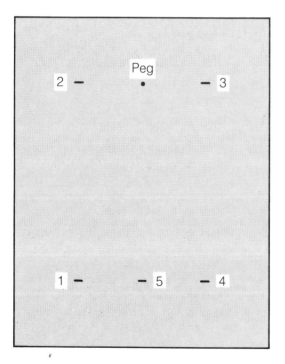

Fig 12   5 hoop setting.

Maintenance

A good croquet lawn should be level, flat, firm and fast. Levelness and flatness are not the same. A gentle gradient will mean that the court is not level but that need not matter very much. Flatness means a smooth surface without irregularities that might cause a ball to bounce as it travels. Flatness is much more important and can only be achieved by good lawncraft. It is beyond the scope of this book to say much on this specialist subject, except to remind you of the American tourist who admired a lawn at a Cambridge college. He asked the gardener how the beautiful surface could be achieved and was told that it was very simple: 'Just mow it and roll it, sir, just mow it and roll it – every day for two hundred years'.

You need not be quite so attentive, but mowing three times a week in May and June, and twice a week during the rest of the summer, with a cylinder mower, will improve the flatness and firmness of any lawn and there is now a wide range of chemicals available from garden centres to give you all the help you need in dealing with weeds, moss, insects and other problems.

Autumn tasks include raking to remove moss and thatch, which are the worst enemies of a firm, healthy surface, and hollow-tining to reduce small humps that are too large for the roller. Rolling should not be used excessively as it will compact the surface and inhibit growth, and most lawn experts regard the weight of the average petrol cylinder mower as sufficient. Larger mounds may need more drastic action, such as rolling back the turf and removing earth to the appropriate extent. In a severe case, it is the subsoil that must be removed, not the topsoil. Dips can be tackled by sifting soil into them in the autumn so that the grass will grow through the following spring.

The speed of a lawn depends on the height and sap levels of the grass, and on the weather. For home play, a grass height of a quarter–inch (6mm) is as low as you need go. At croquet clubs, the blades are sometimes set at half this height, but it is not a good idea to go this low unless you know what you are doing, and can treat the lawn effectively if the grass seems to be suffering from the greatly reduced leaf area available for photosynthesis.

'Sappiness' or lushness depends on the amount of nitrogen in the feed and the depth of the water-table. A croquet court should not be a deep green colour, no matter how attractive this may look. The best courts from a playing standpoint are a paler colour, even straw-coloured in a dry spell. The advent of artificial watering has proved a mixed blessing for croquet in Britain. We normally get quite enough rain and there are far too many slow courts. A fast court is important for developing touch. It is no great test of skill for any good player to complete a break on a really easy-paced lawn.

EQUIPMENT

The Hoops *(Fig 13)*

Every croquet club worthy of the name uses only championship hoops. These formidable pieces of metal stand 12in (30cm) high above the ground and are secured by 'carrots' that sink 8in (20cm) into the earth so that the hoop forms a rigid obstacle. So-called 'tournament' hoops are very inferior and if you are prepared to make an investment to enjoy the game at home, purchasing championship hoops is a priority. Championship hoops are not cheap, with a set of six in cast iron costing rather more than a set in aluminium. The latter are much lighter and slightly less robust, but have much the same playing characteristics as their traditional cousins. A championship hoop has uprights ⅝in (1.6cm) in diameter, with an internal gape of 3¾in (9.5cm), exactly ⅛in (0.3cm) wider than a croquet ball. You certainly need precision to run a hoop from any distance but it is amazing from what angles hoops can be scored. The hoops are painted

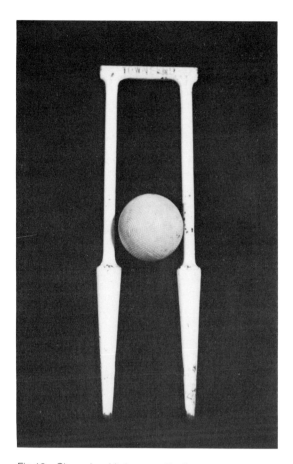

Fig 13   Championship hoop and ball.

white but hoop 1 (and 2-back) has a blue crown and rover (and hoop 5) has a red crown.

The Peg

The winning peg is made of round wood 1½in (3.8cm) in diameter and stands 18in (45.0cm) clear of the ground. It carries a detachable top portion to hold the clips (*see* below). It is an item of equipment that you could make yourself if you are keen to economise. It need not be painted, but the traditional decoration consists of stripes in blue, red, black and yellow, with a white base.

The Clips

There are four plastic or metal clips, coloured to match the balls, which are used to indicate the score by being placed on the hoop each ball has to run next. The clip is placed on the top of the hoop if the ball is on the outward circuit, the first six hoops, and on an upright if it is on the return circuit.

The Balls

The game is played using four coloured balls. The usual colours are blue, red, black and yellow. In double-banking, when two separate games are played on one lawn simultaneously, the second game uses green, pink, brown and white. The balls are 3⅝in (9.2cm) in diameter (plus or minus 1/32in (0.08cm)) and weigh exactly 16oz (0.454kg) (plus or minus ¼oz (7g)). In a tournament, the balls will also be tested for rebound (between 30 and 45in (75 and 112.5cm) when dropped from 60in (150cm) on to a steel plate, 1in thick, set rigidly in concrete) and consistency of rebound (all balls in a set must display rebound heights that do not differ by more than 3in (7.5cm)).

The standard tournament ball is made from a composition core with a plastic cover, and a number of manufacturers are attempting to produce a durable homogeneous ball with similar playing characteristics. Another investment you should make, if you are to enjoy home croquet, is to buy a set of four tournament balls. The extra weight will make them travel much more smoothly and predictably over a less than perfect surface, and will allow you to develop the full range of strokes.

Mallets *(Fig 14)*

A range of modern championship mallets are shown. Note that several have square heads and plastic faces. The only significant advantage of a square-headed mallet is that it will stand up on its own, which can sometimes be useful.

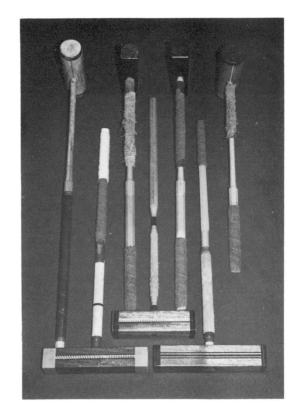

Fig 14   Championship mallets.

Plastic faces are more durable than wood and protect the mallet against mishits. Such mallets weigh between 2lb 12oz (1.25kg) and 3lb 12oz (1.7kg) with most within 2oz (56g) of 3lb (1.36kg) and have a shaft length between 30in (75cm) and 40in (100cm) depending on style (*see* Section 2).

A mallet is your most personal item of equipment and a tournament player may well play with the same one for a lifetime. They are certainly not cheap, but the good news is that the cheaper ones, being made from modern materials, are actually more popular with the leading players than the more expensive, traditional mallets made from lignum vitae and other hardwoods. If you are only going to play at home, a standard weight, standard length mallet is all you need, and the average family could make do with two, especially if metal shafts are specified to cope with the occasional difference of opinion on the lawn. A potential tournament player would be well advised to borrow a few to try out before buying.

Dress

Croquet is played in flat-soled shoes to avoid damaging the court. Modern tennis shoes are very suitable and offer a wide range to suit every taste and pocket. Good shoes are important, as croquet is played on the feet and after a day of tournament play you will be grateful for the support and comfort of well-fitting footwear.

Tournament play requires whites which can mean anything from cream flannels, long-sleeved shirt and panama hat (if you are so inclined) to shorts, short socks and a T-shirt. Shorts and knee-length socks are a popular combination, and fencing breeches offer the same advantages (no trouser flaps in the way of the mallet), and greater warmth on a cold day. Rain does not stop play until the court becomes waterlogged and, as a well-drained court can absorb an astonishing amount of rain without this happening, waterproofs are essential. Bowlers are equally hardy and, being more numerous than croquet players, are well catered for in sports shops.

GENERAL INFORMATION

Joining a Croquet Club

It will be apparent that some items of equipment are not cheap. However, apart from your mallet and shoes, you need spend no more than the annual subscription of your local croquet club to have the use of all the items mentioned above, as well as access to coaching and the social benefits of the game. Your national croquet association will provide you with the names of your nearest clubs. A list of national associations is given in Appendix V.

The Laws of Croquet

Although this book describes the principal laws of various games in some detail, it is desirable to have your own pocket-sized copy of the laws. Your club or national croquet association will be able to supply you with the official laws, and may also publish simplified versions for garden use, and detailed commentaries for those who wish to take a deeper interest.

Equipment Manufacturers

A list of equipment manufacturers in Australia, Canada, England, New Zealand and the USA is given in Appendix I.

4 A Typical Turn

In subsequent chapters we explain how to master a variety of strokes. We will urge you to practise those strokes and we suggest methods of practice. The aim of this chapter, however, is to give you a flavour of the game, a glimpse of the promised land. Here we offer a preliminary answer to the question 'what is croquet?'.

A game of croquet is, in fact, a race. Each side tries to be the first to get both of its balls through all the hoops in the correct order, and to hit the winning peg with them. To win the

Fig 15   What do I do? David Thatcher ponders.

race speed and stamina are not required, guile and skill are. Physical attributes are relatively unimportant, but clarity of thought and the ability to concentrate are vital if you wish to improve quickly.

Croquet is sometimes described as 'snooker on grass'. As in snooker, you can play either singles or doubles. Instead of a cue, you use a mallet. Strokes can be played to vary the amount of forward spin on a ball, much in the way a snooker player varies the way he addresses the cue ball. A croquet player needs to understand angles to play strokes involving more than one ball, in order to get one or both of them to predetermined places on the court.

If you like winning, you must learn to play breaks. If one player stays on court for a long time, you know he or she is making a successful break.

Defensive play is equally easy to recognise. We are all familiar with the cat and mouse play of top snooker pros, when the cue ball remains close to one end of the table, whilst the reds or the next colour are up at the far end. Defensive situations in croquet see all the balls close to the boundaries of the court, with turns alternating rapidly between the players. As in snooker, you can wait for your opponent to make a mistake, or choose a position in which you risk an attack, knowing that if it fails you may leave an easier situation for your opponent.

A snooker player can win with one long break, but in croquet you need two breaks for the perfect win, as you have to give your opponent a turn when you end a break with one ball. The main difference between the games is that in croquet it is never possible for you to amass such a lead in points that your opponent cannot win. There are many

28

examples of games where one side has scored all the hoops (but not pegged out) before the other starts, and is still beaten.

SIDES

A game of croquet is played between two *sides*, using four balls: red and yellow v. black and blue, or pink and white v. brown and green. Red, yellow, black and blue are known as the *first colours*. They are the traditional colours of the four balls used to play croquet. Now, however, due to croquet's increased popularity, two games are often played simultaneously on one court. This practice is called *double banking* and pink, white, brown and green are used as *second colours*.

In singles you play both the balls of a side, in doubles you play one of the balls of your side and your partner plays the other.

TURNS

The sides play in alternate *turns*. In singles, the player in play is known as the *striker*, and the player off the lawn is known as the *outplayer*. When your turn comes to play, you (the new striker) may play either of your two balls. The ball you choose to play is then referred to as the *striker's ball*.

In a turn, a striker is initially entitled to one stroke. In order to earn bonus strokes, the striker's ball must either:

1. Run its hoop, *or*
2. Roquet another ball.

A turn is one stroke, plus bonus strokes (if gained). Bonus strokes consist of one extra stroke each time the striker's ball runs its hoop, i.e. the next hoop it requires in the correct direction, and two extra strokes each time the striker's ball *roquets* another ball, i.e. hits another ball from which it is entitled to gain bonus strokes. Bonus strokes cannot be

accumulated. If the striker's ball runs its hoop and then makes a roquet in the same stroke, the result is two bonus strokes, not three. It is possible, however, to gain a long sequence of bonus strokes. The longest possible turn is one stroke plus ninety bonus strokes (ninety-one strokes).

Thus we see that turns can vary greatly in length, and might take anything from twenty seconds to over forty minutes to complete. The most common turn consists of one stroke, but once one bonus stroke has been gained, others normally follow.

THE TURN *(Figs 16 to 24)*

As we have explained, real croquet games are won by making *breaks*, constructive turns in which at least two hoops are run. The following situation is typical of the middle of a game. Here Ray (who always plays with red and yellow) is playing Bab (who always plays with black and blue). Bab's last turn has just ended with the balls in the position shown in Fig 16. Ray now steps on to the court with the choice of playing either red or yellow in this turn. As red and yellow are close together, and are near red's next hoop (hoop 4), Ray elects to play with red. Red is thus the striker's ball for this turn.

Stroke 1: In the first stroke of any turn, the striker's ball is entitled to roquet any of the other balls. Here Ray strikes red with his mallet so that it travels the two yards (1.8m) across the court to yellow and roquets it. This stroke is played gently so that yellow comes to rest as close to the front of hoop 4 as possible (*see* Fig 17). Because he not only roqueted yellow, but also projected it close to a predetermined spot, this is called a *rush*. As a result of the successful roquet, Ray earns two bonus strokes.

Stroke 2: The first bonus stroke is a two-ball stroke, or *croquet stroke*. Ray prepares for the stroke by picking up red and placing it in contact with yellow, so that a line through

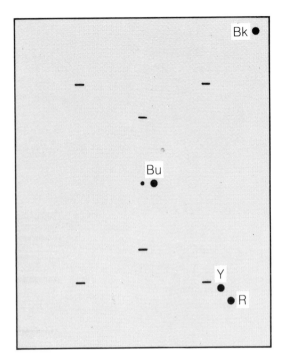

Fig 16

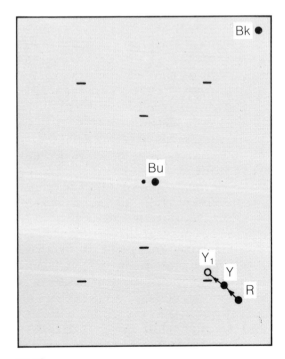

Fig 17

their centres passes to the side of the hoop (*see* Fig 18). Ray plays the croquet stroke by striking red so that yellow – impelled by the force transmitted through red – is sent to a spot beyond, and to the side of, the hoop, and red comes to rest right in front of the hoop, in a position to run it. This type of croquet stroke is called an *approach stroke*, as its main objective is to get the striker's ball in front of the hoop. It is important to understand that a player may only hit his own balls with his mallet, and during a turn he may only hit the ball he played in stroke one of the turn (red in this case). In a croquet stroke, the second ball (yellow here) must be caused to move by the motion of the striker's ball, not by the mallet.

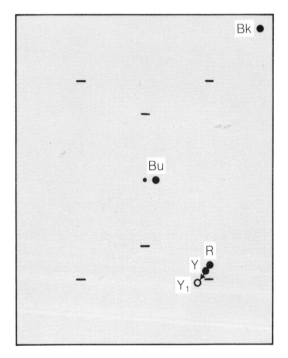

Fig 18

Stroke 3: The second bonus stroke is a one-ball stroke known as a *continuation stroke*, and may be used to make another roquet or, as in this case, to run a hoop. Ray plays this stroke by striking red gently so that it passes through the hoop and comes to rest just past yellow (*see* Fig 19). He has now earned a further bonus stroke – a continuation stroke – and the right to roquet all the other balls on the court again. Running a hoop thus has the effect of 'wiping the slate clean'.

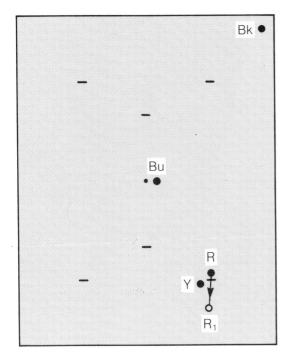

Fig 19

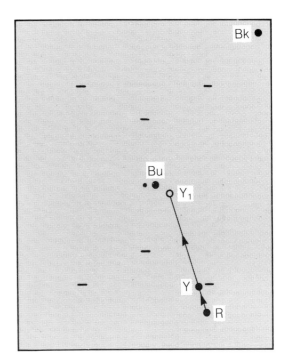

Fig 20

Stroke 4: In his second stroke Ray deliberately chose to send yellow to the right-hand side (west) of hoop 4. Because he did that, and because of his accuracy in running the hoop with yellow to a specific spot indicated in Fig 19, he now has the opportunity to play a rush, projecting yellow into the centre of the court, near blue. Fig. 20 shows how red is hit directly towards the centre of yellow, and yellow is rushed (a *straight rush*) to a position a few yards east of the peg. As a result of this roquet, Ray gains two more bonus strokes.

Stroke 5: As soon as Ray makes a roquet, he may pick the striker's ball up, provided there is no possibility that it will hit any of the other balls. If, however, there is a chance it may cannon into one of the other balls, it must be allowed to run its course. Such a cannon does not constitute another roquet but is a legal movement of that other ball. In our example there is no chance that red will hit blue or black, so Ray picks it up soon after it hits yellow. For the croquet stroke Ray places red in contact with yellow as shown in Fig 21. On this occasion Ray aims his mallet along the line joining the centres of red and yellow. By doing this he ensures that both balls will travel in the same direction. He plays a reasonable stroke, yellow ending nicely by hoop 6 and giving red the chance of a rush on blue to hoop 5.

Stroke 6: The striker's ball is entitled to roquet each of the other three balls once between hoops, and so now red, in this continuation stroke, may roquet blue. Ray needs to do more than just roquet blue, though, in order to have a good chance of running hoop 5 with red. He wants to rush blue close to hoop 5, preferably just south of it, so that the ensuing approach stroke will be as easy as possible.

31

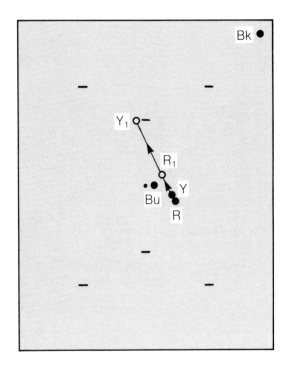

Fig 21

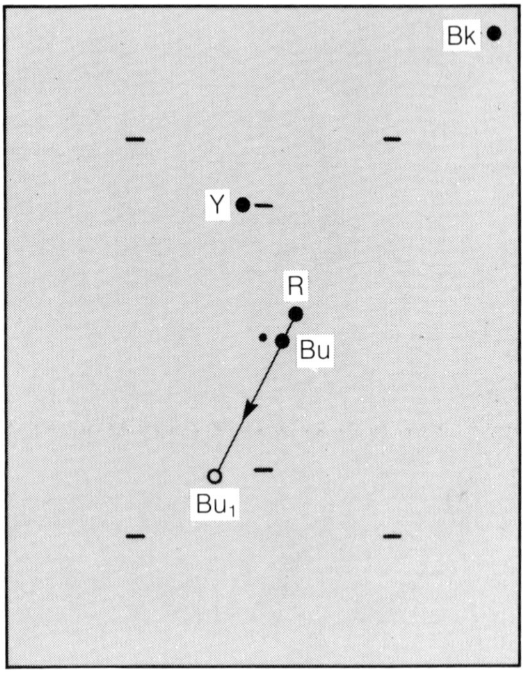

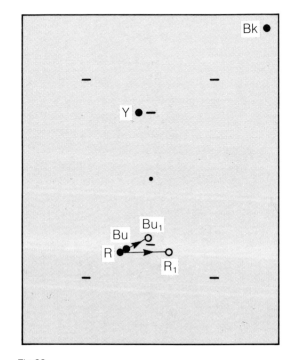

Fig 22

This time the line between the centres of red and blue (the rush) does not point towards Ray's target for blue, but somewhat to the west of it (*see* Fig 22). He must thus try and hit red on to the right side of blue, so that blue is projected somewhat leftwards, towards hoop 5. Such a stroke is called a *cut rush*. In this case Ray does not play the stroke well and blue stops about three yards (2.7m) to the west side of hoop 5, instead of close by it (*see* Fig 22). Two more bonus strokes are gained, however, for the roquet.

Stroke 7: Because of his previous poor stroke and because there is no other ball near hoop 5 he can use, Ray is now committed to playing a difficult approach stroke if he wants to get red in position to run its hoop, and thus have a chance of playing a break (remember, yellow is in a nice position close to hoop 6). He must play a croquet stroke with *roll* (topspin) to send red and blue equal distances, trying to get red in front of hoop 5 and blue behind it. Unfortunately for Ray this approach stroke is

Fig 23

also poor. Red goes too far past the hoop and has no chance of running it (*see* Fig 23).

Stroke 8: In his continuation stroke, Ray is unable to run hoop 5 with red. He is not allowed to roquet blue or yellow again in this turn until hoop 5 is run. He is now left with just two alternatives:

1. He could try to roquet black to win two bonus strokes, and attempt to continue the turn, but this is a long, difficult shot which would help Bab if he missed (can you work out why?).
2. He could accept that this will be his last stroke and play red away from blue to a better place on the lawn.

In our example, Ray chooses the second of those two options, and hits red towards yellow, a positional shot (*see* Fig 24).

It is now Bab's turn but, unlike Ray, she has no easy roquet with which to start her turn. It is likely that she will only get one stroke before

Ray gets the chance to play another, longer turn. Can you understand now why Ray played stroke 8 in the manner indicated?

Ray controls the game at the moment. He has made a *leave*, and he will have an easy roquet at the beginning of his next turn, provided Bab fails to make a roquet. This leave also requires Bab to hit a long roquet to gain any bonus strokes. When a side has such control of a game, it is said to have the *innings*. If Ray had shot red at black in shot 8, he would have handed the innings to Bab on a plate if he missed. Ray felt he had a less than even chance of roqueting black with red. Should he have been fortunate enough to make the roquet, he felt there was virtually no chance of approaching hoop 5 from corner 3. In balancing his options, he felt the risk of missing black far outweighed any reward, and thus chose to play as indicated.

In this turn Ray mounted an attack. The fact that three balls were brought into the middle of the court, and that one player played a number of strokes in sequence, is an indication of an attacking phase in the game. He made one hoop (and thus scored one point), but was unable to construct a break.

RECOGNISING BASICS

Confused? Obviously croquet is not the simple game it is often portrayed to be. Like every serious sport it has developed its own language – turn, striker, outplayer, roquet, rush, croquet stroke, approach stroke, roll and innings are some of the terms we have introduced in this chapter.

Not only is a player faced with a large number of tactical decisions during a game, but also the variety of strokes that can be played is infinite. No two games are ever the same. It is the challenge of confronting a series of interesting problems within the context of head-to-head competition, played in pleasant company and surroundings, that encapsulates the appeal and fascination of croquet.

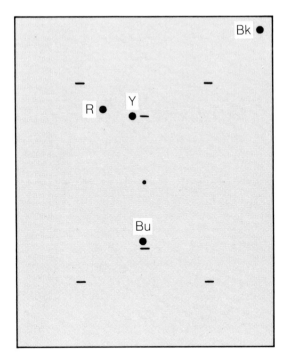

Fig 24

In many ways, however, the game is simpler than it appears. For example, all strokes can be classified into just two categories: *single ball strokes* and *double ball strokes* (croquet strokes).

Single Ball Strokes

The main types are:

1. *Positional shots*: a simple hit to a specified position on (or off) the lawn, for example stroke 8 above.
2. *Roquets* or *attempted roquets* (also referred to as *hits* or *shots*): in the example above, blue would probably try to roquet red or yellow after stroke 8.
3. *Rushes*: when a ball is roqueted to a predetermined place, for example strokes 1, 4 and 6 above.
4. *Scatter shots*: when, in the last stroke of a turn, the striker's ball deliberately hits a ball it is no longer entitled to roquet, in order to move that ball to a place on the lawn less favourable for the next striker.
5. *Hoop running strokes*: for example stroke 3 above.

Croquet Strokes

Strokes 2, 5 and 7 above are examples of croquet strokes, which can be played in many ways (*see* Chapter 6), but in all croquet strokes both balls involved must move, and neither should go off the lawn – if either of these things happens, the striker's turn automatically ends.

5 Single Ball Strokes

The key to any player's game is his *swing*. It should be straight, even-paced, consistent, have a smooth follow through and be capable of producing easily the maximum power required. Almost as important is *touch*, the ability to monitor accurately and apply the correct amount of power required in a given situation. Watch how top players invariably play a very soft stroke at the start of a game, when sending a ball off the east boundary near corner 4. They are attempting to monitor the speed of the court at the earliest possible opportunity.

A good swing and a delicate touch are best developed by practising single ball strokes. Ideally a player should master the various types of single ball strokes before going on to play croquet strokes.

PREPARATION

Stance

The mallet should always be swung so that it travels more or less parallel to the line of the feet, never across the body as in the style of golf. This is because it is vital to guide the mallet along as straight a line as possible, to ensure maximum accuracy when hitting a ball towards its target. There are two ways in which to achieve this: side style and centre style.

Side Style *(Fig 25)* The mallet is swung outside the body. The head should nevertheless still be over the line of swing and thus the weight of the body must be supported by the foot nearest to the mallet, whilst the other foot is used for balance.

Fig 25   Side style – one foot for support, one for balance: William Prichard.

Centre Style   The mallet is swung between the legs. Generally the feet are kept side by side but some players prefer to have one foot slightly in front of the other. Some keep their feet close together, others have them wide apart. Choose what gives you a stable but relaxed position.

Advantages of Side Style
1. Its great advantage is that it allows a free backswing, and thus enables those with weaker arms and wrists to achieve the power required for long shots by using an extended swing.
2. By using a long-handled mallet, a more erect stance can be maintained – an important consideration for those liable to back ailments.
3. It does not restrict ladies' dress. Side style was predominant in the era of the long dress.

Fig 26   Centre style – mallet swung naturally along the eyeline: David Peterson.

Advantages of Centre Style *(Fig 26)*

1. Its main advantage is that the mallet is naturally swung along the eyeline when aiming at a target, and most people find it more accurate for shooting and hoop running.
2. It is completely natural to swing the mallet in a straight line when playing centre style. To ensure a straight swing using side style requires practice.

Grip

How should the mallet be held? The simple answer is to find a way that feels comfortable. By all means study the various types of grip used by good players, or illustrated in our photographs, and try them out, but don't just copy your club coach or the best player you know. Choose the way that works best for you – the odds are it will be the way you held a mallet the first time you picked one up.

For single ball strokes, try to grip the mallet as high up the shaft as feels comfortable, without sacrificing your ability to play the longest shots. This will give a more erect and comfortable stance and a more elegant style.

Experiment!

It is essential that you experiment with various stances, foot placings and grips at an early stage. You must be sure you have found a suitable style, and develop the power of your swing, before you attempt to master croquet strokes. There is no reason why you shouldn't use side style for strokes requiring more power, and centre style for hoop running and more delicate strokes requiring accuracy.

HITTING A SINGLE BALL
(Figs 27 to 29)

1. Stand on an area of flat lawn (or carpet!), away from any obstacles, and practise swinging your mallet.
2. Try to relax – bend your knees.
3. Keep your eyes on the area of lawn in front of your feet, where the mallet reaches the bottom of its pendulum-like swing, and should lightly brush over the grass surface.
4. Keep your head still.
5. Try to develop a smooth even-paced swing.
6. On the upstroke, push your upper arms away from your body and follow through with the mallet. Imagine that you end the swing by hitting the underside of a hanging bucket some three feet (90cm) clear of the ground. The swing should end with your arms extended, but not stiff. When you have learned to swing the mallet smoothly so that it glides over the surface of the grass at the bottom of the swing, get some balls, and . . .

Fig 27   The follow through – note the upper arm position: Keith Wylie.

7. Address the ball. This means that the base of your mallet should rest *lightly* on the grass, with the centre of its face half an inch (1.25cm) behind the centre of the ball. The ball should be at least twelve inches (30cm) in front of your feet, to allow plenty of room for your backswing. Your eyes should be focused on the back of the ball.

8. Gently swing back and complete the stroke as above.

Fig 28   The address – knees flexed, eyes over back of ball: John Walters.

Fig 29   The backswing (centre style) – standing well back from the ball makes an extended swing possible: Phil Cordingley.

To start with, just try to hit the balls short distances. Once you are hitting the balls consistently cleanly, start trying to develop your touch. Choose a hoop or the peg as a target and try to hit the balls so that they come to rest as close as possible to that target. As your touch improves, choose more distant targets. Finally, make sure you can consistently hit the ball the length of the court.

Ball off the Boundary *(Fig 30)*

The actual boundary is the inside edge of the line round the court. Where there seems to be more than one line, it is the most recently marked one that counts. A ball is considered to be 'off' when any part of it touches an imaginary vertical wall raised from that inside edge. In Fig 30, balls B, C and D are all off the boundary.

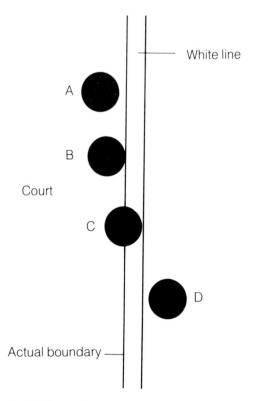

Fig 30   On or off?

The Yard-line *(Figs 31 & 32)*

The *yard-line* is an imaginary line one yard (90cm) inside the court from the boundary line. Once a ball goes off-court, it should be replaced immediately on the yard-line, directly opposite the spot where it first touched the boundary.

Fig 31   Replacing a ball on the yard-line.

The *corner spot* is an imaginary spot one yard (90cm) from each boundary near each corner of the court. If a ball goes off-court in a corner it should be replaced immediately on the corner spot (*see* Fig 32). The area between the yard-line and the boundary line is called the *yard-line area*. When you first get a mallet, measure its exact length and work out how to use it to replace balls accurately on to the yard-line.

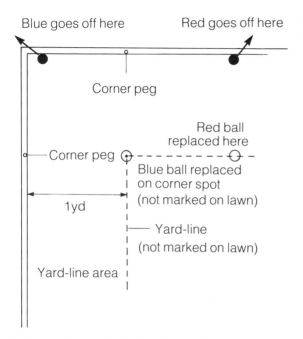

Blue goes off here   Red goes off here

Corner peg

Red ball
replaced here

Corner peg

Blue ball replaced
on corner spot
(not marked on lawn)

1yd

Yard-line
(not marked on lawn)

Yard-line area

Fig 32   Replacement of balls on the yard-line.

Fig 33   Stalking – an exercise in concentration:
Richard Hilditch.

Aiming *(Fig 33)*

There are three main aiming shots in croquet:

1. Aiming at another ball (roquet or scatter shot).
2. Aiming at the peg (peg out).
3. Hoop running.

For all aiming shots, stand two or three yards (1.8–2.7m) behind your ball, so that if you look at the target, your ball lies in a direct line with it from where you stand. Then walk up to your ball, along the line of aim, take up a comfortable stance and address the ball. This act of walking along the line of aim is called *stalking* the ball. If you stalk the ball correctly, your feet will end up in the correct position. As the position of the feet determines the line of swing, this is of paramount importance.

Most players take a final look at the target after they have addressed the ball. If, at this stage, you don't think you have lined the shot up properly, then stalk it again. Do not shuffle your feet around on the spot.

When you eventually strike the ball, keep your eyes on the ball's position and do not look up to see if you will hit the target until you have completed your swing.

Practice

In this chapter, and subsequent ones, we will suggest practice routines. As a general rule, you should always set yourself a target when practising, otherwise your practice could become ineffective and you will be unable to monitor whether or not you have made any progress.

When you practise shooting, it is imperative that you stalk each shot carefully. Try to discover the range within which you can be almost certain of hitting. Start by shooting at balls two or three yards (1.8 – 2.7m) away. As your shooting improves, extend your distance from the target. To force yourself to concentrate, make yourself hit ten in a row at what you consider to be your maximum 'certainty distance', before extending that distance or finishing the practice.

Even when practising croquet strokes, it is possible to set precise targets: for example, play split shots from a specific place and try to get each ball to stop within five feet (1.5m) of a specific hoop.

Hard or Soft?

If you watch other players, you will soon notice that some always hit attempted roquets or peg outs very hard, whilst others hit these shots relatively softly.

Very few courts are without the odd slope, and by hitting hard you are more likely to ensure that the ball is not diverted from its course by gentle borrows. Some courts, however, are so bumpy that hard hitting may result in balls bouncing over their targets! It is also considered easier to control your swing and keep it smooth and straight if you are hitting more gently. Gentle shooting is also to be recommended where a court doesn't have an efficient boundary fence.

Local conditions may dictate whether you shoot hard or soft, but, especially as you progress to shooting at longer range targets, it is worth experimenting to find out which style suits you.

RUNNING HOOPS *(Fig 34)*

It is vital to stalk a ball you want to run a hoop with. In the case of straight hoop shots, you should line your ball up with the centre of the hoop when stalking. It is in hoop running that a good follow through action is most beneficial. Following through helps put forward spin on a ball, just as a snooker player does by hitting slightly above centre on the cue ball. If your aim is not completely accurate, and the edge of the ball hits the side of the hoop, this added

spin could make the difference between running the hoop or sticking in it. Watch other players running hoops and you will soon see examples of this spin at work.

A ball hit hard moves forward initially by skidding across the surface of the grass, and thus for most hoop shots it is best to hit the ball gently, so that it is spinning and not skidding when it reaches the hoop. An excellent way to develop a gentle hoop running action with good follow through is to put your mallet head deliberately through the hoop after the ball on short, straight hoop shots.

Start your practices with short hoop shots, from about one foot (30cm) away, then practise two and three-foot (60 and 90cm) hoop shots. Don't waste time practising longer hoops, just make certain that you are reliable from within one yard.

Fig 34   The hoop stroke – a classic follow through: Roger Murfitt.

When Has a Ball Run its Hoop?

A hoop has two sides – the playing side and the non-playing side. In Fig 35 we see a ball in position to run its hoop in the correct direction.

If a ball stops so that any part of it lies within the hoop, it is said to be 'in the *jaws*'. If you try to run a hoop with your ball, but play a bad shot so that it ends up in the jaws, any one of three situations could arise, as shown in Fig 36.

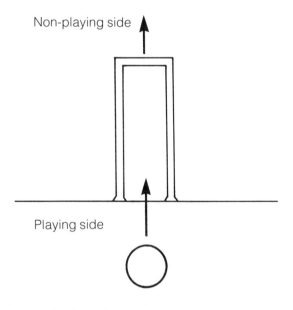

Fig 35   Playing and non-playing sides.

In A, the ball has not started to run the hoop. If you gently slide the side of your mallet down the non-playing side of a hoop and it doesn't touch any part of the ball, then the ball has not started to run the hoop. In B, the ball has started to run the hoop but has not completed running it. In C, the ball has run (scored) the hoop. If you gently slide the side of your mallet down the playing side of a hoop and it touches no part of your ball, then the ball has run the hoop.

It should be emphasised that in a match you should always let your opponent, or a referee, do this 'mallet test' if the position is too close to judge by sight alone.

Running Hoops with Control

Whenever your ball is straight in front of a hoop and very close to it, you should be able to run the hoop with control, to end in a precise position on the non-playing side of the hoop, usually close to another ball.

Beware of over-confidence when faced with an easy hoop. You must stalk the ball very carefully so that you can run the hoop without your ball hitting either upright. Once you have stalked the ball, try to forget that the hoop is there and concentrate on hitting your ball to a specific piece of grass beyond the hoop. Far too often beginners concentrate solely on getting through the hoop and, in consequence,

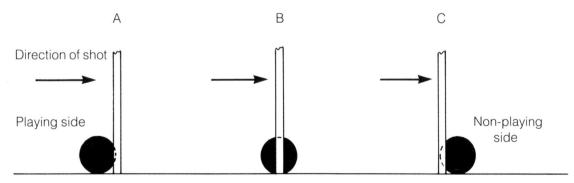

Fig 36   In the jaws – three variations.

their ball ends a long way past the ball lying on the non-playing side which should have provided an easy roquet.

When, however, you are trying to run a hoop from more than two feet (60cm) away, you should just concentrate on running the hoop. If, in trying for control, you hit the ball gently from that distance, it is too liable to be affected by any small bump or slope in front of the hoop, and may stick in the jaws.

A good practice involves placing a coin straight behind a hoop on the non-playing side. Practise running the hoop to finish as close to the coin as possible. Vary the position of the coin from one to six feet (30cm to 1.8m) past the hoop.

Running Angled Hoops

(Figs 37 & 38)

The upright of a hoop is called a *wire*. The two wires are connected at their tops by the *crown* of the hoop. If you are standing straight in front of the hoop, the wires are separately referred to as the left-hand wire and the right-hand wire. Otherwise the upright nearest to you is called the *near wire* and the upright furthest from you is called the *far wire*.

If you are trying to run a hoop with the ball not quite straight in front of it, the aiming procedure is different from that for running straight hoops. It is no good aiming the centre of the ball at the centre of the hoop, because the near side of the ball will hit the near wire, and the ball will either bounce off across the front of the hoop, or will stop in front of it. To run an angled hoop you must just miss the near wire with the near side of your ball. The far side of your ball is bound to hit the inside of the far wire but, as long as you have played the shot with follow through (thereby imparting spin to it), the ball will run through.

To aim, look at the near side of your ball and stalk along a line that shows it just missing the inside of the near wire. *Remember to follow through.*

Try this exercise: place a ball eighteen

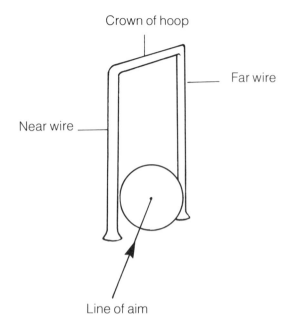

Fig 37   Running an angled hoop.

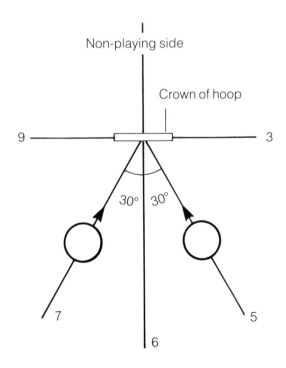

Fig 38   Angled hoop practice.

inches (45cm) away from a hoop at the five o'clock or seven o'clock position. Practise running hoops from these angles. Only count the shot as successful if the ball finishes at least two feet (60cm) clear of the hoop on the non-playing side. Once you have mastered this exercise you can attempt running even wider angled hoops and you can work out for yourself the maximum angle from the straight position at which hoops can be run. Remember, gentle strokes impart more spin!

The Three Vices

If you do not run hoops consistently, it is likely you are suffering from one or more of the three vices. All are vices of omission. You are not:

1. Keeping your head still.
2. Stalking the ball properly. Are you getting far enough back behind the ball? Are you lining the ball up with the correct target, i.e. centre of ball to pass through centre of straight hoop; near side of ball to just miss inside of near wire for angled hoop?
3. Following through with your mallet.

FAULTS *(Fig 39)*

Foul or illegal strokes in croquet are known as *faults*. The penalties for making a fault are: the end of your turn, any balls moved as a result of the stroke are replaced to their positions before the stroke was played, and any points scored as a result of the stroke are not counted.

Ignorance of the laws is not only no excuse, it is a self-imposed handicap. Because players always act as their own joint referees, it is your duty, upon taking up the game, to learn its laws. Duty aside, however, it is in your interest to do this. Knowledge of the laws, especially the faults, will help you to avoid costly blunders and help you to recognise illegal play by your opponents.

Fig 39   Did Stuart Packer (and do you) know at -least four faults likely to occur here?
(Answer on page 48)

Buy yourself a book of the laws (a simplified version will do to start with) and study the section on faults carefully. Carry it with you and don't hesitate to interrupt your opponent if you think a fault has been committed. Refer to your book of the laws, or seek the help of a tournament referee or experienced player, if one of you is not sure how to continue.

Some players, out of a false sense of etiquette, in awe of a more experienced opponent, or using the excuse 'it's only a friendly', say nothing when they notice questionable or obviously illegal play by an opponent. This is a bad habit. Avoid it for the following reasons:

1. If your opponent is less experienced than you, or a beginner like you, he may not realise he has done something wrong. You will help him to improve his understanding of the game by indicating his error. Insist on the penalty. That way he will be less likely to forget the

point you have taught him.

2. Never assume that because a player is better than you, or has been playing longer than you, he knows the laws better than you. As long as you interrupt him politely, another player has no reason to object to you exercising your rights as a joint referee.

3. If as friends, or regular opponents, you consistently ignore each other's faults, you are not only setting a bad example for others, but you are also not playing the game properly. We're sure you would not move a knight in a straight line during a game of chess, so why ignore croquet's laws, thereby devaluing the game?

Crush Strokes *(Fig 40)*

A fault that occurs regularly, and one which you should make a particular attempt to understand and avoid, is the *crush*. A crush stroke can occur when you are trying to run a hoop from only a few inches away. If you 'crush' the ball through the hoop, by forcing the mallet after it, so that the mallet, ball and hoop are in contact simultaneously, this is a fault. It is not a fault to hit the hoop with your mallet. It is the act of squeezing the ball through after it has hit a wire, rather than allowing any spin to try to get it through, that is illegal. A crush can also occur at the peg, although this is rare. For such simultaneous contact to be illegal, the ball must be between the mallet and hoop or peg. It is not a fault to touch the peg or a hoop with the side of your mallet whilst striking the ball with the mallet face.

Because of its very nature, you should be aware if there is a possibility you could commit a crush with your next stroke. If you are playing a match, get a tournament referee or, if one is not available, an experienced player to watch the stroke. If you are playing a friendly, get your opponent to come and watch it. Mark the position of any balls likely to be moved in the stroke, in case you do commit a fault and the balls have to be replaced. Use

Fig 40   A crush – black is touching the upright and the mallet face.

small coins or golf markers to do this – make sure you always have some available.

POSITIONAL SHOTS *(Fig 41)*

Sometimes, instead of playing a shot to run a hoop, or hit a ball or the peg, we play to send a ball to a particular place on the court. Often you may want to join your partner ball on the yard-line but not to hit it, nor leave the two balls close together in case you create an extra large target for your opponent. Decide beforehand exactly how far apart you want your balls to be. Then choose the place on the boundary where you want your ball to go off, so that when replaced on the yard-line, it will be where you want it. It is difficult just to aim at a piece of line, so look for something fixed, off-court, that lies on the line you want, such as a tree or fence post, and aim for that. It is a mark of experience when you see a player concentrating on what appears to be such a relatively unimportant shot. They will have undoubtedly paid the price of casualness in such circumstances in the past, having presented an opponent with too easy a target.

Another common positional shot is to try to hit the ball to a spot from which it is possible to run your hoop. This is called *taking position*. If you are approaching the hoop from in front or behind, this will rely purely on your touch. If your ball ends on the playing side, it is almost certain to leave you a relatively straight hoop shot, the only question being whether you are close enough (perhaps less than five feet (1.5m) away) to stand a good chance of running the hoop in your next turn. Approaching the hoop from the side is more difficult. Players commonly make the error of trying to get too close to the hoop. To maximise the possibility of ending in the 'fan of success', you should be prepared to settle for a longer hoop shot. If you settle for a position three feet (90cm) from the hoop, you have double the chance of attaining hoop position than if you try to get eighteen inches (45cm) away.

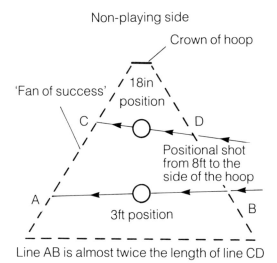

Line AB is almost twice the length of line CD

Fig 41   The 'fan of success'.

A good way of practising hoop running and positional shots is to try to run the first six hoops and hit the peg in as few shots as possible. Start by placing a ball on the yard-line in front of hoop 1. With your first stroke, try to achieve a position a couple of feet (60cm) in front of hoop 1. With your second stroke, try to run it and so on. Count every stroke you take. This is an excellent exercise for good players and beginners alike. A good score for a beginner would be less than 22. The 'perfect' score is 14, although lower scores are possible. It is fun to practise alone or in pairs, as you can try to beat your personal best or beat the score of your partner. As you become proficient, extend the course to all twelve hoops and the peg. The perfect score for this is 26, but any score of 30 or below is excellent.

SCATTER SHOTS AND RUSHES

In both of these strokes you are using the striker's ball to project one of the other balls to a certain place on the lawn, just as a snooker player projects a red or a colour using the cue ball. The differences between these strokes are:

1. Where the striker's ball goes may be important in a scatter shot, but this does not apply in the case of a rush, because it then becomes a *ball in hand*. It is picked up, in order to place it next to the projected ball for the croquet stroke that follows.
2. Because a rush is a roquet, you cannot commit the fault known as a *double tap*. This fault is committed when the striker's ball is hit twice in the same stroke, or remains in contact with the mallet after the striker's ball has hit another ball. This is most likely to occur when the striker's ball is hit into another ball very close to it, and rebounds on to the mallet, or stays in contact with it. The laws exempt strokes where a double tap is caused due to the making of a roquet. When wishing to

scatter a ball close to the striker's ball, however, you must consider whether it can be done without fear of making a fault. Where two balls almost touch, a rush will be possible, but a scatter shot will not.

Despite these differences, the mechanics of playing these two strokes are exactly the same. The following text is equally applicable to scatter shots.

Straight Rushes *(Fig 42)*

In a straight rush, you are trying to project the object ball along a path which is an extension of the line between the two balls. You should:

1. Stalk the shot.
2. Be careful to aim for the centre of the object ball.
3. Address the striker's ball normally, keeping your eyes on it and your head still.
4. Hit the striker's ball just as you would when playing any single ball stroke.

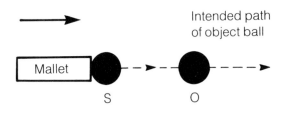

Fig 42 Straight rush.

Concentrate on direction to start with and gradually increase the strength of your rushes, until you can rush a ball from one end of the court to the other. Start by practising 'dolly' rushes, those with only a small gap, perhaps nine to twelve inches .(22.5–30cm), between the balls. When you have mastered them, extend the gap to two or three feet (60–90cm).

The Magnet Effect *(Fig 43)* Do your attempted rushes ever hit the top, and not the centre, of the object ball, and thus fail to rush it the required distance? Does the striker's ball ever bounce over the object ball without touching it? These are very common problems encountered by beginners.

You may get a 'bouncer' because the lawn is bumpy and, having hit a small bump, the striker's ball flies into the air. Make sure, if your lawn is bumpy, that you find a flat section on which to practise rushes.

A more common reason for bouncers is the magnet effect. For some inexplicable reason the object ball seems to attract many beginners irresistibly. By the time they hit the striker's ball they are leaning forward. Thus their weight is on the front part of their feet and, without realising it, they have tilted the mallet face downwards. The result is that they hit the striker's ball slightly into the turf, not straight along the surface of the lawn. Consequently the ball is projected into the air by the turf as it

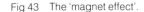

The mallet shaft is tilted forward and the player is hitting down on the ball

Fig 43 The 'magnet effect'.

springs back into shape. Ask beginners to hit balls across the lawn and they will stroke them smoothly, but put a rushable ball two feet (60cm) away and the striker's ball suddenly seems to develop hiccups!

What is the solution? Some players advocate taking half a step back from the normal position when addressing the ball, in order to compensate for any leaning forward during the stroke. See if that works for you.

The proper solution, however, is to concentrate solely on the striker's ball once you have stalked the shot, keep your body still but relaxed and just swing your arms with an even pendulum swing. Avoid jerky motions.

Cut Rushes *(Figs 44 to 46)*

Sometimes you will want to rush a ball to the left or right. For those of you who watch or play snooker, the principle involved will be obvious. If you want to cut rush a ball to the left, you must aim the striker's ball at the right-hand side of the object ball. If you want to cut rush a ball to the right, you must aim the striker's ball at the left-hand side of the object ball.

Fig 45   Cut rush to right.

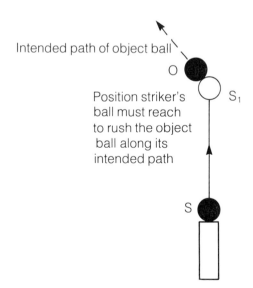

Intended path of object ball

Position striker's ball must reach to rush the object ball along its intended path

Fig 44   Cut rush to left.

You should only deliberately play cut rushes when the gap between the striker's ball and the object ball is small. If it is much more than eighteen inches (45cm) you risk missing altogether. Practise cut rushing balls to a target (hoop or peg) a few feet away which only requires a slight cut to the left or right. As you improve, either extend the distance to the target, or increase the degree of cut required.

You should soon notice that as you increase the degree of cut by hitting the object ball further from its centre, more strength is required to get it to travel a given distance. This is because, with an increased degree of cut, the striker's ball does not strike the object ball so fully and thus less of its energy is transmitted to the object ball. When a straight rush is played, nearly all of the energy of the striker's ball is transmitted to the object ball, and the striker's ball stops almost immediately. In a cut rush, the striker's ball retains part of its energy and it therefore shoots off to one side.

47

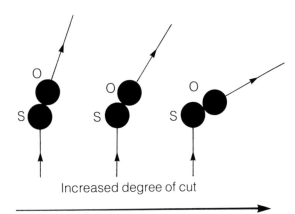

Increased degree of cut

Fig 46   Increasing the degree of cut.

GOLF CROQUET

Golf Croquet is to Association Croquet what pitch and putt is to golf – an excellent game for helping a beginner to develop some basic skills, and later on a game to play occasionally for some light-hearted fun. It has the advantage of being very easy to learn – within ten minutes of starting you should fully understand how to play – and it is also not without its tactical subtleties. The rules are listed in Chapter 9.

Use Golf Croquet to develop your single ball skills. It will give you plenty of practice at hoop running, positional shots and scatter shots. Once you have mastered these skills, move on to Association Croquet. Do not dwell on Golf Croquet. The real rewards of croquet come from playing the Association game, so don't settle for grape juice when you can have wine!

THE TOSS

The tossing rule applies to Golf Croquet, Two-ball games and to Association Croquet. Toss a coin to start the game. The side winning the toss then has one of three choices:

1. To play first.
2. To make the other side play first.
3. To choose which colour ball(s) to play with.

The side losing the toss then has the remaining choice, for example if the winning side chooses to play first, the losing side will have the choice of colours.

The four probable faults in Fig 39 are:

1.   Hand on mallet head (Rule 32.a.i.).
2.   Hand or arm on leg (Rule 32.a.iv.).
3.   Bevelled edge (Rule 32.a.v.).
4.   Double tap (Rule 32.a.ix.).

6 Croquet Strokes

We have already learned that if you make a roquet, you earn two bonus strokes. The first bonus stroke is the croquet stroke, and the second is the continuation stroke. This three-stroke sequence – roquet, croquet, continuation – is the key stroke sequence at the heart of the game.

Following the roquet, the striker's ball is picked up and carried to the place on court where the roqueted ball has come to rest. It may be that the roqueted ball was knocked into the yard-line or off-court. In that case the roqueted ball should be replaced on the yard-line. Then the striker's ball is placed anywhere round the roqueted ball, in contact with it, ready for the croquet stroke.

When you make a roquet, you don't have to worry about either ball involved going off-court. You simply pick up the striker's ball and/or replace the roqueted ball on the yard-line and continue your turn. The opposite is true when you play a croquet stroke. You must ensure that neither ball goes off-court or your turn ends.

Croquet strokes can be divided into two categories:

1. *Straight croquet strokes*, where both balls are sent in the same direction.
2. *Split shots*, where the two balls are sent in different directions.

Other variables that extend to infinity the number of different croquet strokes possible are the strength of stroke played and the amount of spin applied.

We will start by examining the use of spin and, for the sake of simplification, we will be referring solely to straight croquet strokes, until otherwise indicated.

RATIOS

Fig 47 shows how you can work out the ratio of a croquet stroke. We see that the croqueted ball has travelled three times as far as the striker's ball, giving a ratio of 3:1. This is the average ratio for a straight drive.

Sometimes a much higher ratio is achieved (*see* Fig 48). The highest ratio that can be achieved is about 10:1. This is called a *stop shot*. Be happy if you learn to achieve 6:1 or 7:1

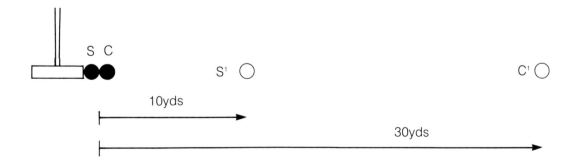

S C

S¹ ○

C¹ ○

10yds

30yds

Fig 47   Straight drive ratio.

S C S¹   C¹

3yds

30yds

Fig 48   Stop shot ratio.

– these are still very reasonable stop shots. Lower ratios can also be achieved : 2:1 is a *half roll*, that is, the striker's ball travels half the distance of the croqueted ball. A *full roll* is 1:1, when the two balls travel the same distance. Some players can achieve ratios of less than 1:1, by making the striker's ball overtake, and go further than, the croqueted ball. Such strokes are called *pass rolls*.

STRAIGHT DRIVES *(Figs 49 to 51)*

Place the striker's ball behind the croqueted ball, so that the line of centres points in the desired direction. The mallet should also be aimed in that direction. Then play the stroke just as if you were hitting a single ball, remembering to follow through. It is important to realise that, at the moment of the mallet's impact on the striker's ball, the base of the mallet is parallel to the ground.

Practise by choosing a target some fifteen yards (13.5m) away and play some straight drives, trying to get the croqueted ball to stop

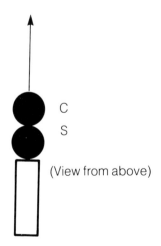

C
S

(View from above)

Fig 49   Straight drive.

Fig 50   Preparing for the straight drive – the base of Spencer Buck's mallet is parallel to the ground, as it will be on impact.

by the target. Mark the position from which you play each stroke, and after each of the first few strokes, work out your own ratio for a straight drive by pacing out the distance each ball travelled. As your accuracy improves, extend the distance of the target for the croqueted ball.

The ratios achieved by individual players vary. It is important to know your own ratio so that, in any given situation where a straight croquet stroke is required, you can immediately recognise whether the striker's ball needs to travel further (tending to a roll) or not so far (tending to a stop shot), as in your normal straight drive.

Your swing should remain as evenly paced as possible. If it slows during the follow through, you could easily commit a double tap. Another fault can occur if you play an exaggerated follow through or accelerate your swing too much after your mallet makes contact with the striker's ball. This is called *pushing* or *shepherding*. The mallet face remains in contact with the striker's ball after the croqueted ball has parted contact with it. The striker's ball is thus given an illegal extra impulse. Because of the danger of committing these faults, some players elect to achieve ratios of 3:1 or so by hitting down slightly on the backward ball and restricting their follow through.

If you are achieving ratios of much less than 3:1 with your straight drives, something is likely to be wrong and you should seek advice from an experienced coach or referee.

STOP SHOTS *(Figs 52 to 55)*

In snooker a player can 'stop' the cue ball, or cause it to spin backwards, by hitting under the centre of it with the cue. Our mallet faces are too large to allow us to do that, but to a certain extent a similar effect can be achieved, as follows:

1. Address the striker's ball as if you are about to hit a straight drive.
2. Take half a step backwards but keep the mallet face next to the striker's ball by gripping the mallet at the very top of the shaft, and resting the heel of the mallet on the lawn, whilst tilting the toe of the mallet so that the bottom of the front face is just below the centre of the ball.
3. Do not follow through when hitting the striker's ball, but try to ground the heel of the mallet at the same instant as the striker's ball is hit.

There is definitely a knack in perfecting this simultaneous grounding and striking. It is best to start by hitting soft stop shots that only send the croqueted ball a short distance, and perfecting the action before increasing power. Concentrate on where you want the heel of the mallet to ground. The action is not a pendulum swing, but rather a downward swing and poking action.

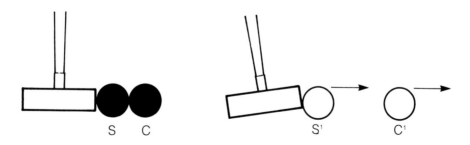

S   C   S¹   C¹

Fig 51 Shepherding.

Fig 52 The stop shot – the toe of David Foulser's mallet is raised.

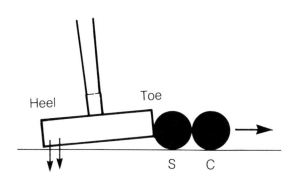

Fig 53 Stop shot – grounding the mallet.

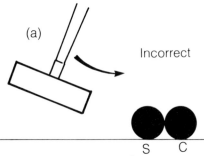

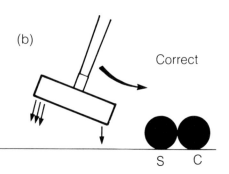

Fig 54 Stop shot – how to swing.

Common Mistakes

You may make the mistake of not getting a clean enough contact with the striker's ball when playing stop shots. This may happen because:

1. You ground the mallet too far behind the striker's ball. You may even not hit it on occasions. Or . . .
2. You raise the toe of the mallet too high and hit the striker's ball above its centre with the edge of the face, and not with the face itself.

This is not a fault unless your shot was hampered, for example if you could not swing freely at the striker's ball because of the presence of a hoop, another ball or the peg, which interfered with your stance or swing.
3. You do not ground the heel of the mallet properly and some follow through is imparted to the striker's ball, in which case lower ratios of 4:1 and below result. This is the most common reason for poor stop shots.

Learn to increase the strength of your stop shots gradually, until eventually you can play a stop shot that sends the croqueted ball the length of the court.

There is something paradoxical about strong stop shots because, in one and the same stroke, you are trying to hit one ball a long way whilst still stopping the mallet and imparting as little force as possible to the other ball. It may take time to master the stop shot, but persevere because the need for this stroke will arise many times in a game. Fig 55 shows one common situation where a stop shot can be used to construct a break.

Here black is the striker's ball, and is for hoop 1. You are taking croquet from yellow on the yard-line of the south boundary and red, which you have not yet roqueted in this turn, lies one foot (30cm) south of hoop 1. You have the chance, by playing a good stop shot, to get black close to red (so that you can roquet it and then have an easy approach stroke to hoop 1) and, at the same time, to send yellow close to hoop 2, which will give you a good chance of making hoop 2 off it, and

continuing. To do this you would need, on a half-size court, to send black 3½ yds (3.15m) and yellow 18½ yds (16.6m), a ratio of 5¼:1.

Once mastered, the stop shot is one you will want to play much more often than the difficult roll strokes. This is because you can control the position of the striker's ball very easily, as you are not sending it far. So, where possible, plan ahead to incorporate stop shots in your play.

ROLLS *(Figs 56 to 60)*

Just as a snooker player can put topspin on to a cue ball, so we can apply topspin to the striker's ball in a croquet stroke. By varying the amount of spin applied, ratios from 2:1 (half roll) to less than 1:1 (pass roll) can be achieved. The following instructions assume that you are a right-handed player:

1. Stand closer to the balls than for a drive. Place your left foot about four inches (10cm) to the side of the two balls. This foot should be flat on the ground and is used to take the body's weight. Your right foot should be about twelve to fifteen inches (30 – 37.5cm) behind the striker's ball and slightly to the left of the line running through the centres of the balls. Both your knees should be bent and you should use your right foot to balance yourself, only the toes being on the ground. In essence you must adopt a crouched side style.
2. Hold the mallet lower down its shaft. Your left hand should be a quarter of the way down the shaft towards the head, the right hand about three-quarters of the way down. The back of the upper hand should face forwards, but the lower hand should grip the mallet palm forwards.
3. Incline the mallet so that its shaft leans forward and its toe points downward, and hit the striker's ball above its centre.
4. Follow through.

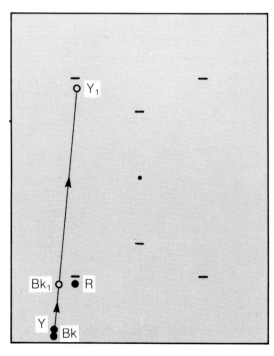

Fig 55

Fig 56　The roll – note how Martin Murray's mallet shaft is held clear of his face by tilting it sideways.

The extra spin on the striker's ball in a roll stroke is caused by the recoil as the turf responds to the downward impact upon it. You can vary the amount of spin applied (and thus the corresponding ratio achieved) by altering the angle of the mallet face and the point of impact of the mallet on the striker's ball. To alter this you will have to alter your grip and stance correspondingly.

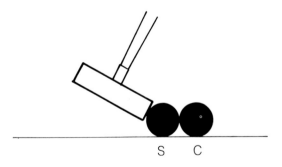

Fig 57　Roll stroke.

Half Rolls *(Fig 58)*

This stroke can be played centre style. The striker's ball should lie just in front of, or between, your toes. Hold the mallet about a third of the way down the shaft and hit the striker's ball just above its centre. It is not necessary to follow through, as the stroke is played with a 'chop' action.

Pass Rolls *(Figs 59 & 60)*

Here you must hold both hands close to the bottom of the shaft. Be careful not to touch the mallet head with your hand during a stroke, as that is a fault. The shaft should lean even further forward than for a full roll and you will thus find it necessary to crouch even lower, and have your feet a little further forward. The crouched position should be retained after impact, ensuring that the angle of the mallet head at impact is correct.

In all roll strokes, the stance is somewhat

Fig 58   The half roll – hands part-way down the shaft and over the balls.

Fig 59   The pass roll – note the position of the hands and mallet head at the address.

unnatural, so it is important to concentrate hard on the part of the ball you intend to strike. Start by practising half rolls. A good exercise here is to play half rolls from the side of hoop 5, trying to get the croqueted ball to end by hoop 6 and the striker's ball to end by the peg. When you can do that fairly consistently, try a similar exercise, this time sending the croqueted ball from hoop 1 to hoop 3. If the striker's ball goes too far, lessen the angle of the mallet face slightly, slide your hands a little further up the shaft and step a little further back. Do the opposite if the striker's ball is not going far enough in relation to the croqueted ball.

Then practise full rolls. Remember to follow through – the ideal action is a scooping action. Start with short rolls and only increase power when you have mastered the technique.

Common Mistakes

1. Make sure you swing the mallet head along a straight line. All too often players swing the mallet across their bodies in a hook action, resulting in a split shot and not the straight croquet stroke they intended to play.

2. Do not change the angle of your mallet during the swing. Many beginners address the striker's ball correctly but then, in the backswing, pull the upper arm backwards and push the lower arm forwards, thereby changing the angle of the mallet face as it strikes the ball. The result is more of a half roll or drive than a full roll. It is essential to extend both arms, not just the lower arm, in the follow through, to maintain the mallet angle in relation to the striker's ball. To do this you must continue to look down at the balls, not

Fig 60   The pass roll – note the position of David Openshaw's feet, legs and body after impact.

forward. Rock your whole body slightly forward as you play the stroke, but do not leave the crouched position.

Fig 61 gives a summary of how to play the various straight croquet strokes.

	STOP SHOT	**DRIVE**	**HALF ROLL**	**FULL ROLL**
Hands	At top of shaft.	Near top of shaft.	A third of the way down shaft.	At least half-way down shaft.
Foot Position	Half a step back from normal stance.	Normal.	Just behind balls.	Front foot by side of balls.
Stance	Erect.	Erect; knees flexed.	Slightly crouched.	Crouched; knees bent.
Mallet Head	Toe of mallet inclined up.	Mallet parallel to ground.	Heel of mallet raised slightly.	Heel of mallet raised.
Part of Ball Hit	Just below centre. 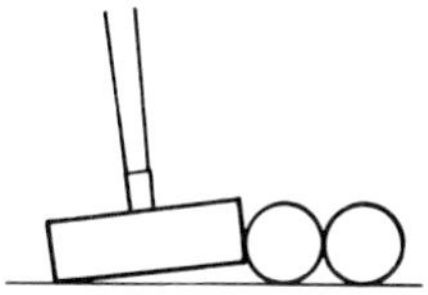	Centre. 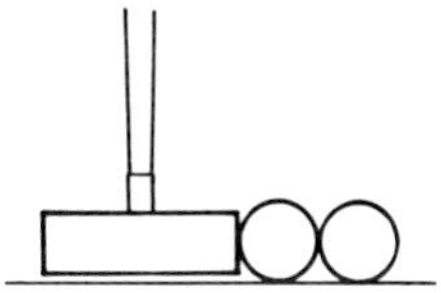	Just above centre. 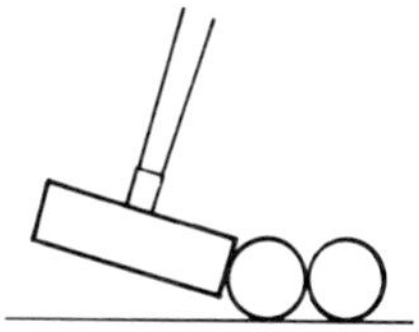	Half-way between centre and top. 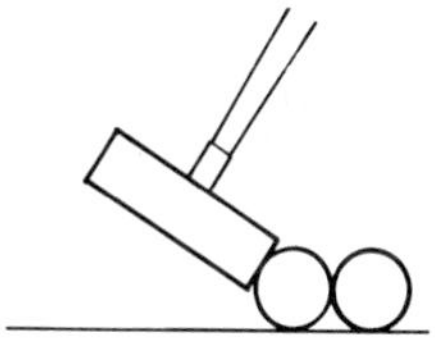
Part of Mallet Face Used	Just below centre. 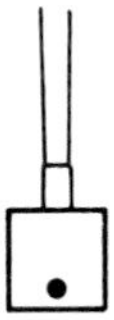	Centre. 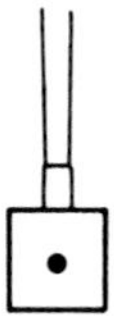	Centre. 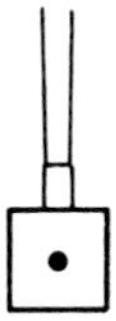	Centre. 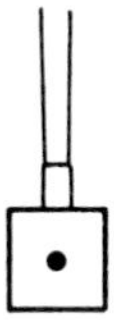
Follow Through	No.	Yes.	Yes (when playing centre style, this shot can be played with a restrained follow through action).	Yes.

Fig 61   Playing your strokes – from stop shots to rolls.

SPLIT SHOTS *(Figs 62 to 68)*

For the sake of simplification you can assume, unless otherwise indicated, that all the strokes we now introduce are played by hitting the striker's ball with the mallet head parallel to the ground, that is, with no component of roll or stop.

It is not possible, in a legal croquet stroke where both balls must move, to get the balls to diverge at an angle greater than 90 degrees. In the diagrams shown we see what is meant by the *angle of swing* and what the effects are when it is varied.

Fig 62 illustrates a straight drive. This has a zero degree angle of swing. The croqueted ball has travelled three times as far as the striker's ball.

Fig 63 illustrates a stroke played with a 20 degree angle of swing. The measurement is taken between the line of centres of the two balls and the line along which the mallet is aimed. Notice, however, that the striker's ball has not travelled along the line of swing.

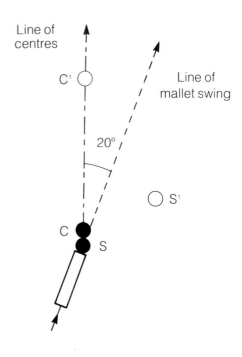

Fig 63   20° angle of swing.

Fig 64 illustrates a stroke played with a 45 degree angle of swing. Notice that the two balls have now diverged at an angle of 90 degrees and that they have travelled equal distances. As we have increased the angle of swing, the croqueted ball has not travelled so far, but the striker's ball has travelled further.

Fig 65 illustrates a stroke played with an 89 degree angle of swing. The directions which the two balls have taken are no different from those in Fig 64. Once you increase the angle of swing above 45 degrees, the directions taken by the two balls do not change, only the distances which they travel. Here, the croqueted

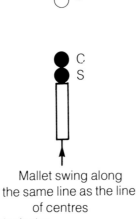

Mallet swing along
the same line as the line
of centres

Fig 62   0° angle of swing.

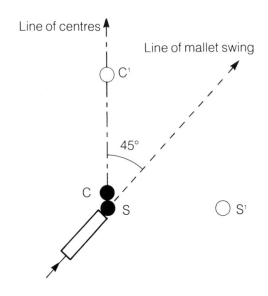

Fig 64   45° angle of swing.

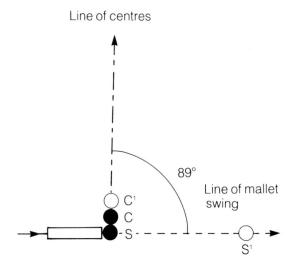

Fig 65   89° angle of swing.

ball has only just moved (it does not have to move from its position, but it must shake) but the striker's ball has travelled a long way. This is a special type of croquet stroke, known as a *take-off*. If you play a croquet stroke with an angle of swing higher than this, the croqueted ball will not move and you will have committed a fault, thereby ending your turn. You are automatically deemed to have made a fault if you play away from the croqueted ball (i.e., at an angle greater than 90 degrees).

Play a few split shots with varying angles of swing and convince yourself of the following facts:

1. The croqueted ball always travels along the line of the centres of the two balls.
2. The striker's ball never travels in the direction in which you swing the mallet, except in straight croquet strokes, or when the angle of swing approaches 90 degrees.
3. For strokes of the same strength, as you increase the angle of swing, so the croqueted ball travels less far, but the striker's ball travels further.

Using the information above, it is now possible to see that split shots should be played as follows:

1. Visualise the two places on the court where you want the two balls to stop. (Remember, it is not possible to make them diverge at an angle greater than 90 degrees).
2. Place the striker's ball behind the ball to be croqueted and in contact with it, so that the line of centres points to the place where you want the croqueted ball to finish.
3. Visualise the spot (x on Fig 68) half-way between where you want the two balls to go and aim your mallet towards that spot.
4. Calculate the type of spin required (stop shot, drive, half roll, full roll, or other – this will only come from practice and experience) and play the stroke with that spin and the required strength. Concentrate on maintaining the correct line of swing for the mallet.

59

Fig 66   A successful split shot. Notice that the mallet is pointed half-way between the final positions of the balls.

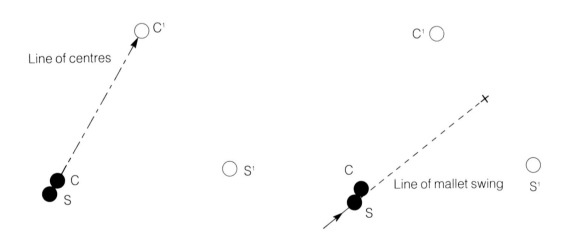

Fig 67   Split shot – placing the striker's ball.   Fig 68   Split shot – aiming the mallet.

Using the hoops, the peg, and other balls or coins as targets, you can make up your own exercises to gain as much experience as possible of playing split shots of all angles and distances.

Take-offs *(Figs 69 to 74)*

Take-offs are croquet strokes played with an angle of swing approaching 90 degrees, with the result that the striker's ball travels much further than the croqueted ball. They are of two types:

1. *Thin take-offs*, where the angle of swing is greater than 80 degrees, and the croqueted ball hardly moves. This shot is played with only one object in mind – to direct the striker's ball to a particular place on the court.
2. *Thick take-offs*, where the angle of swing is between 60 and 80 degrees. The striker's ball travels much further than the croqueted ball, but the latter is moved to a noticeable degree. Whilst the final position of the striker's ball is considered to be of primary importance, the opportunity is taken to move the croqueted ball sideways.

The figures quoted above do not represent hard and fast boundaries of definition. Thick take-offs merge gradually into thin take-offs at one end of the spectrum, and into split shots at the other end.

Let us examine two situations where the distinction becomes clearer: in Fig 69 red is taking croquet from yellow and is for hoop 3. Black is of little use but blue is right next to hoop 3. Red wants to get as close to blue as possible, so that it can roquet it and use it to make hoop 3. Yellow cannot be sent anywhere useful, so red plays a thin take-off and concentrates on getting close to blue. One advantage of playing a thin take-off is that it is almost like playing a single ball stroke, and most players find it much easier to estimate the strength of stroke required to get the striker's ball to a particular location than when

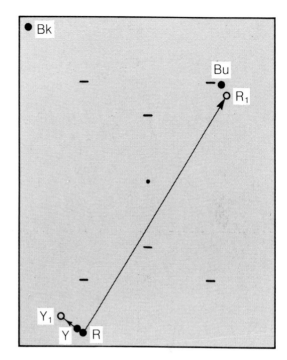

Fig 69

playing other croquet strokes.

In Fig 70 red is still going for hoop 3, with black and blue positioned as before. This time, however, it is taking croquet from yellow in a position that cries out for a thick take-off to be played. The main priority is still for red to end up close enough to blue to have an easy roquet on it, but this time an attempt should be made to nudge yellow sideways so that it ends close to hoop 4. One good thick take-off and you will have established a three-ball break as, after making hoop 3 off blue, yellow is waiting to be used to help you make hoop 4.

Thin Take-offs *(Figs 71 to 73)* Fig 71 shows how you can use your mallet to determine where to position the striker's ball. Lay your mallet on the ground so that the shaft points to the target (usually another ball) and part of the base of the mallet is touching the ball about to be croqueted. Then place the striker's ball so that it touches both the base of the mallet and the other ball. It is vital that the two balls are

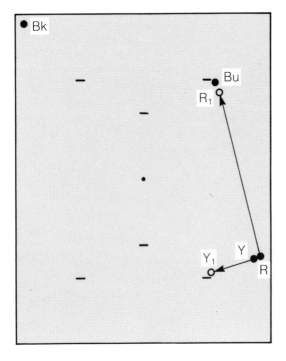

Fig 70

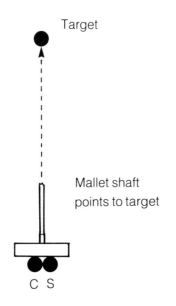

Target

Mallet shaft
points to target

C S

Fig 71   Thin take-off – placing the striker's ball.

touching, otherwise a bad shot or a fault is bound to ensue. When you have positioned the striker's ball, pick up the mallet carefully, so as not to disturb the balls. Such a use of the mallet is perfectly legal but, with experience, you should soon be able to position the striker's ball for take-offs by eyesight alone.

Fig 72 illustrates how to aim the mallet. Ideally you would like to aim directly at the target, but that would result in the other ball not being moved. To avoid that fault, aim slightly inwards towards the other ball. As you know from the section on split shots, the striker's ball will not travel along the line of aim of the mallet, but along a line at right angles to the line of centres of the balls.

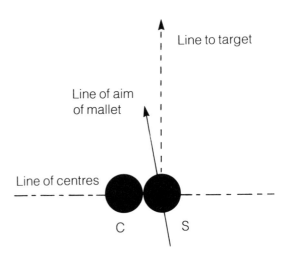

Line to target

Line of aim
of mallet

Line of centres

C   S

Fig 72   Thin take-off – aiming the mallet.

All that remains is to gauge the strength of the stroke. Because the ball to be croqueted will offer so little resistance to the striker's ball, the latter will travel just as in a single ball stroke, so gauging the strength is a relatively easy matter. Practise thin take-offs to the peg or another ball from ten yards (9m) away and, as

Fig 73　A thin take-off.

you become proficient at judging direction and strength, gradually increase the length of your take-offs. To start off with, you will probably move the croqueted ball quite far to the side, but eventually you should be able to play very thin take-offs, sending the striker's ball twenty yards (18m) whilst only moving the croqueted ball a few inches.

On a less than perfect surface you may often find it difficult to position the striker's ball for the shot so that it remains in contact with the other ball. Solve this problem by creating a slight depression where you want the striker's ball to rest, using your two thumbs together and pressing gently down into the turf.

Pull　We have introduced a theory that in split shots with angles of swing of 45 degrees or more, which naturally includes all take-offs, the striker's ball will always travel at right angles to the line of centres between the two balls involved in the croquet stroke. When you practise short take-offs you will notice

little wrong. When, however, you play a lot of take-offs of fifteen yards (13.5m) or more, you should notice a pattern emerging. When you play the stroke with the striker's ball placed to the left of the croqueted ball, the striker's ball will end up a couple of feet to the right of the target. When the striker's ball is placed on the right of the croqueted ball, the striker's ball will end up a couple of feet to the left of the target. Even in thin take-offs of thirty-three yards (29.7m) (from north to south yard-lines on a full-sized court), the deviation known as *pull* will only be four or five feet (1.2 – 1.5m) and so is unlikely to be serious. As the angle of swing decreases, however, and you consider thick take-offs and split shots, the amount of pull increases, so you must know how to amend your aiming procedure.

As a rough guide, thin take-offs are affected by pull at the rate of about eighteen inches (45cm) per ten yards (9m) travelled by the striker's ball. Thus, if you have a twenty-yard (18m) thin take-off to play, and you decide to position the striker's ball at the left of the ball to be croqueted, lay your mallet so that the shaft points three feet (90cm) to the left of the target.

It is worth mentioning here that you should avoid placing the striker's ball always on one particular side when playing thin take-offs. Sometimes there is only one sensible side to choose (for example, choosing the left-hand side in Fig 69 risks sending yellow off-court) and you do not want to develop a state of mind which reduces the likelihood of your playing a good stroke when forced to play from your 'wrong' side.

Awareness of pull, and how to counter it, is most important when peeling or when playing thick take-offs. The cause of pull is explained in Chapter 15.

Thick Take-offs *(Figs 70 & 74)*　The lower the angle of swing (given strokes of identical strength and spin), the further the croqueted ball will travel, and the greater will be the effect of pull on the striker's ball. Try to master thin take-offs, and be certain you understand the concept of pull, before practising thick take-offs.

Start practising thick take-offs by calculating the amount of pull on strokes the length of the court for varying angles of swing:

1. Line up a take-off from the yard-line on the south boundary to a target ball on the north boundary, using the method shown in Fig 71.
2. Play a thick take-off with a 70 degree angle of swing, hard enough so that the striker's ball

goes off the north boundary. Note how far wide of the target the striker's ball was when it passed to the side of the target.
3. If, for example, the amount of pull was eight feet (2.4m), repeat the stroke but position the striker's ball so that it is aiming eight feet (2.4m) to the side of the target (to the left if the striker's ball is on the left, to the right if the striker's ball is on the right).
4. Once you have fine-tuned your aiming allowance for pull, pay attention to how far to the side the croqueted ball travels when the striker's ball is hit the length of the court using a thick take-off with a given angle of swing.
5. If, for example, a 70 degree angle of swing results in eight feet (2.4m) of pull and ten yards (9m) of travel for the croqueted ball when the striker's ball travels the length of the court, you should allow for four feet (1.2m) of pull and five yards (4.5m) of travel when sending the striker's ball just half-way along the court (*see* Fig 74).

Mastery of thick take-offs requires a lot of practice. Not only must you learn to calculate the pull factor and how far the croqueted ball will travel, but, due to partial resistance from the ball to be croqueted, it becomes much more difficult to judge how hard to hit the stroke in order to get the striker's ball to a precise location on the court. However, any effort you invest will be amply rewarded. The thick take-off is a key break building stroke and opportunities to make use of it occur frequently during every game.

APPROACH STROKES (*Figs 75 to 78*)

If the hoop running stroke is croquet's equivalent of a putt in golf, then *approach strokes* are the equivalent of chips from around the green. Strokes 2 and 7 in Chapter 4's typical turn (*see* pages 29, 30 and 32 and Figs 18 and 23) were examples of these – croquet strokes where the main objective is to get the striker's ball in front of its hoop. The

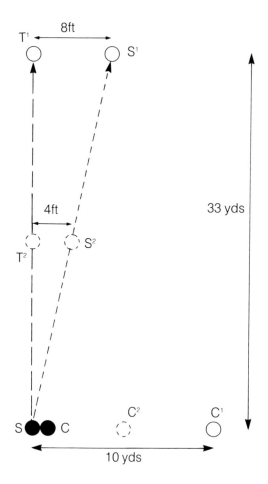

Fig 74   Thick take-offs.

Fig 75   The result of a perfect approach, giving every chance of a good rush to hoop 4.

secondary objective of approach strokes is to send the croqueted ball behind the hoop so that, when the striker's ball runs the hoop, it has a ball waiting for it that will give it an easy roquet and, hopefully, a rush to a useful position on the court.

In Fig 76 a thin take-off has been played and the striker's ball has ended up in a good position, a couple of feet (60cm) straight in front of its hoop. When, however, it runs its hoop, it will have no ball close by to roquet. How much better if a drive had been played, as in Fig 77.

As a rough guide, try and send the croqueted ball five to ten feet (1.5–3m) past the hoop, so that you need not be afraid of running the hoop firmly if the striker's ball is out of safe range to play a controlled hoop shot. If, in Fig 77, the distance to the hoop from which the approach stroke was being played was two feet (60cm), a stop shot would be required (striker's ball to travel one foot (30cm), croqueted ball to travel seven feet (2.1m)). If the distance was eight feet (2.4m), a half roll approach would be required (striker's ball to travel six feet (1.8m) croqueted ball to travel thirteen feet (3.9m)).

If you are approaching a hoop from the side, a split shot, often applying roll, will be required. When approaching a hoop from behind, a take-off should be used. In the latter case, the croqueted ball is already where you want it (behind the hoop), so you need only concentrate on positioning the striker's ball. In such short take-offs pull is negligible and can be ignored. Such take-off approaches from behind the hoop are known as *backward take-offs*.

In your early croquet career you should concentrate on practising and improving your 'short game'. Every golfer knows that more shots are wasted on and around the green than in getting to it. Similarly in croquet, the rewards are proportionately greater for practising and improving your short game, rather than becoming the master of, for example, a full court pass roll which, spectacular though it may be, is rarely required.

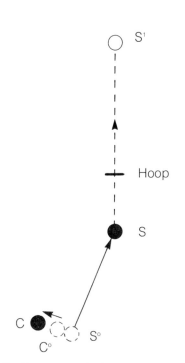

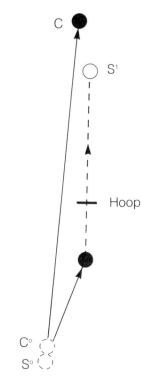

Fig 76   Hoop approach – incorrect.

Fig 77   Hoop approach – correct.

Fig 78   A backward take-off: George Latham making sure the line is right!

TWO-BALL GAMES

Two-ball games are a useful introduction to Association Croquet and provide plenty of opportunities to practise the various types of croquet strokes. *See* Chapter 9 for details of how to play.

7 Attacking Play

Your mental approach to croquet will have a significant bearing on how much you enjoy the sport, how skilful you become and, ultimately, how successful you are. 'Fortune favours the brave' should be the motto of all croquet players. We urge you to adopt an attacking philosophy. Those of you who are prepared to lose some games in the early part of your croquet careers, in order to test your skills to the limit (and thus to extend them), will be richly rewarded later on.

Unfortunately, too many players take the view that their main objective should be to prevent their opponents from making any progress. This 'play safe' strategy inhibits them from experimentation in game situations and retards the development of their skills, to say nothing of increasing the tedium of the games they play. Proponents of this 'Aunt Emma' defensive school of thought are left wondering why their early success against fellow beginners who experiment evaporates, and why they cannot beat single figure handicap players in handicap games.

Attacking play means creating, and playing breaks.

BREAKS

Two-ball Breaks (Figs 79 & 81)

The simplest form of break, a *two-ball break*, involves using only the striker's ball and one other. In Fig 79 Ray is playing a two-ball break. Red, the striker's ball, has just run hoop 4 and has a straight rush on yellow to hoop 5. Ray plays this well and yellow comes to rest close to hoop 5. He takes croquet from yellow with red and has an easy approach stroke to get in

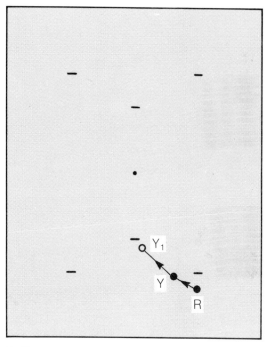

Fig 79

position for hoop 5. Fig 81 shows the position after that approach stroke.

Ray runs hoop 5 with red but does not get a rush on yellow to hoop 6 and consequently fails to make further progress. He has played a two-hoop, two-ball break, that is, he has scored two hoops by means of using only two balls.

Although this is the simplest form of break to understand it is the hardest to play, as every shot must be extremely accurate. Ray's turn ended because he made a slight mistake in running hoop 5 too hard and did not gain a rush to hoop 6. To sustain a two-ball break, it is vital that you get a good rush after every hoop. It is usually a better tactic to utilise your control of two balls to construct three or four-ball

Fig 80   Attack! Carl von Schmieder in predatory mood.

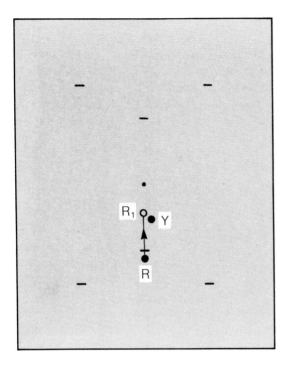

Fig 81

breaks which, once started, are easier to sustain.

The two-ball break illustrates the first important principle of break play. To score a hoop you need a ball other than the striker's ball near the hoop, so that the striker's ball can use it to play an approach stroke to the hoop. In our opening example, Ray had yellow available near hoops 4 and 5, from which red could take croquet, but had no ball near hoop 6 and thus was unable to make that hoop.

There are two ways of positioning a ball, other than the striker's ball, near a hoop you want to make in that turn:

1. By rushing it there.
2. By putting it there well before you need to use it. In this case it is called a *pioneer*. Sometimes your opponent may be generous enough to leave you a pioneer at the hoop you want, but normally you have to put it there yourself, as you will see.

Three-ball Breaks *(Figs 82 to 89)*

Fig 82 shows the initial layout (*see also* Figs 83 and 84). This time Bab is in play, blue is the striker's ball, taking croquet from yellow at hoop 1. Black is the pioneer for hoop 2.

Bab plays an approach stroke, runs hoop 1 and roquets yellow again. She now takes croquet as shown in Fig 85. She plays a big split roll, sending yellow as a pioneer to hoop 3 and blue to black. She roquets black with blue, plays an approach stroke, runs the hoop and roquets black again. She now takes croquet from black again, as shown in Fig 86. She plays another split shot, sending black as a pioneer to hoop 4 and blue to yellow.

The second important principle of break play is now emerging: when you have made a hoop, send the ball you used as a pioneer for that hoop as the pioneer for the *next but one* hoop.

If the striker makes a mistake when playing a break, causing her to end her turn before she

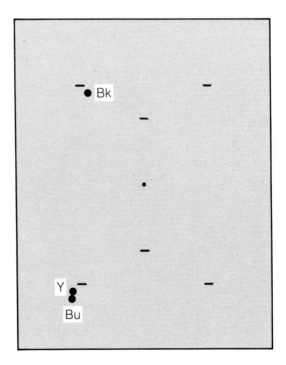

Fig 82

Fig 83   A three-ball break, sending a pioneer to hoop 2.

Fig 84   A three-ball break, roqueting the ball at hoop 1.

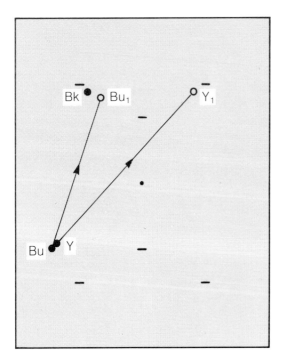

Fig 85

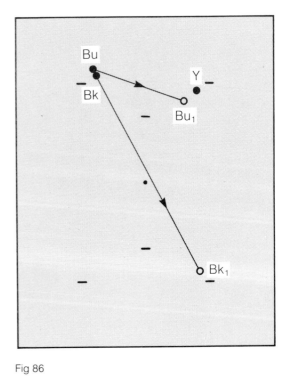

Fig 86

would wish to, she is said to have *broken down*. Thus, in the example above, if Bab broke down before hoop 6 she will have made a five-hoop, three-ball break.

The three-ball break shown here is easier to sustain than a two-ball break, but it can be improved by avoiding having to play so many difficult big split shots. If, after hoop 1, you can get a rush on yellow towards corner 2, you could rush yellow off the west boundary near hoop 2, as shown in Fig 87. You now have a much easier croquet stroke to play than the big split roll shown in Fig 85. All that is required is a straight drive, sending yellow to hoop 3 and blue to black, as shown in Fig 88.

Similarly, a rush after hoop 2 to a position on the north boundary near hoop 3 will leave you a much easier shot to send blue to yellow and black as a pioneer to hoop 4, as we see in Fig 89. Try to work out where to aim rushes to after the subsequent hoops.

Thus you have learned the third important principle of break play: use rushes to make the

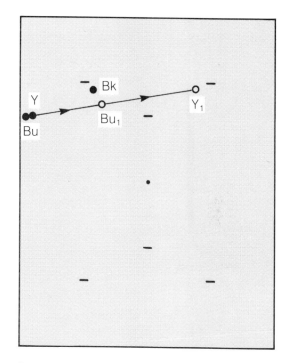

Fig 88

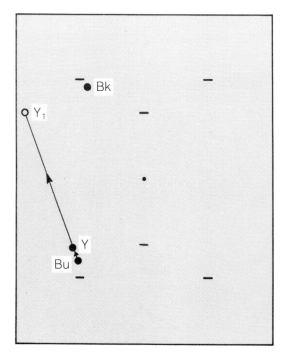

Fig 87

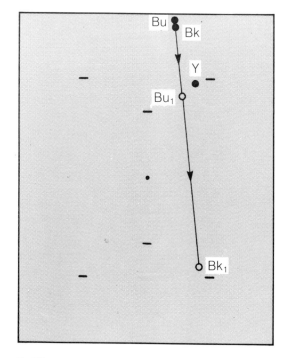

Fig 89

croquet strokes in the break easier.

One result of applying the third principle is that your pioneers will generally become more accurate – the easier the stroke you play, the smaller will be the margin of error when playing the stroke. The logical result of more accurate pioneers is easier approach strokes and, thus, a higher probability of scoring the hoop in question.

A three-ball break is therefore less demanding to sustain than a two-ball break. We next find Ray playing the easiest break of all.

Four-ball Breaks *(Figs 90 to 93)*

Fig 90 shows the initial layout. Red is the striker's ball. Ray plays an approach stroke, runs hoop 1 and roquets yellow again. He places red in contact with yellow as shown in Fig 91 and plays a half roll, sending yellow as a pioneer to hoop 3 and red to blue.

Red roquets blue and plays a take-off to black, as shown in Fig 92, leaving blue near the

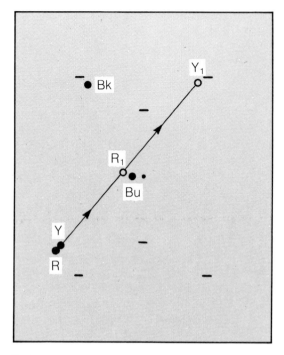

Fig 91

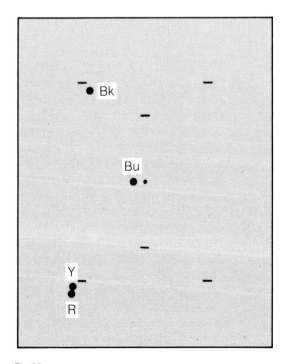

Fig 90

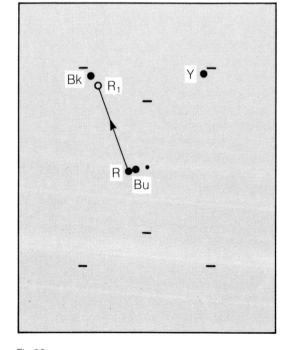

Fig 92

peg. He roquets black with red, plays an approach stroke to hoop 2, runs it, and roquets black again. He places red in contact with black as shown in Fig 93, and plays a half roll, sending black as a pioneer to hoop 4 and red to blue.

Blue is roqueted, Ray plays a take-off to yellow, roquets it with red, and the break continues. If he manages to make all twelve hoops he is said to have made an *all-round four-ball break*.

You should have noticed that one ball (blue in our example) remains close to the peg. Ideally it should always be the same side of the peg as the hoop you have just made. You can manoeuvre it around the peg when playing take-offs from it, or when roqueting it. Because this ball remains in the centre of the court and the break revolves around it, it is known as the *pivot*. The reason it should be kept close to the peg is so that rolls of a ratio lower than half rolls never have to be played. Can you then understand why, after hoop 3, it

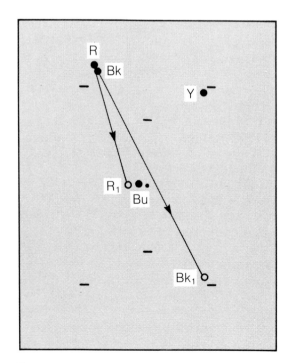

Fig 93

is best to move the pivot three yards (2.7m) or so south-east of the peg?

Only the following types of strokes are *necessary* constituents of a four-ball break: roquets, hoop shots, half rolls, thin take-offs and approach strokes. You need to practise these strokes, and become reasonably competent in playing them, if you wish to play successful four-ball breaks.

You can use any rushes obtained in the course of your break to rush the pioneer closer to the pivot and thus avoid having to play a half roll. Depending on whether you prefer to play drives or stop shots, you will accordingly rush the pioneer a few yards behind or just behind the pivot. The one advantage of playing stop shots in your break is that you will be delivering the pioneer to the next hoop from a position much closer to the hoop than if you played a half roll or drive, thus improving the accuracy of your pioneer.

Precise positioning of your pioneers will improve your break by making subsequent strokes easier. The best position for a pioneer to the outer hoops (1 to 4 and 1-back to 4-back) is just within the corners of the *inner rectangle* (*see* Fig 94). This is the rectangle which has hoops 1 to 4 as its corner points.

You might think that, at hoop 3, it would be better to have the pioneer in front of the hoop. It is important to remember, however, that you will be playing a take-off from blue to yellow, intending to get a rush on yellow to as close to hoop 3 as possible. If you put yellow in the Y1 position in Fig 95 you will have to play a take-off about ten feet (3m) longer than that required to get a rush on a pioneer in the Y position (2 – 3ft (60 – 90cm) inside the corner of the inner rectangle).

Short take-offs will, naturally, be more consistently accurate than longer ones, which is why all pioneers to the outer hoops should ideally be close to the corners of, but inside, the inner rectangle.

We are now in a position to state our fourth, and main, principle of break play, which encompasses the three principles already

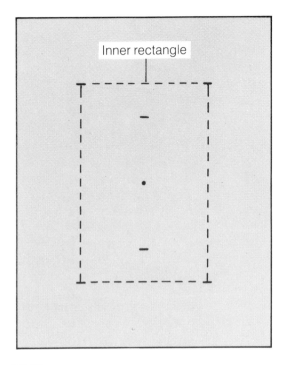

Fig 94

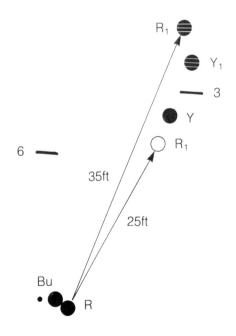

Fig 95 Positioning your pioneer.

stated: play every stroke in such a way that the subsequent strokes become shorter and easier.

BISQUES

'This is all very well,' you are no doubt thinking, 'but it will take weeks of practice before I can play the strokes well enough to make attempting to play breaks worthwhile. After all, one mistake, the whole thing is up the spout, and I've handed my opponent a good position on a plate'.

This would be true but for the fact that all the early games of your croquet career should be (and will be if you join a good club) played according to handicap rules. One of the great advantages of croquet is that it has a handicap system which works very well. It is possible for relative beginners to play the best players and have an exciting game.

Official handicaps in England range from −2 (best) to 18 (beginners), although some clubs extend the range upwards to 24 or 32 to cater for the differences between beginners when they play each other. Why use minus values? Why not have the range from 0 to 20? The reason is to give a special status to those players who achieve a minus handicap – they are players who regularly create breaks from difficult positions, invariably complete breaks with control and often attempt complex man-oeuvres such as triple peels (see Chapter 15).

How does the system work? If a 15 plays a 7, then the 15 will receive 8 free turns (15−7), known as *bisques*. Bisques are generally represented physically by white sticks, about a foot (30cm) long, which are taken to the court and stuck into the ground near where the outplayer will be sitting (see Fig 192). As each free turn is used, a bisque is removed from the row.

A bisque can be used at any time in the game, following your normal turn. You could, for example, after playing the first ball on to the court to a position in front of hoop 1, take a bisque and try to run hoop 1. Because, however, a bisque gives you a new turn, it is not normal to start using your bisques until all the balls have been played on to the court – you can then roquet each ball after taking a bisque and get a large number of strokes for each bisque you take.

Some beginners get confused and think that because they roqueted a ball, say blue, in the turn before taking the bisque, they will not be able to roquet blue in the bisque turn. In practice you remain on the court when taking a bisque, and merely indicate to your opponent that you wish to take one, waiting for them to remove it from the ground before you continue. Nevertheless, it is easier to visualise what a bisque represents by considering that you have left the court at the end of your turn, but come back on immediately for your bisque turn. Thus you can always roquet the other three balls again after taking a bisque and any balls off-court or in the yard-line area must be replaced on to the yard-line before you start your bisque turn.

You may take bisques one at a time, at odd moments during the game, to rectify mistakes you have made, such as sticking in a hoop or missing a short roquet on an opponent's ball. The attacking way to use bisques, however, is to take them one after another, to give yourself a number of turns in succession with a view to creating and playing a break.

Half Bisques

Above handicap 8, handicaps go up in intervals of one, i.e. 8, 9, 10, 11 and so on. Below handicap 8, however, handicaps are at intervals of a half, i.e. 8, 7½, 7, 6½, 6 and so on. So, for example, if a 12 plays a 6½, the 12 will receive 5½ bisques; if a 9 plays a −1½, the 9 will receive 10½ bisques.

What, then, is a half bisque? A half bisque, physically represented by a shorter white stick, gives you a new turn but has a restriction imposed upon it, in that you are not allowed, in that turn, to score a point (you cannot hit

the peg to peg out, run a hoop or project another ball through its hoop or peg it out).

At most you can only have one half bisque in a game. Many players keep their half bisque until late in the game, in case they need to regain the innings to avoid losing. The best use for a half bisque, when you also have full bisques, is to help you set up a four-ball break before using your full bisques immediately afterwards to play the break.

Control of Handicaps

When you join a club you will be given a handicap by the club handicap committee, who will thereafter monitor it and alter it when necessary. If you enter a recognised tournament, open to players from different clubs, your handicap will then be subject to alteration by the official handicapper of that tournament. He or she will usually be a nationally appointed handicapper, who will consult with other national handicappers present at the tournament and the host club handicap committee.

Club handicap committees do not normally alter the handicaps of players who regularly play in such Open tournaments, but rather use those players as guides to the grading of handicaps within their own clubs.

The Class System Players are said to belong to one of four classes, depending on their handicaps and corresponding ability (without use of bisques). The boundaries between the classes are vague, but here is a rough guide:

A Class (handicap below 2): often create and play all-round breaks from difficult positions. Attempt complex peeling manoeuvres (*see* Chapter 15).
B Class (2 – 6½): regularly make long breaks from easy positions.
C Class (7 – 11): usually make one break of 5 or 6 hoops in a game.
D Class (12 and above): rarely make more than 3 hoops in a turn.

Creating Breaks Using Bisques

Here we offer some advice to C and D Class players. Let us imagine that in the first round of your club handicap tournament you are drawn to play an A Class player. There you are, with a fistful of bisques, just having won the toss. What should you do?

The winning strategy against A Class players is simple – the first turn you have when there are four balls on the court, you should start taking your bisques in a row to set up and play a four-ball break. If you play well, you should be able to play one ball all the way round with half your bisques, and use the other half to play the second ball round and win. You have not got time to play a few turns 'to get the feel of the lawn' before taking your bisques. If you do that, the A Class player will hit in, play one ball round, and you will be the one under pressure. If you get your ball round first, it will be the A Class player under pressure, and that pressure can tell.

Having won the toss, you must make the A Class player play first. That way he or she will have to hit in on turn three, and play a three-ball break if they are to get a ball round before you. You get the first opportunity to play with four balls on the lawn.

The playing of the four balls on to the court and the few strokes thereafter is known as the *opening*. We will now examine the classic handicap opening against an A Class player.

Let us say the A Class player chooses red and yellow. In the classic style, red is played from A-baulk and hit off the east boundary, a couple of yards (1.8m) north of corner 4. You should now play your ball, say blue, from A-baulk, and hit it into the court so that it comes to rest three or four yards (2.7 – 3.6m) north and slightly west of hoop 4. This stroke alone will make the A-class player realise they have a match on their hands and not, as possibly anticipated, a leisurely stroll through to round two. The usual reaction is to play yellow from B-baulk into corner 2, which says 'All right, I

know you are going to take your bisques straight away, but let's see how many you waste setting up a four-ball break from this position'. As Fig 96 shows, it certainly looks daunting.

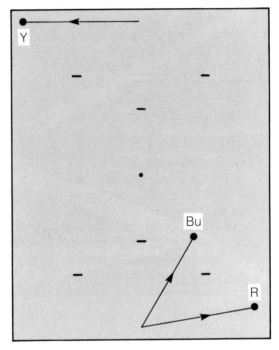

Fig 96

Did you notice how each of the first three strokes was played to send the balls well away from the baulk lines? Never leave your balls near either baulk line when your opponent still has a ball to play on to the court.

Play black from A-baulk and shoot at red. If you miss, take your half-bisque (if you have one) or a full bisque (if you haven't). Now play a straight drive (see Fig 97), concentrating on sending red as close to hoop 2 as possible. Black should stop close to blue – now you should see why we advised you to position blue there in the first place.

Now roquet blue and play a straight croquet stroke, concentrating on getting blue as close as possible to hoop 1, the position of black being relatively unimportant. Then shoot black at yellow. Fig 98 shows the position,

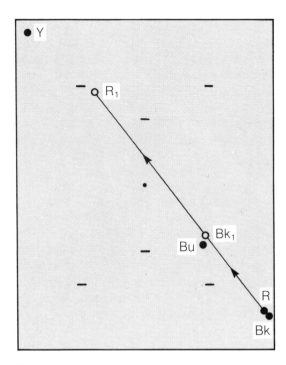

Fig 97

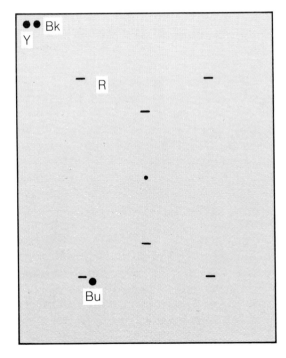

Fig 98

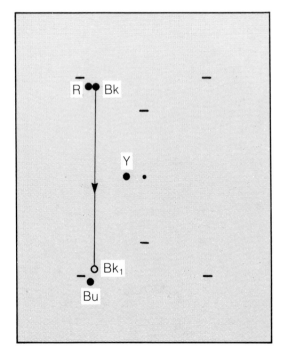

Fig 99

assuming black just missed yellow:

What we have done so far is to establish pioneers at hoops 1 and 2, so naturally yellow is to become our pivot. Take a bisque if you missed yellow and roquet it. Now play a croquet stroke to send yellow close to the peg and black to red. If you hit the long shot at yellow, you will now need to take another bisque because you haven't run a hoop since you last roqueted red. Roquet red, play a thin take-off with black to blue and your four-ball break is set up – you are ready to go (*see* Fig 99).

At best you can set up the four-ball break from that daunting position for only one bisque, and if you miss the long roquets, but play your croquet strokes well, it will only cost you one and a half or two bisques. If you are a D Class player, you should be happy to set up the break in these circumstances for three bisques.

When you are playing a B or C Class player and you have more than a couple of bisques, you must be on the look-out for opportunities to set up breaks cheaply. There is no need to use your bisques right at the beginning of the game, as these players do not threaten to beat you in a couple of turns. Unless a golden opportunity comes earlier, look for the chance to set up a break using bisques when your ball is for hoop 3 or 4. This strategy has two advantages:

1. You will start your break having got used to the pace of the court.
2. The 'run up the middle', from hoop 4 to hoop 1-back, is the easiest part of the break, as the distances between the hoops are much shorter than between the outer hoops. Thus the strokes required should not be as long or difficult as starting a break from hoop 1.

Fig 100 is a good example of how to set up a break in this position. Here black is for hoop 3. Yellow is about two yards (1.8m) from both the north and west boundaries. What should you (handicap 12) do? A couple of our friends

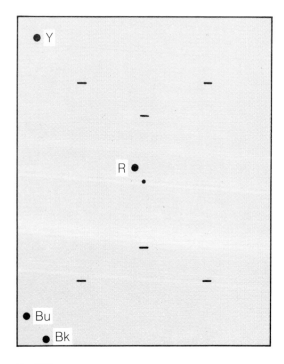

Fig 100

might do something like this:

1. Aunt Emma would roquet blue, play a thin take-off to red and rush or roll red to hoop 3. Whilst this is a fairly disaster-free tactic, it yields at most one hoop forty per cent of the time.
2. Hothead Harry would roquet blue and play a split shot, trying to send blue to hoop 4 and hoping to get black a rush on red. A fine tactic for an A Class player, but a recipe for disaster for Harry. At best, with his level of skill, blue will be a poor pioneer and black will get some kind of rush on red. At worst, blue will be sent off-court, or black will be three yards (2.7m) or more away from red, and Harry will miss the roquet in trying to play a rush. This tactic at least has the merit of trying to construct a break, but lacks the realism of adapting tactics to your own skill level.

You are more aware of your own limitations. Have you spotted yet how to set up a good break for one bisque, using no stroke of more than moderate difficulty? Bab will demonstrate . . .

She roquets blue and then plays a roll, sending blue vaguely towards the peg, but concentrating on getting black close enough to red to roquet it. Because she is only concentrating hard on the position of one of the two balls, the stroke is more likely to be successful than if she were trying to place both balls accurately. She then roquets red with black and plays a straight croquet stroke, not worrying about the position of black, but concentrating solely on sending red as close as possible to hoop 3. We see the position now in Fig 101.

She now shoots at yellow, misses, but is unconcerned, as she knew she would get a good rush out into the court. She rushes yellow towards blue, croquets yellow to hoop 4, roquets blue and only has to play a thin take-off to red to complete the setting up of the break.

The key to that puzzle was the position of yellow. If yellow were actually in corner 2 (on

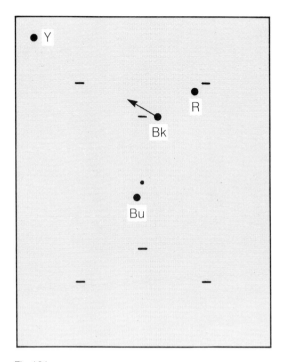

Fig 101

could well cost you another bisque, it is worth playing the roll stroke in order to use red as the pioneer.

Let's look at another situation. In Fig 102, black is the ball you want to get a break for. It is for hoop 4, and for one bisque you should be able to set up a good break. You already have, courtesy of your opponent, a reasonable pioneer at hoop 5 (yellow). Black, blue and red are all yard-line balls. What you should not do is shoot black at blue, because if black misses and ends up south of blue (as is likely from the angle of the shot) you will have wasted a great opportunity.

Instead, aim black about three or four feet (90 – 120cm) to the left of blue, so that when you replace it on the yard-line, you can take your bisque and you will have a good rush in the general direction of hoop 4. 'Hang on!', you may say, 'do you expect me to rush blue within a few feet of hoop 4, so that I am certain of making the hoop after my approach stroke?'. No, but you ought to be able to rush

the yard-line), we would not recommend that play, because a long and very difficult half or three-quarter roll would be required to send yellow to hoop 4 and black to blue. To have to play such a difficult stroke with the end position of both balls being important would put you back in a Hothead Harry situation.

Always keep an eye out for balls just in from the yard-line, as they offer excellent break building opportunities. You can shoot at them from a long way off, knowing that if you miss you will have a good rush into the court.

Some of you may think you spotted an alternative and easier way to construct the break in the example above: having roqueted blue, send blue directly to hoop 3 in the croquet stroke, then shoot black at yellow. True, this obviates the need to play the roll stroke to red but, by laying the hoop 3 pioneer from near corner 1, it is unlikely that that pioneer will be very accurate. In contrast, you ought to be able to lay a very accurate pioneer from the position of red. As a bad pioneer

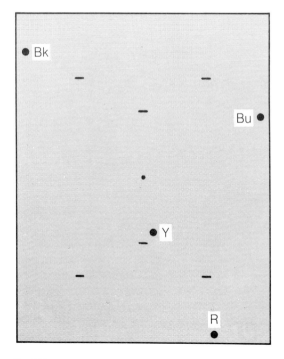

Fig 102

blue within a few yards of hoop 4, making sure in the process that you cut blue into the court.

The key here is the position of red. You have no need to play an approach stroke to send a ball behind hoop 4, because red is already there. Thus, if you can rush blue to the position shown in Fig 103, all that is required is a thin take-off to get black in front of hoop 4, then you can run the hoop hard, roquet red and you have your four-ball break.

Remember the position of red. A ball behind hoop 2, hoop 4, hoop 2-back or hoop 4-back is almost as good as a pioneer when you are approaching those hoops and want to construct a break.

If you are only receiving one or two bisques in a game, save them for emergencies or high profit situations. A good example of a high profit situation is when you stick in a hoop during a good four-ball break, and your opponent is for the same hoop, with an easy roquet.

In Fig 104 both red and black are for hoop 4.

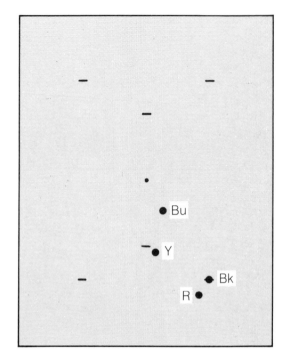

Fig 104

If you (black) take a bisque, you have a good chance of making four hoops or more, whilst if you do not take a bisque, red will have a similar opportunity. Taking the bisque could make a difference of 8 points or more, and this is therefore a high profit situation that should not be missed, even if you only have one bisque. The theorists can argue until the cows come home about the psychological advantage of keeping your bisque until as late in the game as possible. Here is a situation that may only occur once in the game and the percentage play is to take this opportunity to get as much for your bisque as possible.

Common Mistakes
(Figs 105 to 108)

1. The most common mistake (known as the 'windscreen wiper') occurs when a bad take-off or half roll has been played, and the striker's ball needs to make a roquet of eight feet (2.4m) or more on the pivot or pioneer.

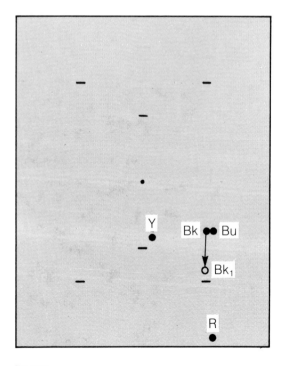

Fig 103

Too often, beginners assume they will make the roquet, shoot firmly and end up missing, with their ball coming to rest ten feet (3m) or so away on the far side of the target, nicely placed for an encore. In trying to save a bisque, two or more end up being used.

The remedy is to establish the maximum distance at which you *never* miss roquets. Be honest – you are probably talking about five or six feet (1.5–1.8m). Then if during a break using bisques, you are required to make a roquet at a longer distance, shoot softly. Aim to go no more than two feet (60cm) past the target, so that you can be certain of making a roquet if a bisque has to be taken.

2. Never give up a break in disgust at your play if you still have bisques left. You may have wasted three or four bisques trying to make a hoop, but, if you were right to take those bisques a few moments ago, it is likely that the situation is still ripe for taking another bisque.

The remedy is to stand back and cool down for a moment to consider whether it is a high profit situation for taking a bisque. On no account leave an A or B Class player a short shot with all four balls still in the middle of the court.

3. Bisques are often wasted by attempting long or very angled hoops. Once again, in trying to save a bisque, two are often needed when the ball strikes the wire and sticks on it.

The remedy is to learn to identify situations where there is a danger of having to use two bisques if a risky stroke does not pay off. Then, do not take the risk. Instead, use one bisque to get a better position and ensure success.

4. Where, near a hoop, a bisque has to be taken, beginners often use it just to position the striker's ball in front of the hoop, instead of getting the full benefit of it to improve the positions of the other badly placed balls. In Fig 105 we see the result of a roll approach from the side of the hoop that has not worked.

The beginner may be tempted simply to hit red into position to run the hoop (*see* Fig 105(a)), take a bisque, run the hoop and hit yellow. Yellow is not, however, in a good

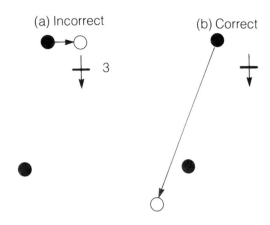

Fig 105   Taking a bisque.

position to give you the chance of a rush towards hoop 4.

The remedy is to use your continuation stroke to hit red to a position behind yellow, as shown in Fig 105(b). Take a bisque and rush yellow three feet (90cm) or so north of hoop 3. That leaves a simple hoop approach to send yellow five feet (1.5m) south of hoop 3 and get red in position to run the hoop.

5. Beginners are far too reluctant to use a bisque in the middle of a break to tidy it up. Instead, they try to patch up a deteriorating position by playing strokes beyond their capabilities and they end up spending bisques anyway, without improving their position.

In Fig 106, Red, the striker's ball, is for hoop 3. It has just played a take-off from blue but has failed to get a rush on the poorly positioned yellow to its hoop. As we can see, black and blue are also out of position. The mistake here would be to roquet yellow and try a long approach stroke to hoop 3, with only a slight chance of success.

The correct play is to invest a bisque to improve the break by playing the following sequence of much simpler strokes: roquet yellow and then play a straight croquet stroke, concentrating on sending yellow to the ideal pioneer position at hoop 3. As you are fairly close to hoop 3, this should be fairly easy, especially as we are not concerned about the

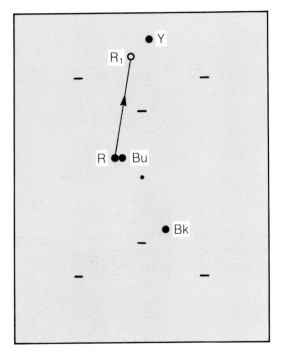

Fig 106

final position of red. Now, as shown in Fig 107, red should, in the continuation stroke, be hit to a position four or five feet (1.2–1.5m) north-west of blue.

Take a bisque and rush blue close to black. Then play a croquet stroke to send blue as your pioneer to hoop 4 (it should be fairly accurate as you will be delivering it from a position relatively close to hoop 4) and try and get a rush on black towards hoop 3 (*see* Fig 108). Rush black to a position level with the peg, play a thin take-off to yellow and you have your break.

6. Do you notice how we are urging you to develop tactics that avoid playing difficult strokes, for example long split shots, long rolls or strokes where positioning both balls is both critical and difficult? The moral is to avoid playing strokes that have a low percentage chance of success. Consider what to do, for example, if your ball is for hoop 2 and you have just roqueted the last ball you are entitled to roquet. You are taking croquet some twenty

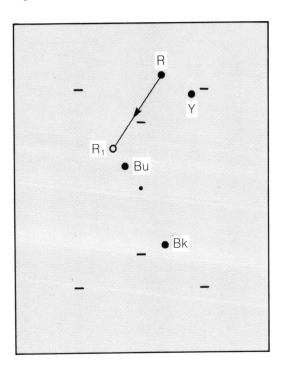

Fig 107

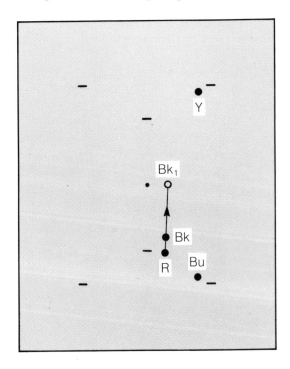

Fig 108

yards (18m) from hoop 2, but the other two balls are in good positions as pioneer for hoop 3 and pivot respectively. Obviously you want to create a four-ball break and it can be done for, at the most, one bisque.

The wrong play (for a C or D Class player) is to try and play a long roll up to the hoop. The chances of getting the striker's ball into position to run the hoop are very low (5 per cent?) and, because you played a difficult stroke in your greed to save a bisque, it is likely that you end up with the croqueted ball some way from the hoop, necessitating a rush in the bisque turn.

The correct play is to play a straight croquet stroke, concentrating solely on positioning the croqueted ball as close to hoop 2 as possible. With your continuation stroke, hit the striker's ball as close to the croqueted ball as possible.

CONCLUSION

If you want to become a good croquet player, you must learn to play breaks. Practise the five constituent strokes of the four-ball break, and then set out the balls as shown in Fig 90. Practise playing a six-hoop break, taking a bisque or bisques when you break down. Keep a record of how many bisques you need to make the six hoops and then try to beat your lowest bisque total in subsequent practices.

When setting up and playing a four-ball break in a match, don't be greedy. Be prepared to spend an extra bisque to set up a tidy break, rather than start trying to make hoops when the break is untidy or one ball is still on the boundary. Attack, but not kamikaze style!

8 Defensive Play

We have urged you to adopt an attacking philosophy when playing croquet. There is a thin dividing line, however, between adventurousness and recklessness. If your croquet armoury is to be complete, you must have an understanding of some basic defensive tactics and be able to recognise occasions when discretion is the better part of valour.

Defensive tactics need to be considered:

1. At the end of a turn in which you have had the innings.
2. Near the end of games in which you have a slight advantage.
3. When you are the outplayer.

LEAVES *(Fig 109)*

The last few strokes of a turn when you have had the innings and have not broken down will determine the position of the balls on the court faced by your opponent at the start of his turn. The position you bequeath to your opponent is known as the *leave*. The act of preparing the leave is known as *laying up*. A good leave will:

1. Not give your opponent the chance of a short shot to regain the innings.
2. Make any shot your opponent takes dangerous, that is, if the shot is missed it will give you an easy chance to construct a break. It will thus tempt your opponent not to take a shot, thereby guaranteeing you the innings.
3. Give you a chance of making progress, even if your opponent plays the best available defensive stroke.
4. Not give your opponent an easy break if he hits any shot.

A good leave is shown in Fig 109. Red and yellow are both for hoop 1, black is for hoop 2 and blue is for hoop 3. Black is wired from both blue and yellow by hoops 2 and 1 respectively, and blue is wired from both black and red by hoops 2 and 1 respectively. How does this leave satisfy the four conditions above?

Firstly, Bab only has two possible shots to retain the innings (black at red or blue at yellow), both of which are very long shots. Secondly, a miss in either case would leave the ball on the south boundary near to red. Red could then easily roquet that ball and stop shot it towards hoop 2 (if it were black) or the peg (if it were blue), going to yellow, and thereby

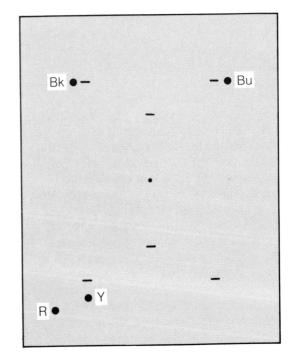

Fig 109

easily constructing a four-ball break. Bab will be very tempted to hit black into corner 4 – this is the best defensive stroke available, as it removes the pioneer for Ray's next hoop and places it well away from the area of the court where Ray will be trying to construct his break.

Thirdly, even if Bab plays black to corner 4, Ray has a good chance of making progress. Red should be able to make hoop 1 easily and, if he can get a rush on yellow after hoop 1 to hoop 2 and can make that hoop, he will have a three-ball break.

Fourthly, if blue should shoot and hit yellow, there are no balls near hoops 3 or 4, so it will be very difficult for blue to construct a break and a long, very accurate rush would be needed to make hoop 3. If black should shoot and hit red, it will not have a ball near hoop 2 and, if you study Fig 109 carefully, you will notice that neither yellow nor blue can be rushed close to hoop 2 because other hoops are in the way.

The leave above satisfies the four principles outlined. It also utilises two elements of defensive tactics to do this – wiring and a trap. Let us now study those and other defensive tactics employed in leaves in detail.

Wiring *(Figs 110 to 114)*

It can be very useful, as we saw above, to use the peg or a hoop or hoops to prevent one or both of your opponent's balls from being able to shoot at some of the other balls following your leave. Notice we say *some*. You must leave each opponent ball a shot at at least one other ball. If you do not, that is, if you wire an opponent ball from all the other balls, then your opponent may claim a *lift* with that ball at the start of their next turn. If, by carelessness, you give your opponent a lift and they claim it, they may play that ball back on to court from either of the baulk-lines. This is obviously a great advantage for them, giving them the chance of a short shot, and should be avoided. Four conditions must be fulfilled for them to be able to claim a lift with a particular ball:

1. You are responsible for the position of that ball: you hit it to that position or it got there as a result of your actions, for example, a fault you made, or, if it shook or bounced away from the side of a hoop, as a result of a stroke of yours that caused the hoop to vibrate.
2. That ball does not have an open shot at any of the other balls on the court. In Fig 110 black is not 'open' to blue because it could not be hit on its right-hand side by the left-hand side of blue. Any part of the relevant ball must be able to hit any part of the target ball.
3. That ball must not be in contact with another ball.
4. It must be the start of your opponent's turn.

One special case is when any part of a ball is in the jaws of a hoop. In that case, it is automatically considered to be wired from all other balls and thus fulfils condition 2 above. If, in laying up, you carelessly send an opponent's ball into a hoop, you must either make sure all the other three balls are well away from the baulk-lines, or, if that is not

Fig 110   Blue is technically wired from black.

possible, voluntarily give up the innings and separate your balls to prevent your opponent having an easy chance of a break.

As long as you take care to avoid giving away lifts, wiring can be a very powerful defensive tactic. When you are completing a break, try and position your two opponent's balls first after making your last hoop. Then try to rush your own ball to a position on court that gives you a chance of wiring one or both of your balls from one or both of the opponent's balls. Similarly, look out for the opportunity of wiring your opponent's balls from each other – watch how good players sometimes *cross-wire* opponents' balls, that is, place them either side of a single hoop or the peg. C and D Class players should not try to construct cross-wire situations from nothing, as their skill levels are liable to let them down and present their opponents with easy roquets, but they should be on the look-out for golden opportunities that occur from time to time, as shown in Fig 111.

Here red is for rover and yellow is for hoop 5. Ray, forced to play with red because it was left near hoop 6, has shot at and hit black, without moving it far. Instead of making rover, he should concentrate on getting a good cross-wire at yellow's hoop. From this position it should be easy. Fig 112 shows the position in more detail.

He should play a thin take-off from black to the position shown (R1). From there he can rush blue into a spot wired from black. Because it is blue's hoop, he takes care not to leave blue in a position where it can run the hoop. With his croquet stroke he should not take off to yellow, or he risks sending blue out of position. If he already has a perfect cross-wire, he plays a short thin take-off, which will just shake blue and will send red to a position from which he can swing the mallet freely, to send it towards yellow in the continuation stroke. If the cross-wire has not been set up, he plays a short stop shot to send blue to a cross-wired position – but only if blue is already close to the cross-wire position. If he played a

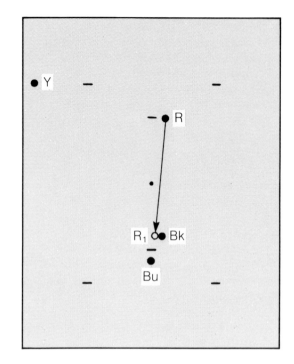

Fig 111

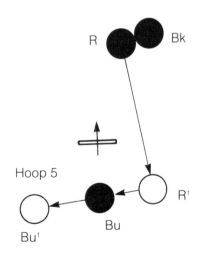

Fig 112   Cross-wiring.

bad rush, he should abandon the attempt and hit blue well away from both black and yellow.

If he does get the cross-wire (*see* Fig 113), he should not aim at yellow with his last stroke. A cross-wire is such a powerful leave that Bab will probably shoot at him in any case, because he is likely to get a break whatever she does. If he shoots and just misses he will give her a big target at which to shoot. Rather, he should aim off the boundary, so that red ends up some four or five feet (1.2–1.5m) away from yellow.

In Fig 114, red is known as the *forward ball* because it has fewer hoops to make than yellow, which is the *backward ball*. Usually you will be keener for your backward ball to make progress, so be alert to the possibility of cross-wiring whenever you hit in with your forward ball and both opponent's balls are near a hoop.

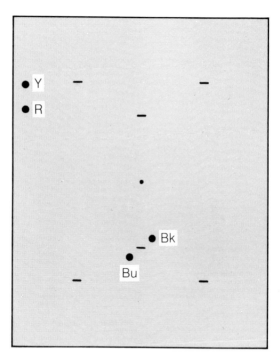

Fig 114

Laying Traps *(Figs 115 to 117)*

Fig 115 illustrates a common leave. Ray has just finished a break with yellow and is laying up for red, which is for hoop 3. He has decided to lay up in corner 3, giving red a rush to its hoop. Fig 116 shows us the position in corner 3 in more detail.

Bab obviously must move black, as it is the ball which would be most useful to red, if left in position. She decides to shoot at red and yellow, but just misses, black ending on the yard-line next to red. What can Ray do now? Red roquets black gently but can only stop shot it out a few yards into court because he must get a rush on yellow to hoop 3. He is likely to make hoop 3 (he would have done that anyway, even if Bab had sent black into a corner) but will still have to work hard for a break. Bab's shot was not as risky as it looked, for that was not the best leave possible.

Fig 117 shows us what Ray should have done (the positions of black and blue remain

Fig 113   A perfect cross-wire.

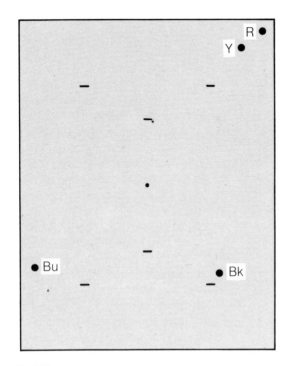

Fig 115

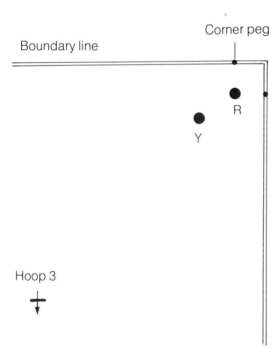

Fig 116   Laying up in a corner – incorrect.

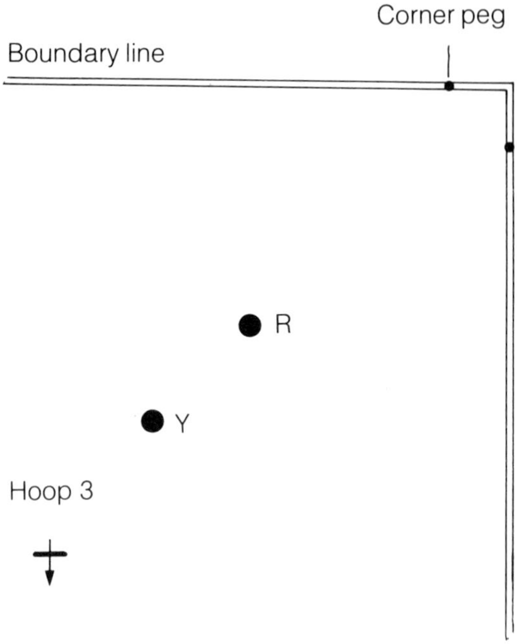

Fig 117   Laying up in a corner – correct.

the same).

Now, if Bab shoots at red and yellow with black she has fallen into Ray's trap. Red roquets black, but now has enough room to stop shot black back to hoop 4 and stop close to yellow. Because yellow is now much closer to hoop 3, it is not vital to get a rush on yellow, although it should still be attempted.

The secret of laying traps is to leave your balls a few yards in from the yard-line. Then, if an opponent shoots and misses, you can use the ball you want to play with to roquet the opponent's ball and stop shot it well into court, still getting a rush on your partner ball where you want to go. A well-laid trap will always give you a good chance of a break if your opponent shoots and misses, but is more likely to benefit you because alert opponents are not so likely to shoot at all against it. One thing to avoid is leaving a double target.

Double and Treble Targets
(Figs 118 to 120)

A double target, or *double* is what it says – two balls left close together, which give your opponent a much better chance of roqueting one of your balls than if they only had one at which to aim.

The perfect double is where the two balls are separated by a space exactly equal to the diameter of a ball. Colonel Prichard, in *Croquet Gazette,* No 144 (Summer, 1977), calculated that the success rate of the average player shooting at a single ball 21 yards (18.9m) away is 23 per cent, whereas their success rate shooting at a perfect double at the same range is 44 per cent. At distances greater than that, it does not seem to matter that the double is not perfect. For example, if you leave two balls together with three ball spaces between them,

you are nearly doubling your opponent's chances of making a roquet. Such an imperfect double is referred to as a *Baillieu double*, being so named after a famous player who sang the praises of aiming at the middle of the space between the two balls at middle or long range, even though you risk passing between them. For all but the best shots, this is good advice.

Thus always leave a gap of three feet (90cm) or more between your balls, and also leave them in such an orientation that neither of your opponent's balls has any type of double to aim at. This restriction is not, of course, necessary if you either manage to wire one of your balls, or line them up one behind the other so that only a single target is offered.

Don't make the mistake of separating your balls as suggested above, but thereby leave a treble. You need to be ever alert to the possibility of leaving a double or treble to your

Fig 118   A double for black.

Fig 119   A treble for blue.

opponent. Fig 120 shows a common position in C and D Class play.

It is Bab's turn to play and obviously it is a good tactic to shoot blue towards black. This not only removes blue, the most useful ball for Ray, from the middle of the court but, by joining up, she puts pressure on her weak opponent to play a good long take-off and make a roquet to retain the innings. What she should not do, however, is to shoot at black. At that range she is most likely to just miss, thereby leaving a double. Then, even if Ray plays a poor take-off, he will have a good target at which to aim. Bab should hit blue off the boundary so that, when it is replaced on the yard-line, it is four or five feet (1.2–1.5m) away from black. Always take care, when shooting from long distance to join up with your partner ball on the boundary, to select carefully where you want your ball to go off-court so that you do not give away a double when it is replaced on the yard-line.

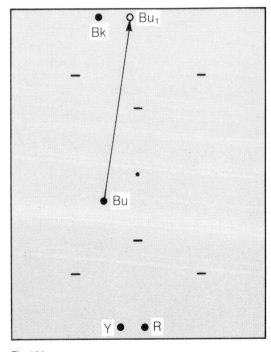

Fig 120

General Principles

We have studied some specific tactics employed in laying up, but, in concluding our study of leaves, it is worth stating the general principles of laying up, some of which have only been implicit so far.

1. Leave your own balls close together, so that you have an easy roquet at the start of your next turn (providing your opponent misses).
2. Leave your opponent's balls well separated and well away from your balls, so that they are forced to hit a long shot to get the innings.
3. Don't join up in the centre of the court. Always lay up near the boundary.
4. Try to leave your opponent's balls in useful positions for you, for example as pioneers to hoops you want to make.
5. Try to leave yourself a rush to somewhere useful, for example to the hoop you want, or to the least useful (and therefore most unlikely to be moved) of your opponent's two balls.
6. Don't leave balls near your opponent's hoop, in case he hits in.

Points 1, 2 and 3 above should always be satisfied. It will not always be possible to satisfy the other principles, but the more you can, the better your leaves are becoming.

ENDGAME TACTICS

Here we assume that you (a C or D Class player) only have a few hoops to make to win, that your bisques have all been used, that you have a lead over a stronger opponent, and that you still have the innings.

Remember the game in Chapter 7 against the A Class player? Let us assume that your bisques got you to peg and 4-back before they ran out. Blue is the ball for 4-back, your opponent has just had a turn and narrowly missed with yellow at red. Fig 121 shows the position.

For once it is time to take a leaf out of Aunt

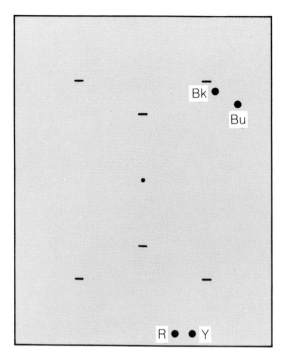

Fig 121

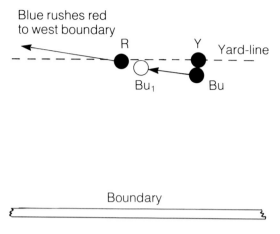

Fig 122   Separating enemy balls.

Emma's book. You must do everything possible to prevent your opponent from gaining the innings. An A Class player can easily beat you in two turns if he manages to get the innings once your bisques have gone.

Start by making 4-back and try to get a rush to penultimate. Only try approaching penultimate, however, if your rush gets you very close to it. Otherwise play a thin take-off with blue to red and yellow, and roquet the ball you end up closest to. This is where you must play to your limitations – don't try to get a rush to penultimate, but settle for splitting red and yellow wide apart. Fig 122 shows the yard-line position in more detail.

Trying to obtain a rush on red to penultimate leaves little room for error, and you risk sending blue off-court. A better percentage play is to try to get a rush on red towards the west boundary. Rush red off the boundary – anywhere off the west boundary will do, but take care not to cut red off the south boundary. Now play a thin take-off to return blue to

black. Take a lot of care with this stroke – you must try to end up within a few feet of black, so that you can lay blue a good rush to penultimate.

Unless you leave a double, it is likely the A Class player will shoot at one of his own balls. If you can progress a hoop at a time to the peg, restricting your opponent to long shots, you have a chance of winning. This is one situation where you will have to risk laying up in the middle of the court. Your priority is to restrict the A Class player to as few shots as possible, so lay up close to your hoops, to make progress as certain as possible.

Similar tactics would be called for against a B Class player, but against fellow C or D Class players you should pay more attention to your opponents' clip positions. If you are of similar ability and you are leading, they may be unlikely to win unless they get an easy break, so try to avoid laying up with two balls next to one of their hoops (particularly that of the backward ball).

These tactics are based on the principle that it is worth being adventurous when you hope to set up a break for a ball that has many hoops to make, but it is not worth risking losing the innings in the critical last stages of a game in order to create a break for a ball that only has two or three hoops to make.

TIME TACTICS

Some games are played to a time limit. If time is called, the following procedure is adopted:

1. The side in play completes its turn.
2. The other side then plays one more turn. These two turns are called the *time turns*, and no bisques may be used in them. If time is called between turns, each side plays one full turn.
3. If neither side finishes in its time turn, the scores are totalled and the side which has scored the most points has won.
4. If the scores after the time turns are equal, play continues until a side scores the next point to win. Any bisques left are reactivated during this period.

One law of handicap play is commonly forgotten in the excitement of time finishes: you may not peg out a *rover ball* (that is, one that has made all of its hoops and is for the peg) unless your partner ball is also a rover.

If time is pressing and you have a lead of more than a few hoops, all you need to do to win is to prevent your opponent from getting a break. You should consider retreating to the boundary away from your opponent's hoops and playing the time out Aunt Emma fashion.

If you have a big lead, it may be worth giving up the innings and encamping your balls in two safe corners. This may allow your opponent to make a few hoops, but they will have great difficulty in constructing the break, without which they have no chance. If your lead is slim, you must keep the innings. Make more hoops if possible, but your priority should be to avoid giving your opponent the innings.

If you are ahead and time is called or time is about to be called, scatter the balls to the four corners of the lawn. Do not, out of habit, end your turn with your balls joined up. A hit in by your opponent when your balls are together gives him the chance of a rush, and one rush gives the chance, however faint, of a break.

OUTPLAYER TACTICS
(Figs 123 to 127)

Keith Wylie, in *Expert Croquet Tactics* (1985), subtly understates a common experience by writing: 'I take it that my readers are not wholly unacquainted with the occasional "previous misplay"'. Such misplay can vary from the annoying, such as failing to leave yourself a good rush, to the disastrous, such as sticking in your opponent's hoop with his ball for that hoop nearby.

Players reactions to the worst disasters likewise vary. It is not, however, the immediate reaction, but how the player responds when they have left the court that distinguishes good and bad outplay (etiquette is another matter).

To remain effective you should try to regain your self-control as soon as possible. By all means analyse your mistake and make a mental note of how to avoid it in future (for example by practice or better tactics), but put it out of your mind as soon as possible and concentrate on what your opponent is doing. Calm down and concentrate on the part of the game which is left, not that which has gone.

Fig 123   Reactions to disaster: Keith Aiton . . .

Fig 124 . . . David Goacher . . .

Fig 126 . . . Alan Sutcliffe.

Fig 125 . . . Fred Rogerson . . .

Bad outplay can be easily recognised. Not only will the player remain obviously agitated, but will probably ignore what their opponent is doing. Common rituals involve cursing oneself or that old faithful, bad luck, in private, or embarking on a public moaning session to all and sundry. Emotionally such behaviour mitigates against the ability to concentrate immediately, if suddenly called upon to play again. It also builds up a negative mental attitude by over-emphasising in your memory your flair for making mistakes, as opposed to your positive playing achievements.

Why, however, is it bad outplay to ignore your opponent? After all, you may argue, knitting, enjoying a laugh with your friends or doing a crossword are good ways of calming down after such a trauma and whilst your opponent is playing their break.

Firstly, you have forgotten your duty as joint

Fig 127   Good outplay: David Openshaw concentrates on his opponent's play.

referee of the game. Your opponent may misplace a clip or play a misplaced or wrong ball, actions which you should forestall or be ready to correct. Immediate recognition of things like misplaced clips or playing the wrong ball can save a lot of time later on. Secondly, it is to your advantage to watch your opponent with an eagle eye, as mistakes like playing the wrong ball, failing to move the croqueted ball in a take-off, or running the wrong hoop are more common than might be expected, but are only likely to be noticed if you are paying attention to the game. Twice in a recent Test Match, wrong ball plays were made without the opponent noticing!

Thirdly, you should study your opponent's play so that you recognise his strengths and weaknesses. This will help you to make a better calculation of the probabilities of him picking up a break from a given situation later in the game, if you are trying to decide whether you dare risk a particular shot, or whether putting a ball into a corner is a better option.

Response to Leaves
(Figs 128 to 132)

If you are the outplayer, you usually have two decisions to make in response to a leave:

1. Which of your two balls to play.
2. What to do with that ball.

Sometimes, when your opponent has not left a good leave, one of your balls may be left with a short shot to regain the innings. In such a case you obviously play with that ball. What constitutes a 'short shot', however, will vary according to your shooting ability and the level of competition. In a game between A Class players, any shot of less than ten to twelve yards (9 – 10.8m) would be considered almost mandatory, even though a miss would give the opponent a certain break, because it is likely to be the best chance for regaining the innings that the player will get in the entire

game. Sometimes the benefit to you of hitting so outweighs the cost of missing that you can ignore the normal defensive considerations. In Fig 128 Ray has to decide what to do in response to Bab's leave. Red is for hoop 1, black for 4 and yellow and blue are both for 4-back.

If Ray does not move yellow, then Bab will have an easy 3-ball break with blue. Not only is there a ball at its hoop, but it already has a rush towards that ball, so she should easily be able to get blue close to yellow and also send a pioneer to penultimate. What however will Bab gain from that? At most probably just two hoops and a good leave. Ray, however, will gain an almost certain 4-ball break if he hits either black or blue with red. Yellow is already at hoop 3 and whichever ball red hits, he should be able to send it to hoop 2 and still get red close to the fourth ball, at hoop 1. The gain for Ray could be an all-round break. In this case, Ray must take the shot with red at black or blue.

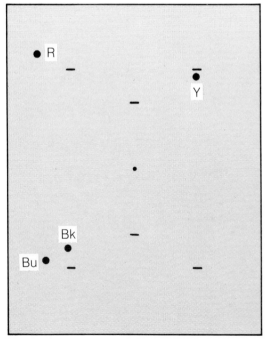

Fig 128

When, however, the opponent has left a good leave, the normal defensive consideration is to move the ball that is of most use to the opponent. In Fig 128, if red were for penultimate instead of hoop 1, the ball to play would obviously be yellow, because that is the ball that is most useful to Bab, being at blue's hoop. Let us consider a couple more examples in which all the balls are for hoop 1.

In Fig 129 red should be moved. A pioneer at blue's next hoop is more useful to Bab than a ball in the middle of the court.

In Fig 130 yellow should be moved. A ball in the middle of the court is of more assistance to Bab, in trying to build a break for blue, than a ball in corner 3.

As a general guide, the following is the order of usefulness of balls to the opposition, and thus the order of priority in which you should play them to more defensive positions:

1. Ball at hoop of opponent's ball.
2. Ball at next but one hoop of opponent's

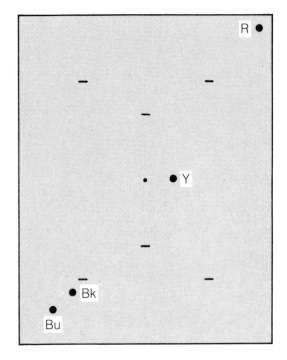

Fig 130

ball.
3. Ball in middle of court.
4. Ball on the yard-line.
5. Ball in corner.

It must be stressed that this is just a general guide and factors such as the position of the opponent's clips, or the nature of any rush the opponent has, must be taken into consideration. In other words, to be a good outplayer and make the correct decision as to which ball to move, you must put yourself in your opponent's shoes and work out how he can use any ball you leave to help him make progress. Consider Fig 131, in which red and yellow are for penultimate, black is for 1-back and blue is for 2-back. At first sight you may say that red is the ball that should be moved, because it is right next to black's hoop. However, if yellow is placed in corner 3, black is only likely to make one hoop because both yellow and blue will be in corners. If, however, red is moved to corner 2, blue has a

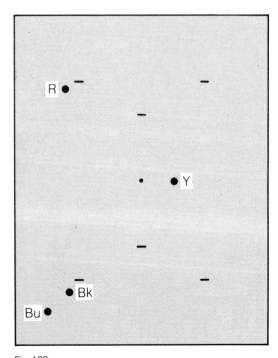

Fig 129

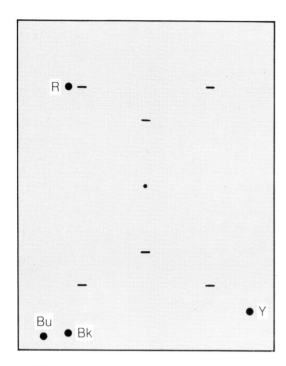

Fig 131

shoot at, will depend on the factors already mentioned, such as length of shot, reward for hitting, what you give away if you miss, whether you have a double or treble to aim at, whether your opponent has laid a trap, etc. You should also take into account how good a shot you are, and whether you think your opponent is playing well enough to make a break if you miss. The state of the court is also a factor. Shots are safer if the court is very flat or very fast (making breaks more difficult to play), but if it is easy paced or undulating, a shot may well not be the best option.

If one of your balls is already on the boundary, well away from your opponent's balls, then your best option may be to join up with it. If you are playing a C or D Class player, you can afford to join up close, maybe a yard or so from your other ball, in the hope that the other player will make a mistake, as we explained when considering Fig 120. Against an A or B Class player you should not join up so closely, because you give them the chance of getting a rush by roqueting one ball and taking off behind the other. A join against a B Class player should be at least four or five yards wide (3.6–4.5m), and against an A Class player should be at least eight or ten yards (7.2–9m) wide.

If you have decided to finesse, the question is, where? The usual answer is a corner, as far from the other balls as possible. If possible, do not go into a corner next to one of your opponent's hoops, the general rule being to play into the corner behind your opponent's break. This is illustrated in Fig 132. Here blue is for hoop 2 and the other three balls are all for rover. Red and yellow are wired from each other.

Red must obviously be moved. A missed shot into blue's trap or a shot into corner 2 would give away a 4-ball break, so the question is, which corner to finesse into? In order, the break passes close to corners 3, 4, 2 and 1, so corner 1 is the place to go.

If you are already close to the corner into which you decide to finesse, aim your ball so

good chance of a break. It has a rush direct to yellow and, by rushing black off the boundary behind yellow, it can then easily stop shot black to 3-back and get a rush on yellow back to 2-back, yellow being in the ideal position, some five feet (1.5m) off the yard-line.

Notice that no shot here is safe for Ray. Yellow at red would give black an easy 3-ball break if missed, and yellow at black would allow black to get a rush into the lawn, if missed, and thus another easy 3-ball break. Any missed shot by red gives Bab an easy chance for a 4-ball break with blue.

Once you have decided which ball to play, you have three options of what to do with that ball:

1. To shoot.
2. To join up with your partner ball.
3. To *finesse* (hit your ball off the boundary, usually into a corner, for defensive purposes).

Whether or not to shoot, and which ball to

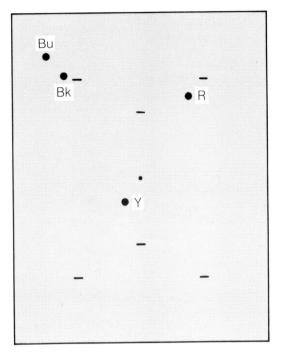

Fig 132

that when it is replaced on the yard-line, it is six to nine inches (15–22.5cm) away from the corner spot. That removes the possibility of your opponent benefiting from a corner cannon (*see* Chapter 17).

CONCLUSION

As in all sports, the excitement of attacking play is what is most enjoyed by player and spectator alike. However, good defensive play can be equally rewarding, not only in terms of its contribution to a player's results, but in its demonstration of the subtleties and strategical and tactical complexities that make croquet such an interesting sport to play.

9 Competitive Variations

In this chapter we first study variations of Association Croquet, that is, those games regularly used in club play, leagues and tournaments. We then examine a selection of games played by Association Croquet players for light relief, as a form of practice or as a means of coaching beginners. Finally, we briefly examine US Six-wicket croquet.

ASSOCIATION CROQUET VARIATIONS

Level Play

Officially referred to as 'ordinary singles play', this is the basic game described in the CA laws book. It is the starting point from which all the other variations are derived. All the rules of play that we have previously introduced, for example roquet–croquet–continuation, faults etc., are rules of level play except where indicated, as in the use of bisques for handicap play. The rules of the variations mentioned in this section are the same as those used in level play, subject to the amendments listed in each case.

Level play is used occasionally in the class events of some tournaments. Players enter the appropriate event according to whether their handicap places them in the B, C or D Class. At weekend tournaments, and in club play, however, games are not commonly played to level play rules.

There are three key rules of level play.

1. The object is for each player to make both his balls score 12 hoop points and a peg point, a total of 26 points, before his adversary.
2. A ball which has scored all 12 hoop points is known as a *rover*. It may then score a peg point by hitting the peg, and is then said to be *pegged out*. A ball that is pegged out is removed from the game.
3. When the striker's ball is a rover, it may cause another rover (his other ball or one of the adversary's balls) to score a peg point and thus be removed from the game.

In doubles you may advise your partner and assist in the playing of a stroke by showing how and in what direction to swing the mallet, and even by placing the balls for a croquet stroke. When the stroke is actually played, however, you must stand well clear of any spot to which the striker is trying to send a particular ball.

Handicap Play

The fact that this is the most common form of play in clubs and tournaments is a tribute to the success of Association Croquet's handicapping system. It allows beginners to play the best players in a well-balanced contest and, because playing better players improves one's game, it is a form of competition that enhances the general standard of play.

The bisque system has already been explained. Apart from the laws relating directly to the use of bisques, handicap play differs in one important respect from level play. You may not peg your own ball out unless your partner ball is a rover or an opponent's ball has been pegged out. Thus, if red is for the peg but yellow is still for 4-back, and you accidentally hit the peg with red when shooting across the lawn, red is not pegged out, unless blue or black has already been pegged out.

This is to stop A Class players pegging their

own ball out if they get the first break in a game. This tactic would effectively devalue the worth of the weaker player's bisques because they could only use them to play a three-ball break. Whilst an A Class player can make progress almost as easily with a three-ball break as with a four-ball break, beginners find them much more difficult and use up many more bisques as a result.

In handicap doubles you add up the handicaps of each side and halve the difference (rounding up to the nearest half) to find the number of bisques to be received by the highest handicapped side. For example, if a −2 and a 9 (total 7) play a 3½ and an 11 (total 14½), the latter side will receive 4 bisques (3¾ rounded up). In a full game a player may not peel the partner ball through more than four hoops – this makes sure that the lower handicapped player must give their partner plenty of play. If this peeling restriction were not imposed, it would be possible for selfish A Class players to try to peel their partners through all of the hoops.

A variation of handicap play is known as the *full bisque* system. In normal handicap play, if a 5 plays a 10, then the latter receives 5 bisques. Under the full bisque system, the 5 would receive 5 bisques and the 10 would get 10 bisques, enabling them both to attempt to play like a scratch player, that is, win with two all-round breaks. There is no doubt that C and D Class players would be well advised to play under this system when playing each other, as it gives them the chance to play long breaks, which is the main way of improving their play.

John Solomon, in his book *Croquet* (B. T. Batsford Ltd, 1966) put in an impassioned plea for the widespread adoption of the full bisque system, arguing that '. . . a handicap is given to a player to enable him to play as well as a scratch player'. While being sympathetic to Solomon's view, and believing that the full bisque system has a place, we cannot agree entirely. Handicaps are given to allow players of differing abilities to compete on equal terms. Blanket application of the full bisque system would remove some of

the attractions of normal handicap play, such as the tactical subtleties of bisque extraction, the chance for B Class players to play breaks under the pressure of having no bisques as back-up and, most importantly, the chance to learn and lay good leaves. The main drawback of the full bisque system, which Solomon did not address, is that laying the kind of good leave that is a key part of the other forms of Association Croquet not only goes unrewarded, but is positively punished because the number of bisques available allows your opponent to regain the innings at will.

Advanced Play *(Fig 133)*

A Class players found level play unsatisfactory because the first player to establish a break made all twelve hoops, cross-wired the opponent's balls at hoop 1 and laid up in corner 3 with a rush to hoop 2, virtually guaranteeing a break for the second ball if the thirty-yard (27m) shot was missed.

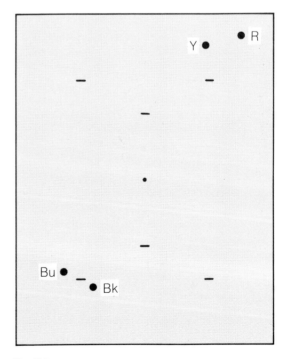

Fig 133

Do you appreciate the power of this leave? Blue is wired from black by hoop 1 and from red by hoop 3, and thus only has a shot at yellow. Black is wired from blue and also from yellow by the peg, and so only has a shot at red. Whichever ball Bab plays, red (for hoop 1) will still have a ball at its hoop. If Bab takes the defensive option and plays black into corner 4, Ray can still rush yellow to hoop 2 and has an easy three-ball break. If Bab shoots and misses, Ray can stop shot Bab's ball to hoop 3, rush yellow to hoop 2 and take-off to the ball remaining at hoop 1, gaining an easy four-ball break.

Although this did not happen all the time, it happened often enough for players to feel it was wrong that the only chance one might get in a game was a thirty-yard (27m) shot. Advanced play rules were developed as a result.

Now, if Ray runs 1-back and 4-back in the same break before his other ball has made 1-back, he must pay the penalty of giving Bab a contact at the start of her next turn. Thus, if Ray plays an all-round break with yellow and lays up for red (for hoop 1), Bab is now allowed to pick up either of her balls, place it in contact with any one of the three remaining balls and begin her turn with a croquet stroke. If black were for hoop 1, she would obviously place black in contact with red and gain an easy four-ball break.

Giving away the innings is generally considered too great a penalty in games between A Class players, which is why the first break by a player in an advanced game usually stops at 4-back.

A further penalty is incurred every time a ball runs 1-back or 4-back (except if it is peeled). In these cases a lift is conceded to the opponent, at the start of their next turn. If, in Fig 133, we now imagine that Ray has made a break with yellow to 4-back, with all the other balls still for hoop 1, and has laid up as shown, Bab is now allowed to lift either of her balls and play that ball from either baulk-line. In this case, Bab would lift black and play it from B-baulk near red. With a shot of only a few feet,

she is almost guaranteed the innings and a break.

Consequently, if you are conceding a lift and are able to end your turn under control, you should leave all the balls well away from the two baulk-lines, which explains why leaving balls in corners 2 and 4 is so popular.

A player entitled to a contact may elect to take a lift instead and either entitlement may be waived if the player prefers to play a ball where it lies.

There is also a form of play called *semi-advanced play*, in which contact is given as above but lifts are only given when 1-back is run. This is, however, a rare variation.

It is also possible to play advanced play with bisques. If a 5 or 6 handicap player wants to practise advanced play and has, as the only possible opponent, a minus player, what should they do? Advanced play would not give the minus player much of a challenge, nor give the 5 or 6 much chance of practising leaves or peeling, let alone winning. The answer is to let the 5 or 6 have the bisques due (say 7 or 8 against a −2), but to make the rule that a half bisque or bisque can only be taken in a turn if a roquet has already been made in that turn. The bisques cannot therefore be used to hit in, only to help play breaks once the bisque receiver has the innings. This maintains the importance of shooting and good leaves, and creates a good game.

Modified Games

People do not always have time to play a full game which, for players outside the A Class, usually takes at least three hours. The laws therefore make provision for various forms of shortened games:

1. *A 22 point game*, where all clips start on hoop 3.
2. *An 18 point game*. Four variations are listed in the laws but two of those have become most common. In one, all clips start on hoop 5. In the other, all clips start on hoop 1, but as soon as

one of the balls of a side runs, or is peeled through hoop 1 in order, 3-back becomes the next hoop in order for its partner ball, and the appropriate clip is placed on 3-back immediately. This variation, commonly referred to as *the 1 and 3-back game*, is for singles play only. It has become a popular variation in handicap singles play because it gives a beginner the chance to make an all-round break using his bisques, whilst it also gives the expert the chance to score all 18 points in one turn, by completing a quadruple peel.

3. *A 14 point game*, where all clips start on hoop 1 and the peg point is the next point in order after hoop 6.

Provision is made in the laws for the modification of advanced and semi-advanced play in shortened games, but A Class players rarely choose to play shortened games, except when playing under handicap rules.

In handicap play, the number of bisques to be given is scaled down in accordance with a schedule published in the laws book. For example, if a 2½ handicap plays an 11 handicap player, the latter would receive 8½ bisques in a full (26 point) game, 7 bisques in a 22 point game, 6 bisques in an 18 point game or 4½ bisques in a 14 point game.

In handicap doubles play, the number of peels allowed by the partner is reduced to three in a 22 point or 18 point game, or two in a 14 point game.

We believe that more use should be made of shortened games, especially for handicap doubles or in handicap singles games involving just C or D Class players. The most exciting part of any game is the ending. Too many full games are started, only to end, unfinished, at a time limit or, worse, having just fizzled out because neither player was playing well and one is forced to leave to go to work, or go shopping, or because daylight has disappeared.

Small Lawn Croquet

Here we refer to Association Croquet played on courts of less than full size. This could be any area smaller than a full court, 35 × 28 yds (32 × 25.6m), where the length:width ratio is kept at 5:4, or the 24 × 16 yds (21.9 × 14.6m) dimensions used for Short Croquet, or the handy 28 x 17½yds (25.6 x 16.0m) dimensions obtained by simply splitting one full court into two half-sized courts.

It is important to realise that Short Croquet, with its special adaptations to the rules, is simply the most modern small lawn game and that any of the forms of Association Croquet mentioned previously can be played on small courts. Having said that, we do not know of small courts ever being used for advanced play. This is not surprising, as they reduce the challenge to the best players, because the reduced distances involved make the strokes required to construct breaks much easier.

We believe that all beginners should be coached on small courts and encouraged to play on them until they have mastered the four-ball break. They will enjoy earlier success in stroke making on small courts, which will encourage them to persevere. With the use of bisques they will be able to make earlier attempts at break play. The much more easily acquired ability to manoeuvre the balls around a small court will enable them to start unravelling the strategic and tactical complexities of croquet much more quickly than if they play on full-sized courts. Small is beautiful!

Naturally some scaling down of the number of bisques received should occur, according to how small the court is. As a rough guide, the number of bisques received should be halved when using a half-size court

SHORT CROQUET

(Figs 135 & 136)

Short Croquet was launched as a new variation by the Croquet Association in June 1985. One reason for its inception was to provide a standardised small lawn game, particularly one that can be played on unused tennis courts, hence the court dimensions of 24 × 16 yds, (21.9 × 14.6m) the hoops and peg being positioned as shown in Fig 134.

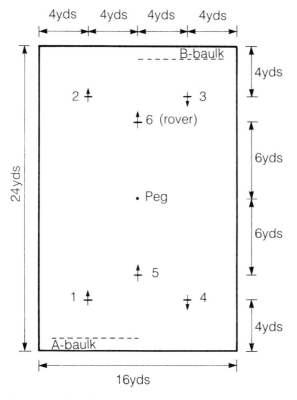

Fig 134   A Short Croquet court.

Perhaps the main reason for its launch, however, was to provide a game suitable for television. It is therefore a 14 point, full bisque, handicap game (hoops 1–6 and the peg), with a modified bisque reception table and requiring that players of handicap 2 and below complete a certain number of mandatory peels.

The mandatory peels are included to make it a challenging game for A Class players. Either ball of its side may be peeled by its partner ball to count as a mandatory peel. When the striker is in a position where the number of mandatory peels outstanding equals the number of hoop points left to be scored by both his balls, he is not allowed to score a point by running a hoop, only by peeling. Each peel on your ball by an opponent from this point reduces the number of mandatory peels remaining by one. If either of your balls is pegged out by your opponent, any mandatory peels you have left are cancelled. If you have any mandatory peels left, you may not peg one of your own balls out (assuming you have that option because you previously pegged out an opponent ball).

Apart from the necessary adaptations to deal with mandatory peeling, the only change from normal is that you may not wire an opponent ball from its partner ball, otherwise you give away a wiring lift. That prevents the type of leave seen in Fig 133 from being used, making it impossible to lay an attacking leave with a shot over twenty yards (18m) for your opponent.

The 'baby' appears to be growing at a healthy rate. 1986 saw the first national Short Croquet tournament, more weekend Short Croquet tournaments, and the first ever televised croquet tournament, the Royal Bank Nations Trophy, held on 7–9 May at the headquarters of Granada TV in Manchester on a specially constructed lawn.

The small court certainly got over one of the main televisual problems, being easily able to show the whole court without the balls, hoops and peg appearing insignificant, special hoop numbering boxes being added for clarity. The scaling down of the court and the halving of the number of hoops to be made also makes for quicker games; two-thirds of the games at Manchester were completed within one hour. Whilst vital for television, this also adds the attraction of making Short Croquet a game that can be played during the lunch-time (for those fortunate enough to have a court near work).

FUN GAMES

Golf Croquet

This is a very popular game, widely used as an introductory game to Association Croquet, but also having its own adherents and championships.

Rules
1. Same course as for level play.
2. All balls must start from B-baulk.

3. Singles or doubles can be played. Red and yellow play black and blue.
4. There are no bonus strokes. Each ball is hit only once per turn. It is a sequence game. The sequence followed is that of the colours on the peg (in descending order): blue, red, black, yellow, then blue etc. Any of the balls can start, but once the first ball has been played, the sequence must come into operation.
5. The first ball to run hoop 1 in the correct direction scores one point for its side. The contest for that hoop is finished and then,

Fig 135   The Short Croquet court at Granada TV for the Royal Bank Nations' Trophy.

Fig 136   Eric Solomon under the scrutiny of the cameras.

from where they lie, the balls are played up to hoop 2. So, if red runs hoop 1, black would be the first ball hit up to hoop 2.

6. If a ball only partially runs a hoop (except if an opponent knocked it there), it cannot score a point by completing the running in its next turn. A hoop must be run in one shot to score a point. If an opponent hits his ball into the jaws, you can knock it through without scoring a point for him, if you wish to clear the hoop.

7. Even if it seems pointless, you must still contest the hoop to be scored. You may not send a ball to the next hoop. If you do so deliberately, your ball must be replaced and you lose your turn.

8. If a player plays the wrong ball or plays out of sequence, the balls should be replaced and play should continue normally. No penalty.

We suggest you start by playing 'best of seven', that is, hoops 1 to 1-back, with four points needed to win. Progress to 'best of thirteen',

that is, the full course with hoop 3 again as a decider, if necessary.

Alternate Stroke Handicap Doubles

Rules as for handicap play, except that the players of each side do not play one ball each, but play both balls of their side together. They play alternate strokes throughout the game and from turn to turn, whether such turns are ordinary turns, half bisques or bisques. For example, if you make a roquet, then your partner plays the croquet stroke and you play the continuation stroke, and so on. The partner of the player who played the last stroke of a turn plays the first stroke of their next turn.

This is a fun way of helping beginners to learn the game and is much more interactive than ordinary handicap doubles. When a good player is paired with a beginner, he is often challenged to play difficult and accurate strokes, for example roll approaches to hoops from ten or more yards (9m or more) away, attempting for position two foot (60cm) straight in front, as he not only has to make up for a previous poor stroke of his partner, but has to make the next stroke as easy as possible, so that his partner won't break down by missing a roquet or failing a hoop. Its appeal as a more serious alternative is limited, because individual players have no chance to make breaks on their own.

Two-ball Croquet

A good introduction to Association Croquet is to play games with just two balls, that is, one ball per side.

The full rules of Association Croquet apply, so you will get the chance to practise the various croquet strokes. Because, however, there are only two balls, the tactics are much simpler and more obvious, and the game is much quicker. If you play hoops 1 to 6 and the peg, the game should only take ten minutes. The full course should take fifteen to twenty-five minutes.

Whoever plays first has three options (we assume that both players will decide to play their balls on to the lawn from A-baulk):

1. To try and run hoop 1 straight away. This is the gambler's choice – if, against the odds, you manage to run it, you can try to take position by hoop 2 with your continuation stroke. A clean miss is not too disastrous, but if you hit the wire you are in the lap of the gods – the ball may bounce away from the hoop, and A-baulk, if you are lucky, but you risk it staying near the hoop with the consequent danger, explained below.
2. To take position in front of hoop 1. This is the worst thing you could do. You offer your opponent a relatively short shot to make a roquet and he will then be able to use your ball to make hoop 1 and maybe, by use of a rush (preferably) or a take-off, he will also be able to make hoop 2 in the same turn.

3. The percentage play is to play your ball on to the court so that it is well away from A-baulk and about ten to fifteen yards (9–13.5m) from hoop 1. It must be in such a position that, if your opponent is tempted to take position, you will not be wired from his ball.

Eventually someone will win the game of cat and mouse around the first hoop and will establish a lead. His tactics will then be simple – to run the remaining hoops in as few strokes as possible. The backward player should initially adopt similar tactics and hope to catch him up. As long as the lead is no more than two hoops, the backward player still has a good chance. If you have a ball in position to run penultimate (hoop 5 in a half game) before the forward player can approach the peg, you are in a strong position. If, however, the lead is more than two hoops, chasing is no longer good enough and you must start shooting and make some roquets.

Pirates

This is an excellent game for practising hoop running and shooting.

Rules
1. Each player uses one ball and up to eight people can play, each one using one of the first or second colour balls.
2. Players shoot at the peg from either baulk and the choice of starting positions is given to the player who gets nearest to the peg, the second nearest getting second choice, and so on. Once the starting order is determined, players start the game proper from either baulk-line, in the normal way.
3. The winner is the first player to score 19 points.
4. When you run any hoop, in any order, you score one point. There is no extra stroke for running a hoop. Note that this rewards the running of controlled hoops. Another variation is to award an extra stroke for running a hoop, but not to allow extra points or strokes if the

same hoop is immediately rerun in the opposite direction.

5. When you hit another ball, you gain the units of points owned by that ball and an extra stroke. For example, if a 4 hits a 13, it becomes a 7 and the other ball becomes a 10. Once a ball gets 10 points, those are secure and cannot be taken away. If your ball hits a ball that is a 0 or a 10, it does not gain any points but still gains the extra stroke.

6. You do not take croquet following a hit but play your ball from where it now lies (or from the yard-line, if it went off-court). You only get another extra stroke for hitting the same ball in the same turn if you hit all the other balls first, and then run a hoop before hitting it again.

Progressive Handicap Doubles

Another handicap doubles variation, to make sure that high handicapped partners get their fair share of play. These fast forty-minute contests, enabling beginners to play with a variety of experienced partners, are well suited to club sessions or croquet gymkhanas.

Rules

1. Players are divided into two groups, with the best or lowest handicapped players in one group and the beginners in the other. All pairings are made up using one player from each group. Initial pairings are decided by lot.

2. 18 point, 5th hoop start games are played.

3. Games last forty minutes and all games in a round start and finish together (use a whistle or bell). If scores are level at the bell, the side to make the next roquet is the winner.

4. Only one peel on a partner ball is allowed per side, per game.

5. Bisques are individually owned and may not be used by the player's partner. Unused bisques may not be carried over to the next game. Allocation per game is as follows:

Handicap	Bisques Received
0 or below	0
½ to 5	1
5½ to 10	2
11 to 16	3
17 to 20	4
21 to 24	5

6. To further encourage very high bisquers, you can 'weight' the points they make, for example 2 points per hoop for handicaps 17–20, 3 points per hoop for handicaps 21–24.

7. At the end of each game, the victorious low bisquer is responsible for reporting the score to the manager.

8. Each player is credited with the number of points scored by their side, for example a 9–4 win means both winners get 9 points and both losers 4. Each group has an overall winner, being the player who, over the number of rounds played, has the highest personal points score.

9. At the end of each round, the winning low bisquer of a pair goes to the next court 'up', whilst the winning high bisquer goes to the next court 'down'. The losing pair stay on the same court, but split up.

Apart from making for a very sociable time, this game rewards attacking croquet because even the players of a losing side benefit if a particular game is high scoring on both sides. This is one example of a newer game, the rules of which you should not be afraid to amend to suit local circumstances, for example the time allowed, whether to use full or small lawns, the details of rules 5 and 6, etc.

Three-ball Croquet

A game that offers a better balance of play than two against one if you are short of a fourth player.

Rules

1. Decide playing order as in pirates.

2. The player who is due to start last plays the

fourth ball on to the lawn from either baulk, and then each player plays their own ball on to the lawn.

3. The players take turns in sequence. You may only play your own ball but may use the fourth ball, as well as opponents' balls, to help you play breaks.

4. Three clips are used, as the fourth ball does not score hoops (but see 6, below).

5. The first player to peg out their own ball, after the fourth ball has been previously pegged out, wins.

6. You can play level but, if A Class players are playing or the players are of different abilities, utilise the Short Croquet bisque table to determine bisques received, or mandatory peels required. If mandatory peels are required, they must be done on the fourth ball and, unlike in Short Croquet, must be peels at specific hoops, that is 4-back to the peg if three peels are required, penultimate to the peg for two peels, or rover to the peg for one peel. If more than one player is required to do peels, the peels are considered to be independent of each other. For example, if one player has already peeled the fourth ball through rover, that does not prevent or release an opponent from his obligation to do his outstanding peel(s).

US CROQUET

As before, only the differences from Association level play rules are listed. We do not have the space to list all the differences from the Association Game, and anyone wanting the full rules should apply to the USCA for an official rule book. We have tried to list the major differences, enough certainly for you to try it out. For peg read *stake* and for hoop read *wicket*.

The Six-wicket Game

Rules

1. The rover wicket is run in the same direction as wicket 5, that is, towards the stake.

2. Balls are played in strict sequence: blue, red, black, yellow, blue, and so on.

3. The blue ball always starts the game. Each ball starts the game from a spot one yard (90cm) in front of wicket 1 (*see* Fig 195, which shows a player placing red for its first turn). Until a ball has run that wicket it cannot gain any bonus strokes, nor may any other ball roquet it. It may be scattered by other balls that have not made wicket 1, but must be temporarily removed if it is likely to impede any ball that has made wicket 1.

4. Once a ball has made wicket 1, it may roquet other balls that have also made wicket 1. However, it may only roquet each of the other balls once between wickets. Once it has roqueted another ball, it is said to be *dead* on that ball, and it may not roquet that ball again until it has run its next wicket. Deadness persists from one turn to another. A special 'deadness board' is used to display the current state of deadness of all the balls in the game. The striker's ball may not hit a ball on which it is dead. If it does so, its turn ends and the balls are replaced to their positions before the stroke was played.

5. Balls are replaced on court only nine inches (22.5cm) in, that is, the yard-line has become a nine-inch line.

6. If you roquet a ball out of bounds (off-court) your turn ends, but you do not become dead on that ball.

7. If, in the same stroke, a ball runs its wicket and goes out of bounds, its turn ends.

8. If, in the same stroke, a ball runs its wicket and strikes another ball, that does not count as a roquet. It must strike a ball in the continuation stroke to make a roquet, immediately after running its wicket.

9. A ball is only out of bounds when it is more than half-way over the boundary line.

10. If, at the beginning of its turn, a ball is wired from all balls on which it is alive, and the adversary is responsible for its position, the striker may place that ball in contact with any ball on which it is alive, and take croquet. (If

this rule is used, you are said to be playing the advanced game).

11. When each ball of both sides passes through wicket 1-back, the opposing side may clear the deadness on one of its balls before starting its next turn, or sooner, if asked to declare by an opponent.

12. A rover ball that is dead on at least two balls can clear its deadness by running any wicket in either direction, and it receives a continuation stroke for doing so, but even after clearing it remains dead on the last ball it roqueted.

In tournament play one to one and a half hour time limits usually operate, with forty-five to sixty second stroke limits, making it a much faster game than the Association game.

The sequence rule makes US doubles play more interactive. It also makes it much easier to lay a powerful leave because it is always safe to lay up with the spent opponent ball. For example, blue plays a break and then leaves black with a rush on yellow to its next wicket, placing itself as a pioneer at that next wicket with red as far away as possible. If, in addition, you remember rules 5 and 6 above, and lay up on the nine-inch line, with a leave such as the one shown in Fig 137 (red to play and wired from blue, black for wicket 2), you can virtually guarantee yourself a three-ball break on your next turn.

The rule prohibiting the roqueting of a ball out of bounds, and the difficulty of getting behind a ball on the nine-inch line for a rush, make it much more difficult to construct breaks than in the Association game, and once a player has constructed a three-ball break, he is often loath to take the risks involved in bringing the fourth ball from the boundary into the break.

The concept of deadness certainly creates a new sphere of strategy and tactics but, because the penalty for breaking down in a break and becoming three-ball dead is so severe, it discourages many players from trying to play

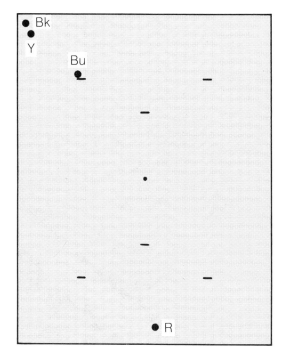

Fig 137

and master three and four-ball breaks. This has been compounded by the fact that most tournaments are played level, but recently the USCA has made a move towards introducing more handicap play. American bisques, however, merely allow a replay of a poor stroke or unsuccessful shot and are thus much less powerful than the Association bisque, which allows an extra turn, with which it is possible to set up a break before taking a subsequent bisque.

The USCA are to be applauded for taking this step to improve the general standard of play in their game, but we believe that changing to an Association type bisque is essential, if they wish the general standard of play of US rules players to match that of those who play the Association game.

US Six-wicket Croquet, like the Association game, can be played on smaller courts, provided the respective dimensions of length:width are kept in proportion.

ADVANCED CROQUET

10 Advanced Play

Advanced play describes the more demanding croquet played in championships and major tournaments, and the special laws under which it is played. The intention of these laws (*see* Chapter 9) is to give the outplayer a better chance to regain the innings by awarding lifts and contacts depending on the progress made by the striker in the previous turn. The practical effect is that the first break by each player will almost always end after 3-back, and the game can be won in two breaks only if the winner has the skill to complete a triple peel.

Advanced play is usefully described as play in which all-round breaks are common in normal playing conditions. Success depends on many factors. Although the physical skill displayed by a croquet champion does not quite compare with that of a professional golfer or snooker player, it is very considerable none the less. Only regular practice will develop and maintain the accuracy to hit half of all thirteen-yard (11.7m) shots taken, to run almost every hoop of less than three feet (90cm) that is offered, and to play split shots that send both balls twenty yards (18m) to within a few inches of their targets. The tactics of advanced croquet are undoubtedly the most involved of any outdoor game, and croquet is one of the few games where a better tactician can hope to defeat a better technician. Lastly, but by no means least, advanced croquet exposes competitors to the same pressures and psychological demands that are experienced by champions of any sport.

This section of the book is intended to give the budding A Class player an up-to-date guide to the principal tactics of the advanced game. It cannot teach you to become a first-class player, as that is something you have to teach yourself with experience, usually painful experience, as your tutor. All that a book can do is to set you thinking on the right lines, and a recent publication, *Modern Croquet Tactics* by K.F. Wylie (K.F. Wylie, 1985), is recommended as stimulating further reading.

11 The Openings

Croquet does not have as extensive an opening repertoire as chess, but a number of distinct ways of starting a game have been developed. In general, the opening represents a battle for the first innings. The winner of the toss has the right to choose who shall play the first turn of the game. It might be thought that he would invariably choose to do so himself, because the first player can join up safely on the third turn. However, A Class players are usually good shots, and the price of joining on the third turn is allowing the opponent to take a shot of about fourteen yards (12.6m) on the fourth turn, which may yield him a break if he hits. It is therefore quite common for the winner of the toss to elect to play second, or even to choose the balls and so thrust the onus of choice on to his opponent.

In this chapter it is assumed that Bab wins the toss and chooses to play first. Ray then chooses red and yellow so that Bab must play with blue and black. The early turns of the game will be referred to as 'turn 1', 'turn 2', and so on. To avoid confusion, Bab will always play black in turn 1 and blue in turn 3, and Ray will always play red in turn 2 and yellow in turn 4.

THE TICE OPENING (Figs 138 & 139)

This is croquet's equivalent of P–K4 in chess. It is almost as old as the game itself, and has retained its popularity because it offers almost equal chances to both players and gives the player who loses the initial exchange reasonable defensive prospects.

In turn 1, Bab plays black to a point on the east boundary, anywhere between one and six yards (90cm–5.4m) north of corner 4, according to taste. In turn 2, Ray plays red to a point on the

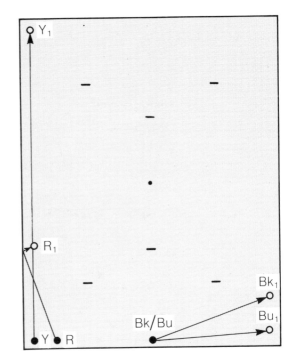

Fig 138

west boundary which is usually between nine and fifteen yards (8.1–13.5m) north of corner 1. This is known as *laying a tice*, because the object is to entice Bab to shoot at red in turn 3 and miss. The length of the tice is a matter of judgement and depends on Ray's opinion of the relative shooting skills of Bab and himself, the state of the lawn, and even the time of day, as many players are at their least confident of hitting first thing in the morning. The opening has two main variations.

Variation A

In turn 3, Bab accepts the tice and shoots with blue at red, usually because she thinks it is too short to be left for Ray. If blue hits, Bab can take-off thickly, to send red about five yards south-west of hoop 2, and blue over to black, so that she can roquet it and lay a short rush towards red on the east boundary level with the rover hoop. Alternatively, she can approach hoop 1 by a thick take-off which sends red several yards north of hoop 1. If Bab fails to get adequate position for the hoop, she can send blue back to black. In either case, but particularly in the first option, Ray must hit a long roquet in turn 4 or Bab will have a good chance of a 3-ball break in turn 5.

In turn 4, if Bab misses the tice from corner 1 and blue ends up in corner 2, Ray will shoot with yellow at red from a point well to the east of corner 1, to ensure that yellow will stay near red if it misses. If yellow hits, Ray should lay a rush to hoop 1, guarding corner 1 from both blue and black. If yellow misses, Bab should shoot at red and yellow in turn 5, unless they are so close together that a miss by blue into corner 1 would give Ray an easy chance of a

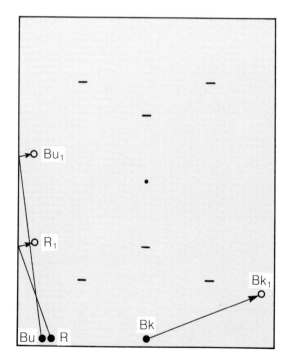

Fig 139

corner cannon.

Bab may try another variation in turn 3, and shoot at the tice from a spot one yard (90cm) east of corner 1, so that if blue misses, it will be replaced only seven to ten yards (6.3–9m) north of red (see Fig 139). Ray has three choices in turn 4: shooting from just outside corner 1 to make a double target of red and blue; shooting from corner 1 to ensure that yellow reaches corner 2 if it misses; or declining to shoot and simply playing yellow a few yards north of corner 1. Unless Ray hits, Bab will have a relatively short shot at an enemy ball, or a safe join with partner in corner 4.

Variation B

In turn 3, Bab declines the tice and plays blue to the east boundary to join black, hoping that Ray will miss the tice with yellow. Bab will usually play blue from the end of A-baulk to a distance from black that will range from one to six yards (0.9–5.4m) and will depend on Ray's calibre. The stronger Ray is, the greater the distance that should be left between blue and black, to minimise the likelihood of a break for Ray if he hits the tice.

Bab may adopt a variation popular among good shots by playing black six yards (5.4m) north of corner 4 in turn 1, and shooting with blue at black in turn 3 from just outside corner 3. If blue hits, Bab has a good chance to set up the same position as the one resulting if she had hit the tice in Variation A. If blue misses, it should have ended up in corner 4, giving a six yard (5.4m) join that should prevent Ray establishing a break in turn 4.

In turn 4, assuming that Bab hit nothing in turn 3, Ray will shoot with yellow at red from corner 1, so that yellow will finish up in corner 2 if it misses, and will thus minimise the likelihood of an immediate break for Bab in turn 5. If Ray hits, he will take-off to blue and black, and either start a break by getting a rush to hoop 1 or obtain a promising leave.

In turn 5, if Ray misses in turn 4, Bab may be able to start a break by playing black, rushing blue to the north boundary and taking-off to yellow and then to red, with the object of obtaining a rush to hoop 1. If blue and black are too far apart to rush, Bab will just hit, and either lay a rush towards red or hoop 1, or take-off to separate red and yellow.

THE CORNER TWO OPENING
(Fig 140)

A drawback of the Tice Opening is the fact that hitting the tice requires a take-off over the full width of the lawn to the east boundary. In the early part of a game, Ray's touch may be imperfect and there is a risk that he will either take-off over the boundary or pull up very short and miss with yellow at the enemy balls. As this disaster usually gives away better break prospects for Bab than Ray possessed, he may reasonably decide to take a tice length of shot at the enemy balls on the east boundary instead. If he hits, the uncertainties of the long take-off are avoided.

In turn 1, Bab plays black to the east boundary. In turn 2, instead of laying a tice, Ray plays red six inches (15cm) south of corner 2, to discourage Bab from shooting at it with blue in turn 3, because of the risk of leaving a double target if blue misses on the right. In turn 3, Bab should play blue about four yards (3.6m) away from black on the east boundary, to threaten a cannon, or at least an easy rush to hoop 1, if Ray misses in turn 4.

This opening is usually favoured by a very strong Ray who believes that he is more likely to establish a break if he hits, than is Bab if he misses. On a difficult lawn it effectively prevents either player getting away on a break and is therefore an appropriate opening for the more skilful tactician.

THE CORNER FOUR OPENING (Fig 141)

If Ray is prepared to shoot at the enemy balls on the east boundary in turn 4, he may prefer to do so in turn 2. This is a lively opening often used as a mild shock tactic by the slightly weaker player to force the issue. The opening divides into two variations, A and B, depending on the result of Ray's shot.

Variation A

If Ray hits in turn 2, he usually rolls both balls to the peg, leaving a double target from both baulks and, with the aid of the peg, leaving no useful rush for the enemy ball. In turn 3, Bab can either play blue defensively into corner 2 or 4, or aggressively by shooting hard or softly at the double. The defensive answer is more usual in advanced play, and is strongly indicated if black has been left any sort of rush towards either corner. In turn 4, Ray is committed to shooting with yellow and should normally do so from A-baulk, to minimise Bab's break chances if he misses.

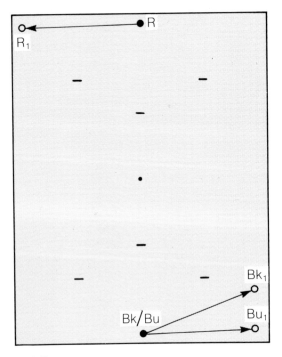

Fig 140

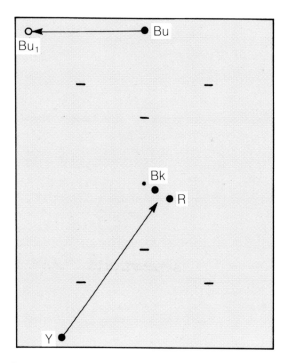

Fig 141

Variation B

If Ray misses black on the right, he may well leave a double target which Bab should shoot at with blue in turn 3. If blue hits, Bab has a chance of a three-ball break and otherwise

transposes into the Tice Opening, Variation A. If Ray misses on the left, or by so much on the right that he leaves no double, Bab can either play blue to corner 2, transposing to the Corner 2 Opening, or shoot with blue at the double target that is available from B-baulk, hoping to end in corner 4 if blue misses. This puts Ray in a tight spot. If he shoots and hits, he may have a break. If he misses, Bab will probably have better chances with the aid of a cannon. On a difficult lawn, it may even pay Ray to decline to shoot.

SUMMARY

The openings described above are the ones you are most likely to meet in tournament play. However, there are several others and innumerable minor variations. Some, such as the Duffer Tice Opening, can be argued to have real merit. Others, such as the Short Tice Opening, are amusing frivolities which catch the fancy of an enterprising player every so often and enjoy a brief popularity before returning to obscurity. There is much to be said for refusing to be hidebound, but at the highest levels of the game, the experts usually remain faithful to the openings they know.

12   Obtaining the Innings

'What is the best way to win at croquet?' the young man asked. 'Hit in, and don't break down', the old man replied. The obvious ingredients of successful croquet, such as creating and playing breaks and constructing sound leaves, are covered in the chapters immediately following. Here we deal with obtaining the innings, which is not often given the attention it deserves by improving players, and yet it is the essential first step towards victory.

The innings changes hands for only two reasons – either the outplayer hits a long roquet, or the inplayer, the striker, blunders. Whenever the outplayer steps on to the court he must decide which eventuality is more likely to give him the innings before his opponent finishes a break or wins the game. The outplayer therefore has only two choices, to shoot or to finesse. Finessing, the attractive jargon for not shooting, can be aggressive or defensive. Joining wide with partner is aggressive, because it threatens a hittable shot if your balls are left untouched and may precipitate a blunder from your opponent in his attempt to separate them. Playing into a corner is defensive, and designed to remove a ball from the opponent's break with the hope that he will overreach himself and break down.

The decision to shoot or to finesse can be reduced to an exercise in probabilities, as there are only three variables, namely the probabilities:

1. That you will hit the shot.
2. That your opponent will establish and finish a break if you miss.
3. That your opponent will establish and finish a break if you finesse.

Consider the position in Fig 142. Ray has a rush to hoop 1 and a ball at each of his next two hoops. Blue and black are only fourteen yards (12.6m) apart and, if the playing conditions are easy and Ray is a very good player, Bab might assess the above probabilities as 40 per cent, 90 per cent and 75 per cent respectively. Thus, if she shoots with blue at black she will miss 60 per cent of the time. This suggests that Ray will make a break to 4-back 54 per cent of the time (60 per cent x 90 per cent) if she shoots and 75 per cent of the time if she finesses. The decision is not difficult. She should shoot.

Estimating the probabilities is not a mathematically precise exercise, but reasonable accuracy will come with experience. The

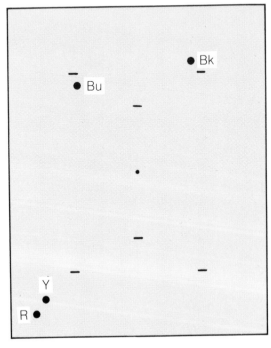

Fig 142

abilities of the players, the difficulty of the playing conditions and the psychological state of the game are all relevant. If the court is uneven and very quick, and the hoops are firmly set, Bab might estimate rather different probabilities, such as 30 per cent, 80 per cent and 40 per cent. In these circumstances, a missed shot will allow Ray to finish a break 56 per cent of the time while finessing will lead to that result 40 per cent of the time. This time, discretion is clearly the better part of valour.

There are situations in which probabilities may be relegated in favour of psychology. In Fig 143, Ray has laid up in corner 4, with blue at hoop 5 and black a few yards north of hoop 6, wired from blue. He had a 4-ball break almost under control at hoop 3, but a bad pioneer at hoop 4 forced him to lay up. Bab has a twelve yard (10.8m) shot at yellow which will give back the break if it is missed, and the probabilities may well favour finessing. However if Bab shoots and misses, Ray will know he was lucky to escape and his confidence will

not be helped by his unforced error and the belligerence of his opponent. If Bab merely corners, Ray will be heartened by such timidity and his confidence may well increase. In such cases, it is usually right to try and punish your opponents for their errors.

Probabilities should also be used to decide with which ball to shoot. If the odds favour shooting, you should take the shot that gives least away if you miss. After all, regaining the innings is the priority and you should not really mind with which ball you hit the vital roquet. However, towards the end of a closely contested game, it may be appropriate to consider the odds of winning the game rather than those of merely regaining the innings. If you hit with the forward ball you must take into account your opponent's chances of hitting in his turn.

If the odds favour finessing, you must decide whether to join wide with partner or to run for cover into a corner. Joining wide is sensible only if the partner ball is on or very near a boundary and is best on difficult courts when a long take-off may be a daunting prospect. In easy conditions, a good player will treat balls separated by fifteen or twenty yards (13.5–18m) as an invitation to set up a good leave. Generally, finessing is defensive and you should seek to play the ball of most use to your opponent into a corner behind his break. This maximises the number of hoops that he will have to make without the benefit of a 4-ball break, and therefore increases the chances that he will break down. In Fig 144, Ray has a rush to hoop 2, and blue and black are near hoops 3 and 4 respectively. If Bab decides to finesse, she should play blue a foot (30cm) outside corner 1. This deprives Ray of the more useful enemy ball, forces him to play a 2-ball break to make hoops 2 and 3, and minimises the chance of a cannon in or near Corner 1.

Successful outplaying is an art. It demands self-discipline and an acceptance that you are going to make mistakes. Sometimes you will itch to have a shot at something when it is

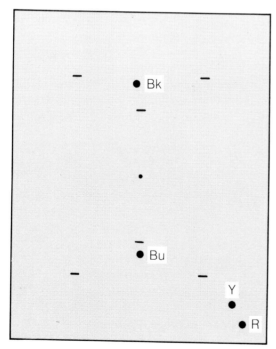

Fig 143

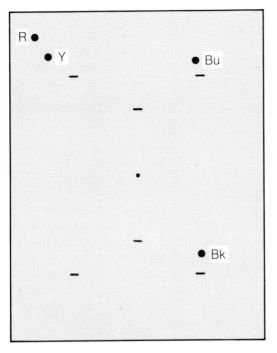

Fig 144

more fruitful to finesse. At others, you will quake at the prospect of shooting into your opponent's leave, but it is clearly the best chance you have. Ultimately, it is probably better to lose by missing a shot than by declining to shoot. There is nothing quite as annoying as seeing your opponent go out from 4-back on a 2-ball break after you have convinced yourself not to take a fifteen yard (13.5m) shot but to go to corner 1 instead. The only sure remedy is to be the inplayer as often as possible.

13 The Break

The art of running several hoops and scoring several points in one turn is fundamental to Association Croquet. This skill of playing breaks is an essential tool for all good players. However, the hallmark of the expert is his ability to develop and establish breaks from unpromising positions.

ESTABLISHING THE BREAK

(Figs 145 & 146)

Once you obtain the innings you must establish a break as soon as possible. You will have three immediate choices:

1. Try for a break which risks the innings if you fail.
2. Try for a break with a good leave available if you fail.
3. Make a leave.

Success in advanced croquet depends on taking the chances offered to you as soon as they appear. A break postponed may be a break lost. Have no sympathy for the player who lays up instead of trying for a possible break and is hit from twenty-five yards (22.5m). It serves him right.

The distinction between choices 1 and 2 is that in 1 you will normally commit your partner ball into the lawn before a break is certain, whereas in 2 it will remain near a boundary until a 3-ball break is established. Choice 1 is correct whenever your opponent blunders in the middle of a break. If he hands you an easy break, you should not consider the possibility of failure. Safeguarding against unlikely disasters is often the best way to bring them about.

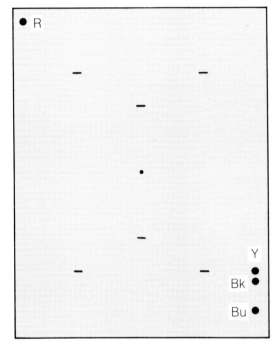

Fig 145

Choice 2 play shows the expert to greatest advantage. He can see possibilities in a position that are not apparent to lesser players. He has the skill to play certain strokes that give him a chance of a break but cost nothing if they fail. Consider the position in turn 5, after a Corner 2 Opening when Ray misses in turn 4 (*see* Fig 145). If Bab is a moderate player, she may see nothing better than the following: make hoop 1 off yellow, with a rush towards hoop 2; split yellow to hoop 3 while going to red in corner 2; roll approach hoop 2 from corner 2. If this fails to give almost perfect position, Bab must retire to partner near hoop 4, leaving a rush to corner 3, and Ray with a thirteen or fourteen-yard (11.7–12.6m) shot

119

for red at yellow and little reason not to take it.

An expert Bab would approach the situation with more vision. Hoop 1 is made off yellow as before, but the rush is directed back towards black. Yellow is croqueted one yard (90cm) south-east of hoop 4, while blue seeks a rush on black towards corner 2. If this succeeds, red is rushed to hoop 2 and back into corner 2 after the hoop is made, and another precision rush on black to hoop 3 soon establishes a 3-ball break from which a 4-ball break can quickly emerge.

If the rush on black to corner 2 crossed the boundary more than two yards (1.8m) away from the corner, Bab would not be without resource. She would roll black two yards (1.8m) north-west of hoop 2 while going to red. A split stop shot will send red two yards (1.8m) north-east of hoop 3, and blue in front of hoop 2. If blue's position is merely reasonable, it may still pay Bab to try for the hoop, in the knowledge that there is a break to be had if she succeeds, and no immediate disaster if she fails. If blue has no position at all for the hoop, Bab can retire behind black with a rush to her hoop and a very powerful leave that virtually forces Ray to send red into corner 1 (*see* Fig 146).

Establishing breaks demands accurate rushing to the right places. Nowhere are mistakes more often made than in the long rush to the first hoop of a turn. If it is essential to obtain a forward rush after running the hoop, you will find that it will improve your chances of success to ensure that the hoop approach is played from the playing side of the hoop. Most experts would prefer to approach from three yards (2.7m) on the playing side than from one yard (90cm) to the side or from behind, particularly on a fast court. A long rush to a hoop should therefore be aimed at a spot about two yards (1.8m) on the playing side, rather than at the hoop itself.

Experts are made rather than born, and most of their expertise comes from hard practice and the ability to learn from the mistakes of others as well as their own. Once

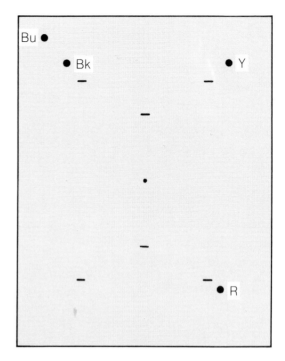

Fig 146

you can successfully rush a ball from one corner to another, or approach a corner hoop from the boundary or the adjacent corner three times out of four, you will see situations in a different light and many more possibilities will present themselves.

MAKING A LEAVE

(Figs 147 to 149)

Sometimes all you can do in the immediate turn is to make a leave with a view to making progress in the next. A good leave offers you the chance of at least a 3-ball break if your opponent finesses, and only long and dangerous shots if he wants to chance his arm. An expert usually prefers his opponent to finesse rather than shoot, as the innings cannot then change hands and he is confident of his ability to extract a break from an unpromising situation. Occasionally, in very difficult conditions, it may pay to tempt the opponent into shooting in order to establish a playable break immediately.

The standard leave is the so-called 'next two' leave. In Fig 147 red is for hoop 1 so blue and black are placed near hoops 1 and 2 and red is left a rush on yellow towards either corner 1 or corner 2. This leave usually forces Bab to play with blue, the most immediately useful ball, and she may shoot at black, relying on Ray making a mess of the rush from hoop 2 to hoop 1. Alternatively, she can shoot at red or yellow if they offer a reasonable target, and red has such an easy rush that a miss by blue will not help Ray immediately, or she can finesse by sending blue to corner 4 if vacant, or corner 1 or 3 otherwise.

Note that blue is placed only slightly south of hoop 1 so that if Bab were to shoot with black at blue and miss, Ray would be able to stop shot black to hoop 2 and make hoop 1 off blue. Black, however, is placed half-way between hoop 2 and the boundary instead of nearer the hoop. This has several advantages

for Ray. First, it lengthens the shot blue at black to over twenty-five yards (22.5m). Second, it may allow blue and black to be cross-wired. Third, if blue moves, yellow can be rushed behind black and stop shotted to hoop 2, while red obtains a rush on black to hoop 1. It is significantly easier to get an accurate rush this way than by the full roll that would be needed if black were close to the hoop.

Fig 148 shows a comparable leave when red is for hoop 2. Note that blue is only two yards (1.8m) west of hoop 2, to allow a stop shot from the west boundary which sends a ball to hoop 3, while allowing red to hold a rush on blue. Black, on the other hand, is placed four yards (3.6m) east of hoop 3. This lengthens the shot with blue at black to twenty yards (18m), gives a possible cross-wire and, if blue misses black, allows red to stop shot blue to hoop 3 and gain a rush on black to hoop 2.

These leaves strongly discourage Bab from shooting at her partner ball. She will be discouraged from shooting at red and yellow if

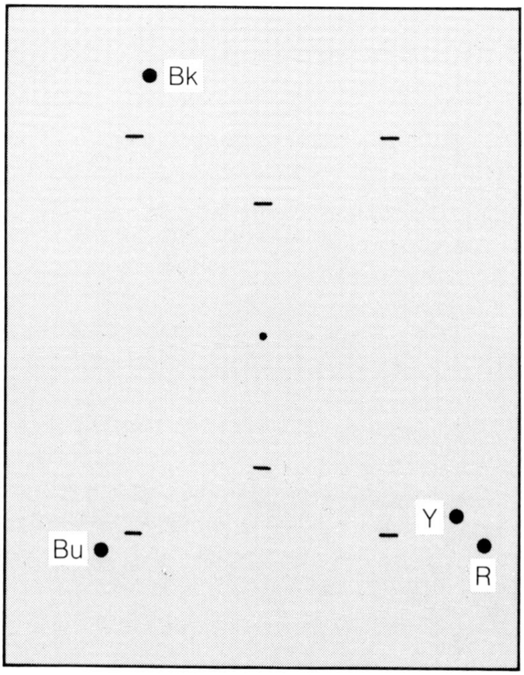

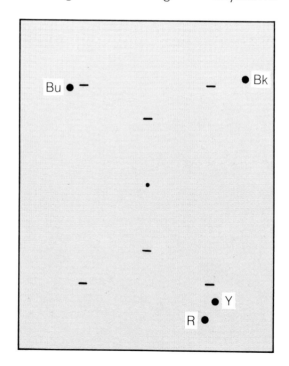

Fig 147

Fig 148

the shot is very long, is at a single target and offers Ray a materially easier break if the shot is missed. In addition, the natural defensive corner should be left vacant to encourage the finesse. The use of the cross-wire to hide one of red and yellow from blue should not be forgotten.

Most non-lift leaves in other situations and hoop positions are simply variations on this theme. The enemy balls are prised off the boundaries by a few yards, in the vicinity of the next two hoops if possible, and ahead of the break if not. The striker leaves a rush either to his hoop or to the less immediately useful enemy ball. Fig 149 shows a typical leave when Ray is for 4-back and peg. Because he can expect to make 4-back off partner with control, blue and black are placed as rather distant pioneers for penultimate and rover.

It is appropriate to end with a word of warning. Never be astonished by anything your opponent does and never feel aggrieved if he takes 'the wrong shot' and hits. In particular, avoid forcing him to shoot unless you want him to do so. It is not a good idea to leave a good shot at hoops 1 and 2 when your balls are for each of those hoops. He must shoot in such circumstances and will do so quite freely as he has nothing to lose.

PLAYING THE BREAK *(Fig 150)*

A break is regarded as established by the time you have three balls under control. Under normal playing conditions, it should be routine to develop a 3-ball break into a 4-ball break. Usually the fourth ball is hiding in a corner, and it is easiest to extract it immediately before making the adjacent corner hoop. Fig 150 shows a common situation, where Bab has just made hoop 3 with blue off black. Red is in corner 4 and yellow has been deliberately placed just south-east of hoop 4 to facilitate the pick-up of red. Bab should rush black as near to red as possible and stop shot black south of

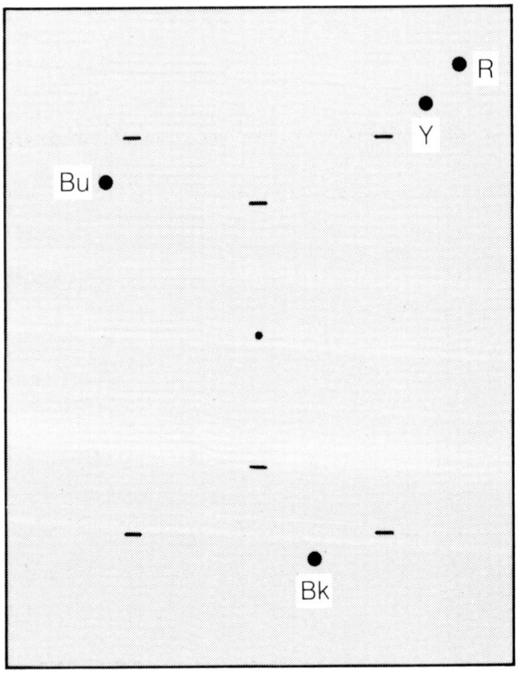

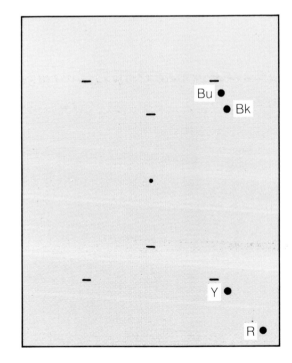

Fig 149

Fig 150

hoop 4. Blue remains close to red, so that Bab can roquet it and croquet it to hoop 5, while sending blue to yellow. All the balls are now in court and a 4-ball break has been established.

It is unwise to extract red in this way if yellow is instead north-west of hoop 4. In this situation, unless playing conditions are very easy, it is safer to send black to hoop 5 and to ignore red until after making hoop 4. There are two methods of extracting the extra ball in this position. The bold line is to rush yellow a little way north-west of hoop 4 after making the hoop, and then to take-off to red. A hefty split sends red to hoop 6 and blue to black at hoop 5, and a 4-ball break is effectively set up. The precision player may prefer to rush to the corner ball after making hoops 4 and 5, and thus develop a ball near 3-back which will be of use at the end of the break, or even to continue the 3-ball break until red can be picked up, before making 3-back.

The split roll method can also be used to extract a ball in corner 1, before making hoop 5, so that all the balls are available in good time for making an effective leave or attempting a delayed triple peel (see Chapter 15).

PLACING PIONEERS (Fig 151)

The hallmark of a good break player is the apparent simplicity and inevitability of his breaks, which flows principally from the accuracy of his pioneers. A good pioneer is placed about three feet (90cm) from the hoop on the playing side, so that a gentle roquet will always leave it in good position and a firmer roquet from the playing side will not send it past the hoop.

Beginners are advised to place pioneers for the four corner hoops inside the inner rectangle (see Chapter 7). However, experts attach great importance to being able to approach every hoop from the playing side. The disadvantage of the beginner's pioneer placement with respect to pioneers for hoops 1, 3, 1-back and 3-back, is that a poor contact

when rushing the pioneer into position prior to the hoop approach will leave the pioneer on the non-playing side of the hoop. In competition play, new, heavily milled balls are often used, and an unsatisfactory contact in a gentle rush is not unknown. In these circumstances, play safe and place all your pioneers on the playing side of every hoop.

More disasters probably occur at 2-back than at any other hoop in advanced play, and most can be traced to inaccurate pioneers and the impending lift. Accordingly, it is now routine for experts to place the 2-back pioneer after making hoop 5. Fig 151 shows the position before Bab runs hoop 5 with blue, with the intention of leaving black at 2-back afterwards. Bab roquets black immediately after running hoop 5, croquets it accurately into position from short range, and makes hoops 6 and 1-back on a 3-ball break. This should obviously not be attempted if the hoop 6 pioneer is inaccurate.

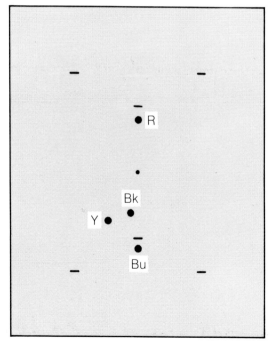

Fig 151

The same tactic may be used to place the hoop 6 pioneer after making hoop 3, but it is much less frequently employed. Hoop 6 does not have the same fearsome reputation as 2-back, and the break is often only partially established when hoop 3 is run. None the less, if circumstances permit, it is worth doing.

The tactics of playing breaks, discussed above, are undoubtedly important, but they take second place to the fundamental skill of running hoops with control, so that you can always secure the rush you need afterwards. Without such control, you will never be a really convincing break player.

You must learn to trust your hoop stroke well enough to run hoops very gently if the need arises. A worthwhile form of practice is to place a ball six inches (15cm) in front of a hoop, and practise running it by as little as possible from each side alternately. As you lose control, you hit harder and the ball sails through by more and more, which in turn forces you to hit harder still. Ultimately, you will stick, although you may get an occasional reprieve when the ball only struggles through and allows you, once more, to run the hoop from a couple of inches. When you can perform this initially tedious exercise successfully for fifteen minutes without a break, you will have run the hoop at least 150 times, and learned the valuable lesson that a gently struck ball has a remarkable tendency to run the hoop if it possibly can.

14 Lift Leaves

The leaves described earlier had two common features. The enemy balls were left no shot of less than twenty-five yards (22.5m), and the striker had a rush to somewhere useful so that he had a good chance of at least a 3-ball break, irrespective of where the outplayer went.

Once you have conceded a lift, the situation becomes more difficult because your opponent can play from either baulk, and can therefore be virtually certain of having at least one shot of fifteen yards (13.5m), or less. Statistically, this represents an improvement in the outplayer's chances of hitting from about 20 per cent to 40 per cent. In practice, the difference is even more significant. A good shot will know that he should hit a fifteen-yarder if he swings correctly, but can only hope to hit the longer shot because the extra ten yards (9m) give the irregularities present in most lawns a much greater chance to influence the path of the ball.

There are other factors peculiar to lift leaves which are best discussed in the context of various examples. In the descriptions that follow, we shall assume that Ray plays with red in the break culminating in the leave.

Fig 152   A precision leave: 1986 British Open Doubles Champions, Nigel Aspinall and Stephen Mulliner.

THE OLD STANDARD LEAVE
(Fig 153)

Ray leaves blue a few yards south-west of hoop 2 and black about three yards (2.7m) east of the peg. Yellow (for hoop 1) is on the east boundary, between one and four yards (90cm–3.6m) north of corner 4, red is two to three feet (60–90cm) north of yellow. Bab's usual options are: to lift either ball and take the short shot, actually thirteen to fourteen yards (11.7–12.6m) at red or yellow from the end of A-baulk; or, to lift blue and shoot at black from A-baulk. In the latter choice there is a further choice. The shot from the east end of A-baulk is about seventeen yards (15.3m), but a miss will leave blue in the middle of the north boundary and readily accessible to Ray if he makes hoop 1. The shot from near corner 1 is about twenty-three yards (20.7m), but misses into corner 3, which may be slightly safer. The thirteen-yard (11.7m) shot should be hit about 50 per cent of the time by a good shot, but is often refused because it is thought to give away too much if missed.

This leave has a long history. It was given the blessing of Solomon and Cotter in the 1950s as a prelude to a standard triple peel (*see* Chapter 15) from the hoop 2 and 4-back position, following a peel of the partner ball through hoop 1 in the course of the first break. It is still the most commonly seen leave after a break to 4-back, even though peeling partner through hoop 1 has gone out of fashion. Its main advantage is that it can be easily set up from almost any position of the balls after making 3-back. It also gives Ray a good chance of a break if Bab misses. Its drawbacks are the relative shortness of the shots left for Bab, and the fact that Bab has an equally good chance of a break if she hits. It is thus a bit of a lottery and you may well feel that after getting round to 4-back you should have a better than 50 to 60 per cent chance of keeping the innings.

THE DIAGONAL SPREAD *(Fig 154)*

Ray makes 2-back off black with yellow by the peg and blue at 3-back. He rushes black to the peg, croquets it two feet (60cm) east and slightly south of the peg, and either takes off from yellow to blue or rushes yellow to blue and stop shots yellow back to the peg. After making 3-back, Ray rushes blue about five yards (4.5m) south-east of black, so that he can croquet it to a spot level with penultimate and about two yards (1.8m) in from the west boundary. Black is now rushed and croqueted to a spot between six and eighteen inches (15 and 45cm) south-east of the peg, and directly wired from blue. Yellow is then rushed to the east boundary level with rover and given a three-foot (90cm) rush pointing directly at the peg.

The point of this leave is that black is wired from blue and hampered from red and yellow. Most players are reluctant to leave a ball in the middle of the court when the opponent has a rush towards it, so Bab will usually lift black to B-baulk, to shoot down the east boundary at

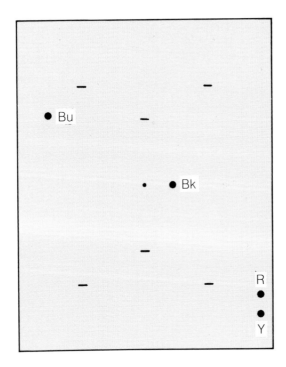

Fig 153

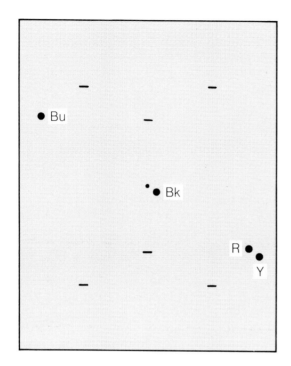

Fig 154

rush on blue to hoop 1. An aggressive player who is good at big roll strokes can go to black after making hoop 1, and send it to hoop 3, while yellow goes to red at hoop 2, giving a good chance of a standard triple. A precision player will usually be content to pick up black before making hoop 4, and will then attempt a delayed triple.

THE NEW STANDARD LEAVE *(Figs 155 & 156)*

Ray ensures that yellow is the pioneer at 2-back and makes 1-back with blue and black close by. Blue is sent to a spot one yard (90cm) off the yard-line and two or three yards (1.8–2.7m) south of 1-back. Black is rushed to a spot north-west of yellow, so that Ray can croquet it to 3-back and make 2-back with control and a rush on yellow towards 3-back. Yellow is croqueted about three yards (2.7m) north-east of 3-back, while red gets position to rush black

red and yellow, a shot of about twenty-three yards (20.7m) which, if it misses, will finish up reasonably safe in corner 4. A hit does not guarantee an immediate break if red, the in-court ball, is hit full, because Bab may have a difficult take-off to get a rush on yellow to either blue or hoop 1. If yellow is hit, the rush is easier to obtain, and this explains why good players always aim at the yard-line ball unless they suspect the flatness of the boundary area. She might take a bolder option and shoot with black from the end of A-baulk at red and yellow. This reduces the shot to about sixteen yards (14.4m) and a hit gives excellent break chances. But a miss gives Ray all four balls and a good chance of a standard triple peel.

This is a very effective leave that should be in every good player's repertoire. It requires only a little organisation and usually forces the opponent to take a shot which is only hit about 20 per cent of the time. If the long east boundary shot is missed, red is rushed to blue and croqueted to hoop 2, while yellow gets a

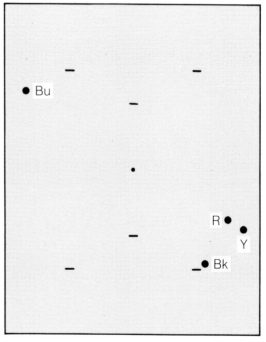

Fig 155

accurately to a spot six inches (15cm) south-east of the hoop. In the hoop approach, black is sent six inches (15cm) north-east of 3-back, and red gets close position to run the hoop gently, so that a tiny roquet and croquet stroke will place black in the position shown in Fig 156. Ray now rushes yellow to the boundary and lays a rush for yellow, either towards blue, or towards hoop 1, or to a spot six yards (5.4m) west of corner 4, according to taste. If the balls are left at least three feet (90cm) apart they will not present Bab with a double target.

Black should be invisible from the end of A-baulk and hampered from red and yellow. In this leave, blue is usually seen as the ball that is more useful to Ray, so Bab will usually lift blue. With no ball left near hoop 2, Bab has a free choice between shooting from A-baulk or B-baulk, and the former should be preferred as it offers the shorter shot and a pick-up for Ray that is not completely straightforward if it is missed.

If Bab does take the shot down the east boundary and misses, the normal continuation for Ray is to roquet red gently, take-off to blue and stop shot it to hoop 2 while attempting to get a good rush on black to hoop 1. If it comes off, the standard triple is there for the taking; if not, Ray can make an excellent leave. A more adventurous variation consists of stop shotting red to hoop 2, while getting a rush on black towards corner 4 and blue. The square stop split is quite easy if practised, and the target for the rush is enormous. This should ensure an

easy rush to hoop 1 and gives Ray a similar position to that reached after a diagonal spread and a miss by Bab into corner 4.

THE VERTICAL SPREAD
(Figs 157 to 159)

Ray has already taken yellow to 4-back and is now taking red to the peg. He makes 4-back off black, with blue and yellow waiting at penultimate. Black is croqueted to rover, yellow is croqueted to a spot five feet (1.5m) south of penultimate and blue is rushed to a spot six inches (15cm) to one side of the hoop and either level with it, or a fraction north. In the hoop approach, blue goes six inches (15cm) in front of penultimate, while red gets close position to run the hoop gently, roquet blue and gently croquet it into the position shown in Fig 158. Ray rushes yellow to rover, leaves it about three feet (90cm) east, and approaches the hoop off black, so that black

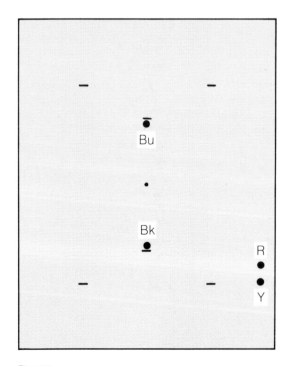

Fig 157

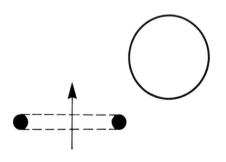

Fig 156   New standard leave – ball at 3-back.

stays by the east side of rover and can be easily roqueted and croqueted into the position shown in Fig 159. Ideally, blue and black will be unrushable to either hoops 1 or 2, and unable to shoot at red and yellow from where they lie. Yellow is rushed to the east boundary, level with rover, or a little south, and given a three foot (90cm) rush on red up the east boundary.

Ray is threatening to rush red to 4-back so Bab will usually lift blue. Her options are:

1. To shoot at red and yellow from B-baulk, making a double target if possible.
2. To shoot at red or yellow from A-baulk.
3. To shoot at black from B-baulk, so that blue will finish in A-baulk if it misses.
4. To play blue a foot (30cm) out of corner 1.

The rationale of options 3 and 4 is that Ray may fail at penultimate on a 2-ball break and concede a lift with a ball in baulk.

OTHER LEAVES *(Figs 160 & 161)*

The 1-back leave and the scatter leave may be useful if you are playing a really good shot. Space forbids giving full details of how to create the leaves, but if you have understood the descriptions above you should be able to work it out. The 1-back leave (*see* Fig 160) achieved modern fame as the 'delayed sextuple leave' pioneered by Keith Wylie. It offers a thirty yard (27m) shot which will not be hit more than 5 or 10 per cent of the time. Having stopped at 1-back on the first break to avoid giving a lift, Ray should aim to reach the peg with yellow, do at least 4 peels and concede a contact, secure in the knowledge that Bab has a very long way to go. If Bab had already reached 4-back, Ray should instead aim to triple peel and peg out Bab's forward ball instead.

The scatter leave is suitable when two crack shots meet. Blue and black are left level with the peg and six inches (15cm) off each yard-line, and red and yellow are left in corners 2

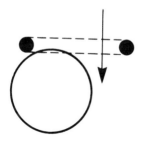

Fig 158   Vertical spread – ball at penult.

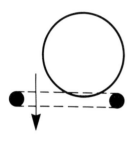

Fig 159   Vertical spread – ball at rover.

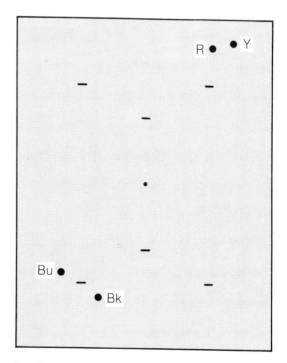

Fig 160

129

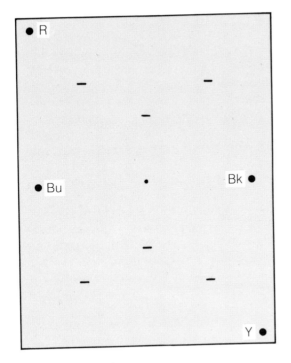

Fig 161   The scatter leave.

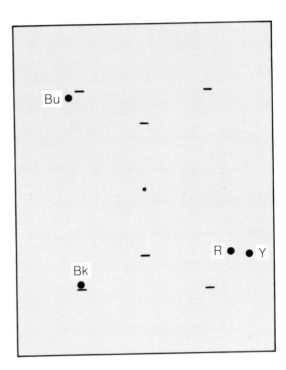

Fig 162   A strongly polarised leave.

and 4. The point is that if Bab shoots at red or yellow, she has no immediate break, and if she shoots at partner, she will leave a double for Ray. Even if she trickles to partner, leaving no double, Ray will still have a chance to hit a sixteen-yard (14.4m) shot to recover the innings.

LEAVE POLARITY *(Fig 162)*

All the descriptions given above have assumed that blue and black were both for hoop 1 and, apart from the vertical spread, that yellow has also not started. Clearly hoop positions will have an important influence on your choice of leave. It is obviously not a good idea to join up near an opponent's hoop. If Bab has one ball for hoop 4, Ray would be well advised to forget the new standard leave and consider instead the mirror images of the old standard leave or the diagonal spread.

However, polarity is most useful when your opponent is for hoop 1 and 4-back or for 4-back and peg. You need to induce him to play with the forward ball, so that a hit will not be immediately fatal or, if he insists on playing with the backward ball and misses, you will obtain a very easy break as a result. The old standard leave and the diagonal spread are easy to polarise by leaving the ball near hoop 2 right on the yard-line. This will suggest to your opponent that you have no certain break and will strongly influence him to lift his other ball.

The vertical spread is naturally very strongly polarised and almost forces the ball at penultimate to be moved. The new standard leave is moderately polarised and most players lift the ball near hoop 2. An example of a very strongly polarised leave, when the opponent is for hoop 1 and 4-back, is shown in Fig 162. However, never forget that your opponent may reasonably conclude that he must either hit or lose the game. In that mood, he will take the shot he wants to take. All you can do is to make it very expensive for him to miss.

15 The Triple Peel

If you reach 4-back with red and your opponent misses the lift, you hope to take yellow to the peg. If you can arrange to send red through 4-back, penultimate and rover as part of yellow's break, you can peg out both red and yellow at the end of the turn and win without further ado. When a ball is sent through its next hoop by another ball, rather than directly by the mallet, it is said to have been *peeled* and may be referred to as the *peelee*. As red has three hoops to make, three peels are needed and, if the break culminates in a successful peg out, it is called a *triple peel* or, simply, a *triple*.

The triple is no longer regarded as a complicated manoeuvre performed only by a small minority of experts. Successful triples are commonplace in every championship and in most A Class tournaments, and the ability to complete a triple should be part of every good player's armoury.

Triples are traditionally divided into two varieties, the standard and the delayed. A standard triple is an ordinary 4-ball break in which the peelee acts as the pivot and remains near the three peel hoops for most of the break. Delayed triples are more adventurous and have been aptly described as 3-ball breaks with added complications.

THE STANDARD TRIPLE

Assume that Ray left a diagonal spread (*see* Fig 154) after taking red to 4-back, and that Bab lifted black and missed at red and yellow from A-baulk. Blue is not far from hoop 2, so Ray now plays with yellow and attempts a standard triple. He begins by hitting black, makes hoop 1 off red and rushes red back to the east

boundary a few yards south of black. He croquets red to hoop 3, and rushes black to blue. Black is croqueted back towards the middle of the lawn, and Ray makes hoop 2 off blue. Blue is sent to hoop 4 and black is rushed to hoop 3. So far, nothing unusual has occurred.

THE 4-BACK PEEL
(Figs 163, 164 & 167)

Black is croqueted to a spot two feet (60cm) south and one foot (30cm) to one side of hoop 3. If blue came to rest to the east of hoop 4, it makes life easier to have black east of hoop 3 as well, and vice versa. Red is rushed to a spot one foot (30cm) north and 6 inches (15cm) to one side of the hoop, so that in the hoop approach, red can be sent one foot (30cm) south of hoop 3 and yellow can easily get close position to run hoop 3 gently. Yellow will probably roquet red in the hoop stroke, so Ray takes croquet immediately and plays a gentle split shot, which sends red through 4-back by a couple of yards and gives yellow a rush on black towards blue at hoop 4.

THE PENULT PEEL
(Figs 165 & 166)

Ray croquets black to hoop 5 and makes hoop 4 off blue. If black has been accurately positioned about three feet (90cm) south of hoop 5, and Ray is a good rusher, he should approach hoop 4 by sending blue just to the east of the hoop. After running the hoop gently, Ray can rush blue to corner 3, croquet it to hoop 6 and get a rush on red to the middle

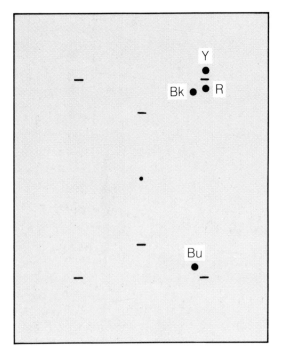

Fig 163

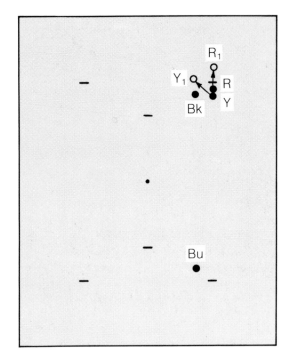

Fig 164

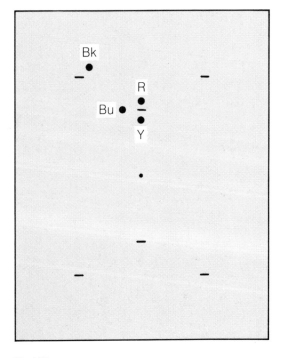

Fig 165

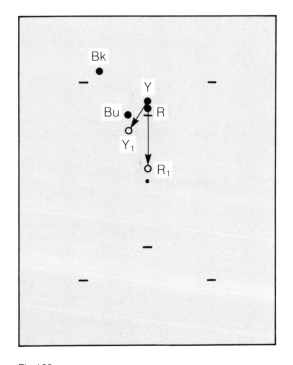

Fig 166

Fig 167   The 4-back peel: Mark Avery.

of the south boundary. Red is then croqueted to hoop 6, and yellow approaches black at hoop 5. An alternative method, useful in easy conditions, is to rush red directly to hoop 6, and take off to black at hoop 5. Its main drawback is the danger of getting cross-wired from black, either before the take-off (by hoop 6, the peg or blue) or by hoop 5 itself.

Having made hoop 5, Ray rushes black just south of hoop 6, croquets it to 1-back and roquets blue. Blue is croqueted to a spot level with, and two feet (60cm) west of hoop 6, and red is rushed to a spot one foot (30cm) south and six inches (15cm) to one side of the hoop, so that, in the hoop approach, red is sent into perfect peeling position, namely one foot (30cm) north of the hoop, and yellow gets close position to run hoop 6 gently. Ray runs hoop 6, roquets red gently, if the roquet did not occur in the hoop stroke, and plays a firm stop shot which sends red through penultimate as far as possible, and gives yellow a rush on blue to the middle of the north boundary (see Fig. 166).

It is unsafe to collect red immediately after making hoop 4 if black is badly placed at hoop 5. Instead, Ray should rush blue south of black after running hoop 4, so that he can croquet blue to hoop 6 and obtain a good rush on black to hoop 5. Ray now makes hoop 5, rushes black into corner 3 and croquets it to 1-back, getting a rush on red to penult. Red is rushed and croqueted into peeling position, and Ray approaches hoop 6 off blue, sending blue to a spot two feet (60cm) west of the hoop unless red is to the east of penult when blue should be sent two feet (60cm) east instead. He runs the hoop, roquets red and attempts the peel. If red is peeled successfully, the triple returns to the original line. If the peel fails, the triple becomes delayed.

THE ROVER PEEL

Returning to Fig 166, Ray stop shots blue to 2-back, makes 1-back off black and rushes it a few yards north of red. He croquets black to a spot three feet (90cm) south of 3-back and gets as good a rush as possible on red to rover. It is unsafe to attempt the peel going to 2-back, unless red is rushed directly in front of rover and not more than two feet (60cm) away. If this does not happen, Ray should be content with playing a take-off, which sends red about a yard (90cm) north of rover, and yellow to blue at 2-back.

Ray makes 2-back off blue and plays a hard stop shot, which sends blue to 4-back and yellow just north of red. Red is rushed into perfect position for the rover peel, namely a foot (30cm) north of the hoop, and peeled using a split full roll which sends yellow just south of black at 3-back. The peel must not be played with a firmer shot using less roll, because red might be sent over the boundary and so end the turn. If the peel is successful, Ray rushes black to the middle of the south boundary after running 3-back so that black can be sent to rover and red can be rushed up the lawn towards blue at 4-back. Red is croqueted to penult and Ray is able to finish with an easy 4-ball break.

THE DELAYED TRIPLE

A delayed triple occurs when any peel is performed later than in the standard triple, but the three peels and peg out are nevertheless completed. Many triples are delayed and the ability to recover safely and successfully from a failed peel or a delayed start to the triple is the hallmark of an expert. The description that follows confines itself to the main lines, although there is no shortage of variations which you will meet or work out for yourself as your experience grows. For reasons which will become obvious, we shall begin with the delayed rover peel and end with the delayed 4-back peel.

THE DELAYED
ROVER PEEL (Figs 168 to 170)

The commonest case arises when a standard triple goes according to plan until the failure of the rover peel before 3-back. This necessitates peeling red through rover immediately before the hoop is made for yellow, and such a peel is known as a straight rover peel. We shall rejoin Ray at this point. If the peel attempt left red stuck in the jaws or within a foot or two (30–60cm) of rover, Ray should make 3-back and rush black towards blue at 4-back, leaving red behind. Black is croqueted to penultimate and 4-back is made off blue. Ray then rushes blue north of black, croquets it to rover and approaches penultimate off black. The ideal position for blue is level with rover and two feet (60cm) to the side. The choice of side is influenced by the position of red. If red is slightly to the west of rover, blue should be to the west as well, and vice versa.

A different approach is needed if the peel attempt causes red to rebound several yards from rover, or if no attempt at the peel has been possible by the time Ray runs 3-back, but Red is accessible in the middle of the court. Ray now makes 3-back with a rush to a spot south of red, so that black can be croqueted a yard south-west of penultimate and red can be rushed up to blue. Ray croquets red close to black and makes 4-back off blue with a rush back towards red and black. Blue is croqueted to rover, ideally level with the hoop and two feet (60cm) to one side, and red is rushed a yard (90cm) north of black. Ray stop shots red accurately to a spot three feet (90cm) north of rover and gets a short rush on black to penultimate. Placing black south of penultimate significantly shortens the vital stop shot that sends red into, or near, peeling position.

The two lines discussed now converge. Ray makes penultimate, rushes black north of rover and croquets it to a spot about eight yards (7.2m) south of the hoop, to cater for the possibility that the peel may not go through cleanly. Whether he should now roquet red or

blue depends on their positions.

If red is north of rover and within three feet (90cm), and blue is level with the hoop and two feet (60cm) or so to the side, Ray should roquet red to a spot one foot (30cm) north of rover and peel it with a firm stop shot that sends red at least three yards (2.7m) through rover and gives yellow a short rush on blue back to the hoop (see Fig 168). In the hoop approach, blue is sent to a spot north of red so that Ray can run the hoop with yellow without hitting red on the way. Ray runs rover, roquets blue and takes off to get an easy rush for yellow on red to the peg.

If red and blue are not so well-placed, Ray should roquet blue first so that he can croquet it two or three yards (1.8–2.7m) south of rover and get a really accurate rush on red to the ideal peeling spot mentioned above. If Ray rushes red within six inches (15cm) of rover, he may choose to send both balls through the hoop in the croquet stroke, a manoeuvre known as an *Irish peel*, which has the

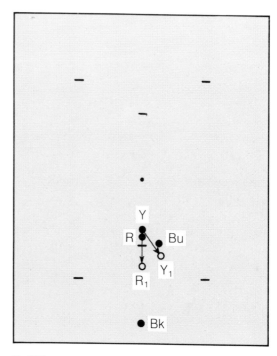

Fig 168

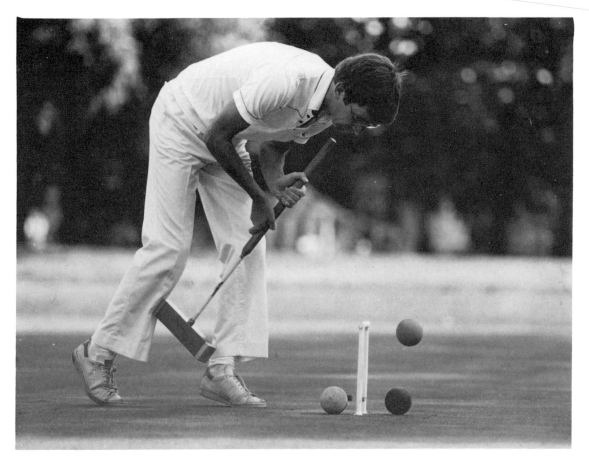

Fig 169　The half jump.

Fig 170　The full jump.

advantage that any contact between red and yellow later in the stroke is not counted as a roquet unless they end up in contact with each other. If the peel is attempted from further away, a stop shot is safest and should be played so that yellow will stop at least six inches (15cm) short of the hoop. Then, if red sticks in the jaws or only goes through by a few inches, Ray can half jump or full jump yellow through rover. Yellow will probably go off the lawn and Ray's foresight in placing black well south of rover now pays off. He hits black, takes off to blue and finishes as described above.

THE DELAYED PENULT PEEL *(Fig 171)*

If Ray is unable to peel red through penultimate after yellow runs hoop 6, he has four opportunities to recover, namely before 2-back, 3-back, 4-back and penultimate. If red sticks in penultimate, it is only technically delayed and can be easily rush peeled down to rover after Ray makes 1-back. Deliberately 'jawsing' the peel is advisable if there is a risk that red may go through by only a few inches. Otherwise, there is a real danger that yellow might be cross-wired from red when Ray tries to get position for a rush on red after 1-back.

The attempt after 1-back is only feasible if red is close to penult, typically after a failed standard peel. Rejoining our example, Ray makes 1-back off black, croquets it to 3-back, rushes red in front of penultimate and plays a big roll, peeling red and sending yellow down to blue waiting at 2-back. The dangers of such a shot on a tricky lawn are not to be underestimated, and such a peel is known as a 'death roll' for good reason. However, if Ray is very lucky, red may stop close to rover and permit him to peel before 3-back. Failing this, he will have to be content with a straight rover peel.

If Ray cannot position red in front of penultimate until after 2-back, he can try a similar peel going to the pioneer at 3-back. If successful, he will have to finish with a straight rover peel unless he flukes red through rover in the penultimate peel. This event is not unknown in play.

If the death roll is too risky, Ray should concentrate on peeling red before yellow makes 4-back. Assume that Ray makes 2-back off blue and rushes it back to penultimate. He croquets blue three feet (90cm) north-east of penultimate as a distant pioneer for 4-back, rushes red into position for the peel and takes off back to black at 3-back. If red was already in reasonable position, it may be safer to rush blue south of black and croquet it east of penultimate, but it is unlikely to make life easier when it comes to doing the peel and

getting a good rush to 4-back. In either case, Ray must get a forward rush on black after making 3-back, so that he can easily position black two feet (60cm) west of penultimate and rush red into perfect peeling position. He now peels gently (lodging red in the jaws is good enough) and concentrates on getting a good rush on blue to 4-back (*see* Fig 171). The break is completed by a straight rover peel.

Ray's last chance occurs when yellow is about to make penultimate itself, the straight penult peel. If the peel before 4-back fails, or red is very close to good peeling position anyway, Ray croquets blue to rover, peels red as firmly as the position of black permits, and makes penultimate off black. Unless red has travelled most of the way to rover, Ray probably cannot afford the luxury of croqueting black south of rover and must be content with using it to get an accurate rush on red. This is even more likely if red is not well placed at penultimate and Ray has to roquet black after blue so that he can obtain a short rush on red

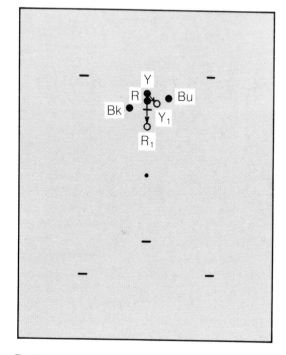

Fig 171

into peeling position. If red is very close to the hoop, an Irish peel may be considered. Otherwise, Ray must be content with a controlled peel and an accurate rush on red down to rover.

Assuming Ray succeeds in rushing red to within two or three yards (1.8–2.7m) of rover, he should go for the peel with a firm stop shot, to give red a chance of clearing rover by a few yards if the peel succeeds, and a chance of bouncing clear of the hoop if it fails. There is no percentage in peeling by a few inches, because the absence of a ball near the south boundary rules out a jump shot.

THE DELAYED 4-BACK PEEL *(Figs 172 to 174)*

If the 4-back peel is not achieved after making hoop 3 with yellow, Ray can safely try again before making hoop 6, after making hoop 6, and before making 4-back, the straight 4-back peel. That last option is the first part of a straight triple, a chancy but spectacular finish.

If red sticks in 4-back, Ray can rush peel it after making hoop 5 and try to roll it into peeling position at penultimate. If successful, the triple returns to the standard form.

If Ray is to attempt the peel before hoop 6, he should position red and blue, the pioneer for hoop 6, near 4-back, before making hoop 5 off black, as shown in Fig 172. If red is already near 4-back, usually because the standard peel attempt has failed, Ray simply leaves it by the hoop while he makes hoops 4 and 5 off blue and black and croquets blue into position after hoop 4. If red was elsewhere when Ray made hoop 3, such as in corner 4, it, too, must be croqueted up to 4-back before Ray makes hoop 5 off black. Having made the hoop, Ray rushes black a few yards south-east of red, stop shots black to 1-back, rushes red into peeling position and, once he has lined up the peel, concentrates solely on getting as good a rush as possible to hoop 6. If the peel succeeds, Ray can continue the triple with a delayed double

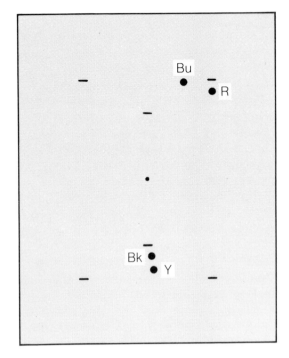

Fig 172

peel.

If Ray is unable to organise the balls before hoop 6, or dislikes the prospect of rushing blue to hoop 6 from near 4-back, he should consider sending black to 1-back as before, croqueting blue to the position shown in Fig 173, and making hoop 6 off red. In the hoop approach, red is sent two feet (60cm) north-east of hoop 6, and yellow is given very close position so that Ray can rush red into peeling position after the hoop (*see* Fig 173). Ray peels going to blue, croquets blue to 2-back and makes 1-back off black. He should try to continue the triple by peeling through penultimate before yellow makes 4-back.

The more traditional method of peeling before 1-back is infrequently seen today but is worth describing. After making hoop 5 off black, Ray croquets black to a spot four feet (1.2m) north-east of 1-back, croquets red to a spot two feet (60cm) south of 4-back, and makes hoop 6 off blue. He rushes blue to corner 3, croquets it to 2-back and gets

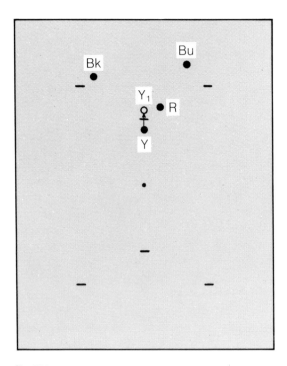

Fig 173

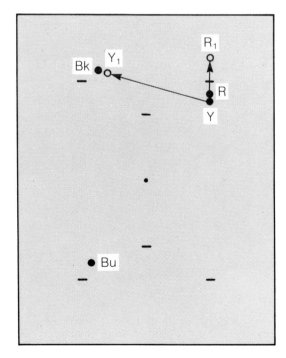

Fig 174

position on red to rush it into perfect peeling position six inches (15cm) south of 4-back. Red is peeled by a take-off in which yellow goes to black at 1-back. If successful, Ray can try the penult peel before 4-back (*see* Fig 174).

THE STRAIGHT TRIPLE

If red can be positioned at 4-back before Ray makes 3-back, he has an outside chance of completing the triple. Having made 3-back off black, Ray croquets it to a spot two feet (60cm) west of penult, rushes blue short of red and croquets it two yards (1.8m) north-east of 4-back. Red is now rushed into perfect peeling position, six inches (15cm) south of 4-back, and peeled with a stop shot. Ray runs 4-back, avoiding a roquet on red, and rushes blue into corner 3. He now has a crucial shot. He must stop shot blue to rover and give yellow a short, straight rush on red to a spot four feet (1.2m) north of penultimate. If the rush succeeds, red is peeled hard down to rover while yellow makes penultimate off black. The turn is completed with a straight rover peel.

The chances of getting an easy rush to penultimate are improved if Ray roquets blue gently after running 4-back instead of rushing it into the corner. This variation requires discipline, as Ray must refuse to be tempted into an attempt at the penult peel unless red is almost dead straight on penultimate and within four feet. If not, the safety of the break must be protected by sending red as a pioneer to rover and abandoning the triple.

Straight triples are now recorded so often during a season that they excite little comment. None the less, they require both skill and luck to complete, and should be embarked upon in a serious match only if you are sure you know what you are doing. At championship level, straight triple attempts are one of the most productive causes of disaster. A famous comment about peeling is worth repeating: 'The most important thing about triples is . . . to know when to give them up'. Boring though it may be, the truth is that for most of us, many more games are won by getting to the peg safely than by doing a standard triple, and many, many more than by persisting with a delayed triple. The best reasons why everyone should try triples are that they are great fun to bring off and they extend your abilities. Another worthy reason is that they are a very effective way of announcing to the croquet world in general, and to your opponent in particular, that you are a force to be reckoned with.

PULL *(Figs 175 to 179)*

There is an important technical point to be made about peeling. If you aim peels by adjusting the balls until the line joining their centres points at the centre of the hoop, you will find that the peelee often sticks in the jaws because it seems to be pulled off its line in the croquet stroke. This 'pull' is a feature of all split croquet strokes, and manifests itself by the balls exhibiting a tendency to narrow the angle between them as they travel across the lawn. It is caused by the milling on the surfaces of the balls imparting side spin. Pull has to be allowed for, and only experience will tell you how much to adjust. It is generally true that pull is most evident on slow lawns, in wet weather, using heavily milled balls, and in split shots that diverge at 45 degrees. The allowance required increases with the distance of the peel, and explains why the easiest peels are from close range and dead straight.

Fig 175   Peeling. The first look . . .

Fig 176   . . . getting down to it . . .

Fig 177   . . . the best view.

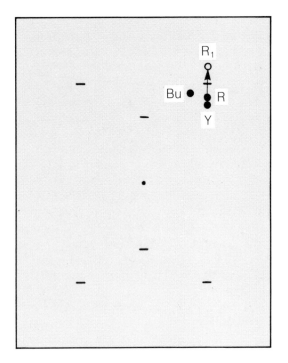

Fig 178

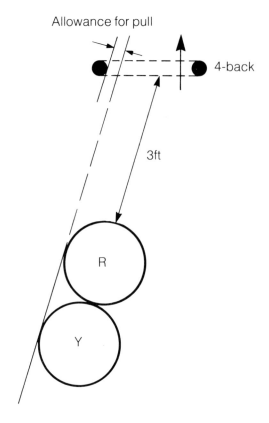

Allowance for pull

4-back

3ft

Fig 179   The 4-back peel – allowing for pull.

In particular, the presence of pull demands accuracy in aiming the peel, and the casual method described above is inadequate, especially for angled peels. You should aim using the line joining the sides of the balls, and you have to get down to ground level to do it properly. This is why so many newspapers and magazine articles feature players in a prone position in front of a hoop!

Assume you are playing yellow and are peeling red at 4-back from a position three feet (90cm) south of the hoop, with blue two feet (60cm) south-west of the hoop (*see* Fig 178). The allowance will be of the order of one hoop upright (the practical unit of measurement in such cases), and the alignment should be as shown in Fig 179. Note that because yellow will move from east to west in the split shot, red will be pulled to the west and, accordingly, it is the west upright of 4-back that matters.

16 The Pegged-out Game

Pegging out your opponent is simply a tactic designed to increase the probability that you will win the game. It cannot guarantee it, and there has been much recent discussion among tournament players on whether it offers any significant advantage to the pegger, the player who does the pegging out.

A little thought will show that pegging out will assist the pegger if, and only if, he knows how to conduct the pegged-out phase of the game properly. If your expert opponent has reached 4-back and peg, and you have reached 4-back and are taking the second ball round, but have no prospect of a triple, then the probability of winning is approximately equal to the probability that your opponent will miss the lift shot, say 60 per cent, if you do not peg him out and are confident of finishing in the next turn. If you do peg him out and separate your balls, a generous estimate of your opponent's chances of hitting the lift and finishing either immediately, or because he hits in subsequently, would be 20 per cent, so your chances are at least 80 per cent.

PEGGING OUT WITHOUT PEELING

The experience of the last twenty years has not significantly affected the wisdom of Solomon's advice on when to peg out your opponent in relation to the position of his backward clip. Always peg him out if he has yet to make 3-back, perhaps if he is for 4-back and your backward ball is for 1-back or better, perhaps if he is for penultimate and your backward ball is for 3-back or better, and *never* if he is for rover.

Having chosen to go for the peg out, it is vital to separate your balls before you leave the court, because you cannot afford to give your opponent a chance of an immediate 2-ball break if he hits the lift. The positions on the west and east boundaries that are respectively two and a half yards (2.25m) north and south of the peg offer nineteen-yard (17.1m) shots from either baulk. It is therefore a little unwise to peg out a good opponent if he is for penultimate as he may simply take position and wait for you to join up. If you shoot at him and miss, or join very wide, he can run penult and take position at rover. If you join up, he has a lift-length shot with an excellent chance of finishing.

Assuming your opponent shoots and misses, how should you proceed? There are two distinct tactics in this situation, namely the wiring method and the break method. The wirer creeps round the court making hoops individually off his partner ball, always rushing to wired spots, and thus preventing the peggee, his opponent, from taking any shot at all. The break method is less subtle. The pegger offers the peggee any number of shots but always at a range of twenty-five to thirty yards (22.5–27m), and at the risk of giving away a 3-ball break if the shot is missed.

As most players do not have the precision needed to obtain perfect wires all the time, it makes more sense to base your game on the break method and take the occasional wire that you find as an added bonus. It is quite easy to make one hoop at a time as far as hoop 4, because it is easy to guard the corners and threaten a 3-ball break. If you are settled into a cat-and-mouse game, with your opponent refusing to shoot, it is important to be patient and to refuse to make hoop 4 until you have a perfect short rush, which gives you a reasonable chance of making hoops 4, 5 and 6 in the next turn. Then you can lie up in corner 2 and threaten a break again.

There are two ways of dealing with the 1-back lift. The first is to make it and separate. The second is to lay up for a peel. This is prudent only if your opponent is not for hoops 1, 2 or 1-back himself, and if he has a shot of at least twenty-five yards (22.5m).

The break method has a significant psychological advantage compared to the wiring method, as it is easier for the pegger to remain positive if he is threatening the peggee. The wiring method can quickly induce paranoia and paralysis in the pegger as he strives to protect his 'won' game. Indeed, it is not uncommon to see the pegged-out phase of a game start, somewhat absurdly, with the pegger's two balls being chased around the court by the single ball of the peggee.

What tactics are available to the peggee? He will only get in by hitting a long shot, or if the pegger blunders in a 3-ball break off the peggee's ball. If the opponent is prone to nerves, it is sometimes profitable to menace his next hoop from the nearest corner. You should never forget the pressure on the pegger, and some strange decisions are often made as a result. If there is a lift due, it is well worth making sure that you get it by staying close enough to the 1-back area to inhibit any attempt at a peel. Of course, you may risk being picked up, if you are too close to the scene of the action or in front of the pegger's break. However, against certain players that may be your best chance of an innings.

If the peggee does obtain the innings, he must make every effort to establish a 3-ball break if he is more than three hoops from home. A dilemma often presents itself at this stage. Suppose yellow is pegged out, and Ray is for hoop 5 with red, and hits blue near 1-back. Black is one yard (90cm) east of 6. Should Ray roll blue to hoop 6 and try to get a rush on black to hoop 5? Or should he leave blue where it is and take off to black? The latter route is obviously preferable, because blue is already in a fairly useful position and, if Ray makes hoop 5 with any sort of north-bound

rush, should give him good chances of establishing a 3-ball break. Clearly, if the roll stroke comes off, it is very comforting to have blue at hoop 6 and an immediate break. However, the odds favour the more patient method and a peggee must expect to have to work for his break.

Another tactic is available to Ray in the position given and whenever he finds himself for an odd-numbered hoop. Instead of going solely for a break, he can give himself an additional chance by leaving both enemy balls ahead of his break. Then, if he fails to get adequate position for his hoop, he simply takes good position wired from the nearer enemy ball (see Fig 180). This 'double squeeze' places the pegger in a dilemma and he will normally send the ball nearer the peggee to a distant corner. Now the peggee can run the hoop hard and attempt to set up a 2-ball break which may, given good play and a following wind, become a game-winning 3-ball break.

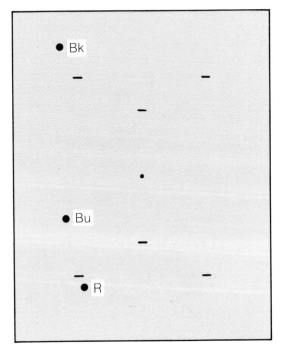

Fig 180

THE TRIPLE PEEL ON THE OPPONENT

The triple peel on the opponent's ball, or TPO, is a spectacular means of taking the battle to the enemy. Let us assume that Ray and Bab meet in the Open Championship in which matches are played as the best of three games. Ray wins the first game and takes red to 4-back in the fourth turn of the second game. Bab is under severe pressure, but she hits the lift and considers her position. If she simply goes to 4-back, Ray will feel free to take the shortest shot available as he is one game up. Can she do better? If she discards 1-back tactics, and can play the pegged-out game well, the TPO is a sound tactic, which will not only give her a good chance of winning the game, but will also restore equality of morale. As neither blue or black are past 1-back when the turn begins, she will concede a contact to Ray at the end of her turn.

The TPO differs from a triple on the partner ball in three respects. First, it is very risky to proceed with a TPO unless it will be a standard triple. Second, it is important to do the rover peel before 3-back to avoid placing the peg out in jeopardy with a straight peel. Third, the break does not end with a simple peg out and a won game, but with a contact leave that needs some forward planning.

Basically, Bab must ensure that blue and black are in opposite corners and as far as possible from Ray's hoop. Assuming that Bab is playing with blue, that red is to be pegged out, and yellow is for hoop 1, she will arrange to have red by the peg, and black three feet (90cm) north-west of the peg before she makes rover off yellow. Having made rover, she rushes yellow a few feet short of red, and pegs out red while getting a rush on black to corner 2. Having placed black as near the corner as possible, Bab plays blue into corner 3, taking care to go right into the corner so that

Ray can gain no advantage by taking a lift instead of a contact.

Faced with this position, Ray's most constructive reply is to take contact from blue and play a big roll, sending blue about ten yards (9m) north of hoop 1, and yellow within range of black in corner 2. A thick take-off will send black along the yard-line north of hoop 2, and may give yellow position to run hoop 1. Failing that, Ray can apply the double squeeze described earlier (*see* Fig 180). Ray should check that blue and black are open, or he may concede a wiring lift instead. If the enemy is wired, he must leave yellow in a runnable position but open to blue and black.

THE 2-BALL GAME

It used to be thought that if your backward ball had a lead of at least four points, it was sound tactics to peg out both your ball and the opponent's rover if you had the chance. The minimum number of hoops lead was increased to six, and then to eight, as it was realised that many more players were capable of playing a 2-ball break for several hoops. Today, the all-round 2-ball break is commonplace in practice games. Against a good opponent, pegging out both balls can be a good way to lose a game, no matter how big your lead is. In a match you will do better to keep both of your balls on the court.

CONCLUSION

No pegged-out game is a certainty, but the tactic should be encouraged as it leads to exciting games featuring good shooting and interesting play. Whenever a crowd gathers round one particular match in a tournament, the most likely reason is that a pegged-out finish is in progress.

17 Yard-line Cannons

A cannon is a description loosely applied to any contact between the strikers's ball and a third ball in a roquet or croquet stroke. Although cannons can occur anywhere on the court, they usually occur on the yard-line, and most often on the corner spots. The expression 'corner cannon' is often used as a general description, but this is erroneous, as a corner cannon is simply a special case of a yard-line cannon. Opportunities for these useful strokes occur frequently, and the tactical advantages they offer make a little practice very worth while.

CLASSIC CORNER CANNON
(Fig 181)

Fig 181 shows the positions of the balls after Ray begins his turn by rushing yellow into corner 1 when the corner spot is occupied by blue. First, yellow must be replaced on either the west or south yard-line in contact with blue, which may not be moved at this stage. Red, having made a roquet, is still in hand and the laws require that blue now becomes in hand as well, and is accordingly temporarily removed. The laws now require that red, the

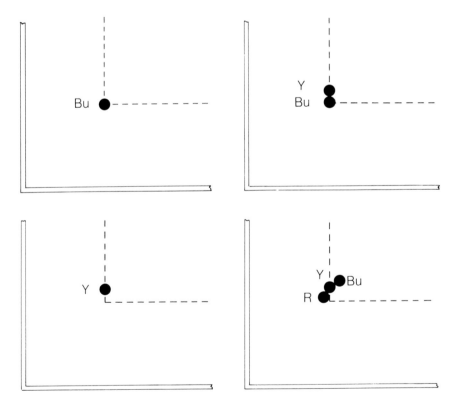

Fig 181   Creating a corner cannon.

striker's ball, and blue, the 'cannon ball', are replaced in contact with yellow, but not touching each other. Exactly where red and blue are placed is entirely up to Ray, and this freedom gives him an opportunity to manufacture an easy 3-ball break if red is for hoop 1. Note that yellow, which is now correctly described as the croqueted ball, has not been moved since it was replaced on the yard-line.

Hoop 1 from Corner 1 *(Fig 182)*

Red and yellow are in contact and the line through their centres points two feet (60cm) west of hoop 2. Red and blue are separated by one and a quarter inches (3.2cm) and point to hoop 5. The croquet stroke is played as a drive using moderate force aimed towards hoop 6. Yellow should finish one yard (90cm) south of hoop 2, and blue should finish one to two yards (90cm–1.8m) south of hoop 1, giving an excellent chance of a break.

You may not use a measurement aid on court, but an easy way of setting red and blue is available. Position red correctly relative to yellow, and place blue on the east side of

yellow so that the line joining the centres of blue and yellow is exactly at right angles to that joining the centres of red and yellow. In practice, this is easy to judge. The distance separating red and blue is now almost exactly one and a half inches (3.8cm). Mentally divide the gap into six quarter-inch (0.63cm) sections and move blue one quarter-inch section nearer to red.

The cannon works because the croquet stroke was played as a split shot and red cut-rushed blue to hoop 1. Although there is considerable loss of energy in the collision between red and blue, the residue is quite sufficient to send blue seven or eight yards (6.3–7.2m) to the hoop. This cannon is the easiest corner cannon of all, and should be familiar to every A Class player. The same arrangement will also give hoop 3 from corner 3, and the mirror image will give 1-back from corner 2 and 3-back from corner 4.

Hoop 2 from Corner 2 *(Fig 183)*

This cannon is similar to hoop 1 from corner 1, although the distance ratio involved is modified;

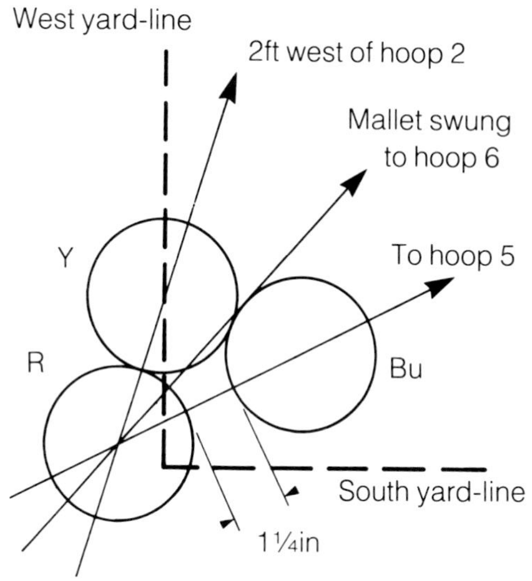

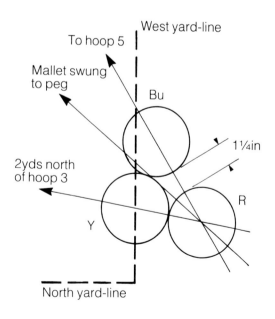

Fig 182   Corner 1 cannon (to 1).

Fig 183   Corner 2 cannon (to 2).

the croqueted ball travels only twenty-two yards (19.8m), and the cannon ball should travel about nine yards (8.1m). Red and yellow are in contact and point to a spot two yards (1.8m) north of hoop 3. Red and blue are separated by one and a quarter inches (3.2cm) and point to hoop 5. The stroke is played as a drive aimed towards the peg. Blue and yellow should finish a yard (90cm) from hoops 2 and 3 respectively. This cannon is only slightly less easy than the previous cannon and will also give 2-back from corner 1.

Hoop 1 from Corner 2

(Figs 184 and 185)

This cannon differs significantly from the earlier ones because the cannon ball travels much further than the croqueted ball. The traditional arrangement of the balls is shown in Fig 184. Red and yellow are in contact and point to hoop 2. Red and blue are separated by an inch (2.5cm) and point three yards (2.7m) west of hoop 1. The stroke is played as a very

hard drive, aimed at a spot four yards (3.6m) south of corner 2. In theory, yellow should finish a yard (90cm) west of hoop 2 and blue about 2 yards west of hoop 1. In practice, it is difficult to achieve even this rather indifferent result consistently, and the modern 'wafer' cannon is much more useful.

The 'wafer' or 'millimetre' arrangement is shown in Fig 185. Red and yellow are in contact and point to hoop 6. Red and blue are separated by as little as possible (hence the name) and point one yard (90cm) west of hoop 1. The stroke is played as a hard drive, aimed also one yard (90cm) west of hoop 1. Yellow will finish three yards (2.7m) north of hoop 2, and blue can be sent right in front of hoop 1. Although the position of yellow is not ideal, this cannon gives a good chance of running hoop 1 with sufficient control, to obtain a forward rush into the vicinity of corner 2, from where a 3-ball break can be established. The same cannon gives hoop 3 from corner 4, and the mirror image gives 1-back from corner 1, and 3-back from corner 3.

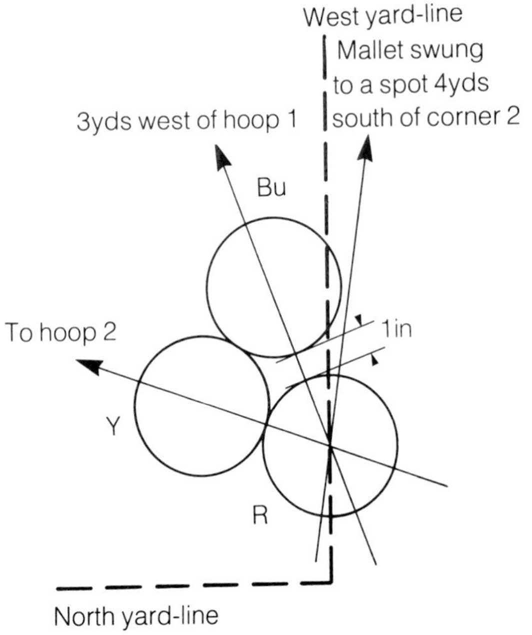

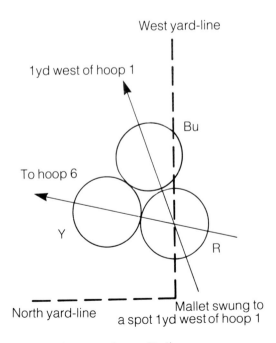

Fig 184   Corner 2 cannon (to 1).

Fig 185   Wafer cannon (corner 2 to 1).

Hoop 1 from Corner 4

(Figs 186 and 187)

This is another cannon in which the cannon ball travels a considerable distance, and which has both a traditional and a modern method of play. The traditional arrangement of the balls is shown in Fig 186. Red and yellow are in contact and point to hoop 2. Red and blue are separated by one and a quarter inches (3.2cm) and point one yard (90cm) north of corner 1. The stroke is played as a very hard drive with perhaps a degree of roll, and aimed at a spot one yard (90cm) north of corner 1. In theory, yellow should finish close to hoop 2 and blue close to hoop 1. However, this is another cannon that it is difficult to play consistently well.

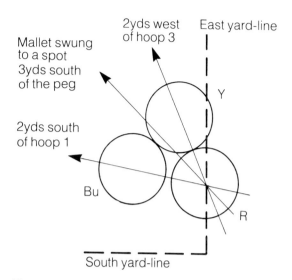

Fig 187   Wafer cannon (corner 4 to 1).

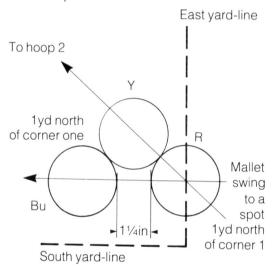

Fig 186   Fourth corner cannon (to 1).

The 'wafer' arrangement is shown in Fig 187. Red and yellow are in contact and point two yards (1.8m) west of hoop 3. Red and blue are separated by as little as possible and point two yards (1.8m) south of hoop 1. The stroke is played as a hard drive, aimed three yards (2.7m) south of the peg. Yellow will finish between hoops 3 and 6 and blue can be sent right in front of hoop 1. The break therefore depends on making the hoop with enough

Fig 188   A corner cannon.

149

control to obtain a rush to yellow, and rushing yellow to hoop 2 from about twelve yards (10.8m). If there is already a ball near hoop 2, the cannon is a gentler stroke aimed directly at hoop 1, so that yellow travels only as far as hoop 4.

TRADITIONAL VERSUS WAFER CANNONS

The fundamental reason why traditional cannons should be discarded in match play in favour of their wafer substitutes is that the traditional cannons do not give sufficiently consistent results to be worth risking in a tight situation. There is little advantage in a shot which may put a ball accurately to the next hoop but one, while leaving the cannon ball several yards short of the hoop you have to run next, making it all too probable that you will fail the hoop and hand the fruits of your endeavours to your opponent. There are two reasons for this unreliability.

1. The large gap separating the striker's ball and the cannon ball, combined with the considerable distance to be travelled by the cannon ball, requires a very forceful shot on all but the fastest lawns. These seem to be fairly scarce, especially in Britain, not only because of the climate, but also due to the advent of automatic watering.
2. Heavy shots are the easiest to mishit. Even if the shot is within your powers, you are likely to be using reasonably new, heavily milled balls in a serious game, and the contact between new balls is notoriously unpredictable.

A tiny error in direction or elevation, whether caused by error or by an irregularity on the surface of the court, can have a dramatic effect on the outcome of the shot.

In the light of the steady increase in the standard of stroke play in the game over the last twenty years, it pays to use a wafer cannon and ensure a good position at the first hoop to be tackled. The break can be established with a couple of accurate rushes, and you are much less likely to leave the earth to the opposition if something goes wrong.

OTHER CANNONS

The cannons described above are the most frequently used but there are many others. The fullest account of these strokes is still to be found in C. D. Locock's *Modern Croquet Tactics* (The Holmesdale Press, 1907).

CONCLUSION

The suggestions given above relating to the type of stroke to be played, and the direction of the mallet, are only general guides. Everyone plays croquet strokes in their own way and one player's half roll may be very similar, in effect, to another's drive. Cannons have to be practised methodically until you have learned what works best for you. You may well find that you have to modify both the stroke and the aiming mark to get satisfactory results.

18 Inner Croquet

Sports psychology is a new name for an old science which, until comparatively recently, attracted little attention in conventional athletic circles. Although everyone recognised that champions displayed special qualities, particularly the ability to perform best when it mattered most, it was customary to ascribe such qualities to talent rather than to training. However, the successes achieved by competitors from the Soviet Union and certain Eastern European countries in the 1960s and 1970s in a wide range of individual and team events, gradually awakened western sporting establishments to the efficacy of mind training in promoting peak achievement. The subject has grown rapidly in the last 15 years, and can now boast a flourishing literature and a place in the sports science curriculum. The sports psychologist is a recognised professional whose skills are in demand by individual athletes, sports clubs and national squads including, indeed, the 1986 Australian International Croquet Team.

Success at croquet requires more than physical and tactical expertise, and there is clearly a third factor at work. Most croquet players have experienced occasional purple patches when it seemed almost impossible to miss a roquet of any length. They have also known the humiliation of missing a short roquet or sticking in rover from six inches (15cm) when the match was within their grasp. Sometimes triumph and disaster can occur within five minutes of each other. The sheer inconsistency of our performance is probably the single most frustrating, and fascinating, part of the game.

The basic reason for such inconsistency is familiar to all competitors and can be summed up in one word – pressure. The pressure of a competitive situation can significantly affect performance, and we talk about nerves, cracking up, blowing it, bottling out, and other colloquialisms which all mean the same thing. Pressure can cause even the most redoubtable of players to commit bewildering errors of tactics and execution. Hardened internationals can play the wrong ball, or stick in a hoop from nowhere. Why should this be so, and can anything be done about it?

THE INNER GAME THEORY

The human body is a very competent machine. It can learn new physical tasks of considerable difficulty, such as playing a musical instrument or driving a car, and can then perform them repeatedly and accurately with little or no conscious control by the individual. Indeed, such tasks are usually performed much better when conscious input is kept to a minimum or eliminated altogether. The novice driver lacks co-ordination and displays considerable anxiety. Every manoeuvre requires active concentration and much conscious effort. The experienced driver is relaxed and can concentrate his conscious thoughts on the tasks he faces when he reaches his destination, while his eyes and ears are alert to external stimuli and allow him to react instantaneously and automatically by making the appropriate adjustments to the controls of the vehicle.

It follows that physical or motor skills are best left to the body's natural controller, namely the mind operating subconsciously in conjunction with the rest of the central nervous system, and that the conscious mind should play as little part as possible. This is the

Fig 189   Concentration: Damon Bidencope.

basic proposition of the so-called 'inner game' theory, and it can be aplied to a wide range of physical activities. Indeed, the principle that the subconscious knows best has led to the application of the theory to non-physical skills such as management, marketing and diet control.

We can now begin to address the basic problem of how to play croquet well under pressure. The inner game theory can be stated in the following form:

Performance = Potential − Interference

Your potential is simply the best performance of which you are physically and tactically capable at a given time. It can always be improved, subject to limits imposed by health, intelligence and time available for practice. For example, if you cannot approach hoop 1 from corner 1 with confidence, and you go away and practice until you can score the hoop four times out of five, you will have increased your potential by that amount.

Interference is the activity of the conscious mind. As pressure mounts, self-doubt rears its head and anxiety grows. The level of conscious thought increases and we describe the physical manifestation of this condition as 'tightening up'. The smooth operation of swinging the mallet is hampered by a flow of well-intentioned, but counter-productive commands to the subconscious. In *The Inner Game of Golf* (Jonathan Cape, 1981), Tim Gallwey gives an amusing account of the internal monologues he noticed when playing tennis. Most croquet players have approached crucial roquets in a similar fashion, with 'hold tight with the left hand . . . ease off a bit with the right . . . breathe slowly . . . don't move your head . . . slow back . . . don't forget to follow through' running through their heads.

Fig 190   Determination: David Goacher.

No wonder they tighten up and miss the shot. After all, the unwanted contraction of only a few extra muscle fibres in the arms is quite sufficent to turn the mallet face off line by one or two degrees, and so cause a fourteen-yard (12.6m) roquet to be missed by several inches.

Improving your potential is a long-term goal. Reducing conscious interference will improve performance without any change in your potential, and can give impressive results very quickly. Learning how to reduce interference can be divided into three stages, namely examining your potential, distracting the conscious mind and reinforcing the subconscious mind. For convenience, we adopt the fiction that the conscious and subconscious minds are separate entities. It would be more accurate to refer to one mind operating at conscious and subconscious levels, but less easy to incorporate in the text.

EXAMINING YOUR POTENTIAL

Find time to practise for half an hour on your own, preferably when the weather is mild and you have nothing important on your mind, so that you are as relaxed as possible. Warm up thoroughly so that your swing is operating smoothly, and then have some fun by attempting to run hoop 1 from the south boundary, first in your normal style, then with your eyes closed during the swing itself, and finally with your eyes open but fixed on the hoop, not the ball. Provided you treat the exercise as a bit of fun with nothing depending on the results, you should find after two or three sessions that shooting blind is no less successful than your normal style of looking at the striker's ball, and that looking at the hoop is more successful. If you are generally reckoned to be a good shot, you should find it quite possible to run the hoop three or four times on the trot. Then try out the three methods in the same order on other tests, namely lift shot length roquets, shots at the

peg from the side boundary and, finally, running hoop 5 from the south boundary.

You may be astonished to discover what your swing can do if left to itself. It is not really very remarkable. Croquet balls are substantial objects which will hold their line on a flat lawn. If you strike the ball correctly on the right line, on flat ground, it is rather difficult for it to miss the target by much, if at all. What should encourage you is the principal point of this routine, namely that it is quite possible to hit a croquet ball perfectly if your swing is basically sound and well grooved. One of croquet's major virtues is that a such a swing is well within the reach of most people. The problem encountered in play is that the swings we actually use are often far less smooth than the ones we can display in practice.

Shooting with your eyes closed or focused on the target ball are respectable alternative methods which you may care to import into your own game on a regular basis. However, there is no need to abandon the traditional method of looking at the striker's ball if you feel more comfortable with it.

DISTRACTING THE CONSCIOUS MIND

An over-active conscious mind does not respond well to being told to go to sleep. It is far more effective to distract it by focusing on something indirectly concerned with the stroke about to be played. The routines described below are simply different ways of giving the conscious mind something to do, so that the subconscious can get on with the shot unhindered. It is worth giving all the routines a try, although each has its own area of special relevance.

Measuring the Miss

Decide to record the accuracy of your shooting by estimating the number of ball's widths by which each shot missed, together with the length of the roquet and the side on which you missed. Be precise, and initially carry a notebook for recording each measurement.

It may sound rather defeatist, but this simple routine can completely alter your attitude. If you are taking it seriously, you will consciously treat each roquet as a statistical record rather than a source of concern and you will find that you are recording a large number of hits. The rationale of the exercise is that the conscious mind spends most of its time passing judgement on anything to hand, and will certainly tell you what it thinks about your last miss, with predictably damaging consequences, unless you can give it something that requires judgement more urgently. Once the conscious mind has expended its initial judgemental enthusiasm on the size of the miss, it is less likely to feel the need to comment on the outcome of the stroke. This is the routine for those who find it hard to avoid castigating themselves for bad shots and gloating over good ones.

You can apply the same techniques to other aspects of the stroke. If you are aware that your head moves too much, or that you sway too much on your feet, you can instead focus on the degree of movement in each shot. If you establish an internal scale, for example from 1 to 10, each shot will give rise to a number that can be recorded with the same beneficial effect as recording the size of the miss.

External Association

It can be most effective to link the stroke causing the problem , such as a long roquet, to a related action which is easy to perform perfectly. If you are aiming at a boundary ball and hit the roquet, your first task will be to replace the roqueted ball on the yard-line. So, when you face a roquet with red at yellow, consciously rehearse the action of replacing yellow on the yard-line as you take up your stance, and synchronise the imagined placement of yellow on the yard-line with the

impact of your mallet and red.

This is an effective piece of 'kidology' for the conscious mind if your main problem is not agonising over the result of the previous shot, but keeping cool in the course of the swing. In principle, you can associate the stroke with anything you wish, but it is usually most effective to link it as closely as possible to the action to be assisted.

Swinging by Numbers

Say 'one' when your mallet reaches the end of the backswing, 'two' when it hits the ball, and 'three' when the ball hits its target or crosses the boundary. The object is to synchronise the words and the events exactly. Whether you say the numbers out loud or to yourself will depend on the privacy of the surroundings or how exhibitionist you feel. In the early stages, at least, it is quite important to make a noise because it makes it easier to check whether you are getting it right.

This routine is very effective. It is harder than it might sound to time your '1–2–3' really accurately and your conscious mind will be fully occupied if you are to succeed. In addition, the imposition of a repeated rhythm makes it easier to swing smoothly. If the rhythm is particularly important to you, it may be more helpful to say 'three' at the end of the swing rather than when the ball hits or crosses the boundary. The advantage of the latter is that it compels you to see the swing as part of a larger stroke, and makes it easier to follow through correctly.

Summary

Distracting the conscious mind is a technique that should be used regularly in match play. It is tempting to treat these routines like pills in a medicine cupboard, and to use them only when things are going badly. You will do better to practise them regularly so that they are always familiar.

REINFORCING THE SUBCONSCIOUS MIND

Distracting the conscious mind is a defensive method of reducing conscious interference. The same objective can also be achieved in a positive way, by strengthening the subconscious control system so that it is better equipped to resist interference. The principal technique is that of mental rehearsal. Sports psychologists subdivide mental rehearsal into at least five variations, but the one of most relevance to croquet players is that of 'instant pre-play', or the forming of an intense mental image of the stroke about to be played and its outcome. The rationale of the technique is that the body and subconscious are capable of being programmed along the same lines as a computer. As soon as you decide to play a particular shot, your subconscious will call from your memory the method of playing the stroke, and will be ready to implement that method at the moment that the stroke is initiated. This muscle memory operates almost entirely subconsciously and explains, for example, why you 'know' how to play a particular croquet stroke without being able to put into words the precise method of hitting the ball, or the force required to achieve the desired result.

The more familiar you are with a particular stroke, the more entrenched is your muscle memory, the more effective is the internal programming of your subconscious, and the greater are the chances that the stroke will be played successfully. If you attempt to play a relatively unfamiliar stroke, the stroke will have to be played using conscious techniques because the available muscle memory will be limited and the internal programming much less powerful.

Even if your muscle memory of a standard stroke, such as a roquet, is well developed, the internal programming of the subconscious can be easily interrupted by conscious interference. Mental rehearsal is beneficial, not only because it supplements the internal programming procedure, but also because, being a conscious activity itself, it displaces other potentially interfering conscious activity.

Instant Pre-play

This technique is relevant to 'closed skill' sports, those that do not involve direct interaction with an opponent. Croquet is an excellent example. It is applicable to a single stroke or to a break, and the time taken by the exercise should be similar to the time taken for the physical activity itself. Obviously, in the course of a match, you are not going to have time to pre-play more than a few shots at a time, but this is all you need, particularly in respect of vital roquets and hoop shots.

Begin by relaxing, using whatever method you prefer. Sitting down and closing your eyes may well be adequate. Then, literally run a film in your mind's eye of the stroke about to be played. See it either from outside yourself or from inside, as seems most natural to you. See it in full, natural colour and at your normal speed. In particular, hear what you would normally hear, and feel what you would normally feel, such as the wind in the trees and on your face, the feel of the mallet as you grip it, and the weight of the head as you begin the backswing. Experience the stroke completely and watch the shot streak to its target. The only rule of this exercise is that the outcome is always complete success.

Don't imagine it is easy to use this exercise. Most people have to improve their powers of concentration significantly before they can complete the pre-play of only one stroke, let alone a break of any length. However, the results are well worth the effort.

CONCLUSION

All champions play the inner game successfully, although they may not describe their particular mental strengths and qualities with that label. They have succeeded in reducing the observ-

155

able effects of pressure on their performances to a minimum. They are said to display the classic badges of success, namely confidence, concentration and consistency.

A croquet champion is no different and, indeed, may be said to have surmounted an unusually difficult hurdle. If the objective of the inner game is to keep the conscious mind out of stroke playing, croquet players are burdened by the fact that the nature of croquet tactics calls the conscious mind into action at regular intervals throughout the game. It would be easier if the entire game could be played at the subconscious level. Perhaps this observation helps to explain why it is possible to become a very good stroke player within a couple of years, as numerous teenagers have demonstrated, but at least five years' A Class experience is usually needed to win a major event. The more experience you accumulate, the greater will be the number of situations met in the course of the game that you can deal with automatically and subconsciously.

The inner game approach is neither magic nor mystic. It recognises the importance of a player's state of mind as a contributory factor to success, and suggests ways in which the optimal state of mind can be achieved. It is hard work but, if you have the patience and the determination, eminently worth while.

INTERNATIONAL CROQUET

19   The World Scene

On 17 July 1986, a meeting was held in London to consider the formation of a World Croquet Federation (WCF). The very fact that such a meeting, attended by representatives from nine countries, took place, is evidence of the burgeoning interest in competitive croquet at world level.

It was agreed that the objects of the WCF would be:

1. Holding world team championships.
2. Holding world individual championships.
3. Awarding official croquet championships.
4. Representing croquet at the World Games.
5. Obtaining sponsorship and government funding.
6. Encouraging croquet in those countries where it is not currently played.

In this chapter our interest lies in the last objective. We feel that the first step in fulfilling it is to undertake a fact-finding mission to ascertain where croquet is played today. Perhaps its wording could be improved, for we are sure the WCF should be encouraging development everywhere. Many of the countries listed below should be the priorities for aid, and should remain so until they have a strong infrastructure of clubs.

We believe that this chapter represents the first attempt to catalogue the full extent of the world croquet scene. Our efforts to substantiate information have not always been wholly successful and in some cases we can only provide second-hand detail. This is partly the case because new information was arriving right up to the time of going to press.

We hope this work will provide a database to which, in time to come, we can add new information about those countries listed and some as yet unlisted. We also hope that the new World Croquet Federation will make use of some of this information to help promote our sport in some of the less well-established croquet countries mentioned. To that end, the Croquet Association welcomes any new information from readers (*see* Appendix V). Contact addresses for most of the countries listed below are also given in Appendix V.

Australia

Croquet in Australia is organised, in the main, at state level. There are just over 150 clubs and about 7,300 registered players, making it currently the world's largest croquet playing nation. The largest clubs are Moorabinda (Western Australia) and Hutt Road (South Australia), with six courts apiece, Warleigh Grove (Victoria) and Marion (Adelaide, South Australia) with five courts each.

Bahamas

Croquet is played at the Lydford Cay club in Nassau. Contact the USCA for details.

Bermuda

One club is in operation, based on three individually owned courts – one at each end of the island and one in the middle. The club has twenty members, who play according to US rules, and each June it holds an invitation tournament.

Brazil

Apparently croquet is being played in Brazil, as the CA has just received a request for some

Fig 191   Warleigh Croquet Club.

assistance from a group of players in Brasilia.

Canada

There are five clubs in Canada, four in Ontario and the Pugwash Mallet and Racquet club in Nova Scotia. Between them they have about a hundred members. Croquet in Canada is organised by the USCA.

China

In 1984, a Japanese team visited Peking to give a demonstration, and their trip has aroused interest in croquet, which is now played in China, especially by retired people. One centre for play is in the Chaoyang district of Peking, where they apparently play on clay basketball courts. It is reported that everyone plays side style, centre style being banned because it looks unseemly. Other areas where croquet is reported to be popular are Hunan province and Wuxi, a city some seventy miles west of Shanghai.

Costa Rica

The Costa Rica Croquet club is based in San Jose. Contact the USCA.

Egypt

Golf Croquet is very popular amongst Egyptians in the Cairo area. Cairo itself has at least ten clubs and there are clubs in Alexandria and elsewhere in the delta area. There is a keen inter-club rivalry and a national championship.

The Gezira club, located on an island in the middle of Cairo, is a large sports club with three full-size courts, which are used throughout the day. Courts are booked for an hour at a time, singles or doubles, and they double bank.

Most, but not all, players are men, and

everyone seems to play with the Irish grip. One adaptation of normal Golf Croquet rules is that they start in corner 4. A recent English Golf Croquet champion, who has seen them in action, reports that the standard of shooting is extremely high.

They use wooden hoops but very good quality balls, which are manufactured at a factory in Alexandria and are very similar in play to Jacques' Eclipse balls.

England

There are approximately 4,000 players and 140 clubs in England. Sponsorship income has risen dramatically in recent years. Much of the extra cash has been used to provide grants and loans for development projects that will result in the provision of new clubs throughout the country.

The emphasis has been placed on development at regional level. Federations have existed for some years in northern England and the West Midlands, but some of the most spectacular development has been promoted by two new regional federations, in the South-west and East Anglia.

England boasts the largest clubs in the world. Cheltenham has eleven courts and Budleigh Salterton and Southwick have ten each. Hurlingham, the palatial headquarters of the CA, has six permanent courts with four extra made available for the Open Championships in July.

Typical of the flourishing clubs of today is Bristol Croquet Club (see Fig 192). Founded in 1897, it languished somewhat during the 1970s, ending the decade with about twenty-five active members. Today it has ninety members and double banking has become the norm on its three courts. Members range in age from fourteen to ninety-three, and their fund-raising efforts recently led to a substantial investment in the first stage of a new clubhouse.

The season lasts from Easter to the end of October, with midsummer play lasting from 10a.m. until 9.30p.m. Club sessions are held one afternoon and evening during the week, but at all other times members turn up as they

Fig 192   Bristol Croquet Club.

wish, or book courts to play friendlies, or take part in club tournaments. Involvement in two local leagues and four national tournaments also ensures a heavy programme of matches with other clubs – twenty-five in 1986! Two two-day weekend tournaments are also run and reflect the national trend by being heavily over-subscribed.

Once membership has been paid for no green fees are payable. A vigorous recruitment campaign is undertaken every spring, with four or five separate coaching courses being held. Dress is casual, although players are encouraged to wear whites for matches against other clubs. 1986 was a particularly successful year for the club, as they scooped three of the five available national team titles.

Finland

A European country where garden croquet is very popular. In the commune of Ylöjärvi, six miles north-west of Tampere, a commune championship was inaugurated four years ago, and the first Finnish Croquet Club, called 'Ylöjärven Krokettiklubi', has just been formed.

France

We understand that there is a club at Fontainebleau. A number of individuals play Association Croquet. Fig 193 shows Jean Louis Mernier and his wife in play at their home at Chateau de Chenonceau in the Loire valley.

Holland

The first Dutch Croquet Club was founded in Vaassen, a small town some forty-four miles east of Amsterdam, on October 13, 1986. Aptly calling themselves the First Dutch Croquet Club, the small membership plans to run a publicity campaign to boost their numbers.

Fig 193   Monsieur et Madame Mernier.

Indonesia

The Indonesian Croquet Association currently has one club, whose thirty members play Association Croquet. The Association president, Jerry Brown, a lawyer from Florida, founded the club at a golf course in Sunter, North Jakarta, in 1984. Four years earlier he had managed to persuade the golf club manager to lay a croquet court there, and since that time interest had slowly grown. Members make their own equipment, some of which is now exported to the USA.

Ireland

Ireland is widely acknowledged as croquet's country of origin. It is therefore sad to relate that since Edwardian times until very recently, only one Irish croquet club existed, namely Carrickmines.

The Carrickmines Club, located in a suburb of Dublin some five miles south of the city centre, was founded in 1908. It had two courts and its pavilion was part of the main exhibition then taking place in Dublin. It was created by one of the Wilsons, a rich Dublin family, for his second wife, who was an avid player. A few years later, tennis was introduced, four courts

Fig 194   Carrickmines Croquet Club.

being laid down. In the course of time the Wilson family sold the clubhouse and grounds to the members for a nominal fee. Two more croquet courts were added later, and today there are thirty-five active players in the croquet section. The annual subscription covers the season from April until October, although they try to keep one court open all year round. Each year the Irish Championships are held in August, and one other week tournament and two weekend tournaments are held. Carrickmines naturally plays host to all Ireland's major international fixtures.

Following a triumphant visit by an Irish international team to Florida in March 1985, and encouraged by the momentum of development both in the USA and England, a decision was taken to form the Croquet Association of Ireland (CAI). The CAI was launched in May 1985 and was immediately successful in obtaining sponsors, Avis Car Rental and Jury's Hotel. By the Autumn it had launched its own publication, *Irish Croquet*.

The main aim of the CAI is to develop new croquet clubs throughout Ireland and an astonishing initial response to its launch saw it growing to an association with eight affiliated clubs by the end of 1986. Two of the most encouraging developments are at Herbert Park, in Dublin, where a club has been launched directly by the CAI, following assistance from Dublin Corporation, and in Cork, where the Rushbrook Club, with its three courts, is seen as a base for developing the sport in south-west Ireland.

Jamaica

Croquet is played at the Jamaica Inn Croquet Club in Ocho Rios. Contact the USCA for details.

Japan

Masura Ikeda established the first club at the University of Tsukuba. It has three full-size courts. There are now twelve clubs and approximately 300 players.

Kenya

About a dozen enthusiasts play regularly in Limuru, approximately twenty miles outside Nairobi. Friday afternoon is 'club afternoon' and they use three private courts in various gardens in the district.

Each year the Oxford and Cambridge Society arranges a competition in which members of the universities, in terms of eight, play 14 point doubles games. In 1986 they played on two three-quarter size courts marked out on the bowling green of the Limuru Country Club, and Oxford emerged victorious.

Mexico

There is a club at Cuernavaca, about forty miles south of Mexico City. For details, contact USCA.

New Zealand

There are 4,200 players in around 200 clubs, which are organised into 19 area associations. In terms of the number of croquet players per head of population, this makes it easily the world's number one amongst the strong playing nations and it is the one country where the media give croquet unquestioning recognition as a serious sport.

The largest club is the St John's Hill Club in Wanganui, with nine courts, a number of other clubs having six courts. The main season extends from the end of September to the end of April. A few clubs keep a court open during the winter. A few weekend tournaments are run but most tournaments are still one week or longer in duration.

Portugal

The Vale do Lobo Golf Club, situated just west of Faro in the Algarve, has one full-size court for use by visitors. We are also informed that croquet is played at the nearby Quinta do Lago Golf club.

Scotland

There are twelve clubs, ranging in size from Edinburgh with sixty-five members, to the Dollar Club with five members. There are about 300 players. The Edinburgh Club was founded in 1950, has three courts and is located at Lauriston Castle.

The Scottish Croquet Association (SCA) was formed in 1974. One of the reasons for its formation was because the Scottish Sports Council refused to award grants to any Scottish clubs unless it was done through an autonomous national governing body. Since that time the SCA has received considerable help from the Scottish Sports Council and, due largely to their help, a national centre for croquet will open in 1987. This is to be located on the Bush Estate near Penicuik, a few miles south of Edinburgh. For the first time, the SCA will have a club with three top quality courts, which can be used for international fixtures, major tournaments and coaching courses. In addition it is hoped that this venture will stimulate interest in croquet in the east of Scotland.

The SCA has managed to attract sponsorship from companies such as the Royal Bank of Scotland and Wilkinson Sword and it boasts an impressive annual fixture list with, in 1986, twenty-four events complementing a busy league programme. Among the annual events is the USCA Cup, played to US Rules, to commemorate Scotland's match in the USA in 1984, and using the trophy won in Florida. One popular fixture is the annual weekend tournament using the courts belonging to the Gleneagles Hotel.

Singapore

It is reported that croquet is played by members of the Singapore Cricket Club and we know that an Asian Championship was held here in 1982, which was won by Jerry Brown from Indonesia.

South Africa

Croquet has been played in South Africa since the 1860s but it was not until 1936 that the South African Croquet Association (SACA) was formed. Membership of the SACA is open to people of all races, colour or creeds without exception and currently stands at about 390, spread over eleven clubs.

Rondebosch Croquet Club in Cape Town is easily the largest in the country. It has about sixty members, ranging in age from fifteen to ninety. It has three courts, all of which are double-banked during summer weekends. The favourable climate permits play to continue all year round. Membership fees vary for single people, married couples and students and green fees are also payable. The club hosts the Western Province Championships each March or April, and every two or three years it hosts the national championships. In addition, a number of weekend tournaments are organised each year.

Spain

The Santa Clara Croquet Club at Jerez de la Frontera in south-west Spain was founded in 1979 by Sr. Bobadilla and his wife. In 1980 they and another member, Sr. Ansorena, visited Hurlingham to gain further information, and in August 1981 two officers of the CA, Robin Godby and Richard Rothwell, visited Jerez to coach the members.

The club has sixteen members and one court. It is open for play all year round. It lies on the outskirts of Jerez, on the road to Seville. Sr. Bobadilla, the club president and owner, says any visitors would be more than welcome. The club motto is 'No dues, no don'ts'.

Sweden

Garden croquet is widely played, using rules similar to US Nine-wicket Croquet. Two groups, however, are hoping to establish clubs playing Association Croquet. The first is in Alingsås, a town about 28 miles north-east of Gothenberg, where the local players hope to introduce the Association game further, in conjunction with a local golf club. The second is in Åkersberga, a town about 19 miles north-east of Stockholm, where a large group of over fifty players hope to have a club established in the very near future, in the suburb of Kuisslinby.

Switzerland

Garden croquet is popular but Switzerland can only boast one Association Croquet club, based at CERN, the European Organisation for Nuclear Research. CERN has 3,500 nationals of twelve West European nations studying particle physics using large accelerators, and is therefore a large village. It is located some five miles from the centre of Geneva, by the Franco-Swiss border.

The CERN Croquet Club was formed in spring 1982 by Norman Eatough. At present the club has one court, in front of the main administration building, although space for a second court is available. Currently the membership of fifteen includes three Swiss, so perhaps it will be some time before a Swiss national team emerges. Nevertheless, a 3–1 victory in the club's first ever match (v. British Airways) has encouraged them to bolster their recruiting efforts. Play is from early May to mid-October and visitors are welcome.

Tenerife

The British Club in Puerto De La Cruz on the north side of the island has one small court plus a bowling green that is available for use as a croquet court on occasions. The club lies on the hillside, about one mile above the harbour.

USA

The USCA boasts around 3,500 associates and 275 clubs, and driven on by the vision of its president, Jack Osborn, a former advertising executive, it is expanding so rapidly that, by the end of the century, it is almost certain to have overtaken Australia as the world's biggest croquet-playing nation.

In July 1986, USCA moved its headquarters from New York to the PGA National Resort Community in Florida, where five full-size courts are being installed, ready for use early in 1987.

Clearly the finance being raised in the USA to promote the sport is going to have a profound effect on its development, both internally and externally. Already two of

Australia's 1986 test team have signed on as full-time croquet professionals in California. The world invitation event at the Sonoma-Cutrer Vineyards in Windsor, California, could prove to be the forerunner of a world individual championship, and the day is not far away when substantial prize money will be offered at such a tournament, bringing croquet face to face with the issue of professionalism.

The USCA's regular publication is *US Croquet News*, but in September 1986 a new regular independent publication, *Croquet Magazine* was launched, with editorial offices in California, another indication of the tremendous interest in croquet that has been generated.

Disappointed that the USCA's application to take part in the 1990 MacRobertson shield contest was rejected, the CA and the USCA have since agreed to instigate an annual international contest for the Solomon Trophy, the first to be held in 1988.

Fig 195   US Croquet at the Breakers Hotel, Palm Beach.

One of the clubs that moved from the 'backyard' to affiliate to the USCA is the Puget Sound Croquet Club in Seattle. In 1979, the then thirty-year-old club decided to change from Nine to Six-wicket Croquet. Located at the south end of the Seattle Seahawks professional football practice field, its membership includes some prominent citizens of the Seattle community.

Annual subscriptions cover the whole season, which runs from May to October. Membership is by invitation, but occasional croquet clinics are run for aspirants. The club now has over sixty members. The club has four full-size courts and in 1986 hosted the USCA Western (Pacific) Regional Championships.

Although there are no strict rules on dress, members are encouraged to wear whites and most do. Many serious club players, like president Lisle Guernsey and his wife, Joy, buy Jaques equipment from England. At a high price per set, they contrast sharply with the nine-wicket garden sets produced by US manufacturers at around one-tenth of the price per set, over 300,000 of which are sold each year.

USSR

Croquet has long been played in the USSR. Tolstoy had a court in his garden in Moscow and Phil Clarke, writing in the *New Zealand Croquet Gazette*, informs us that the garden game is still played on a number of private lawns. Croquet is actively played in some of the embassies in Moscow but, more interestingly, he reports that 'cosmonauts, on returning to earth, are encouraged to play croquet. Scientists say that croquet, above all other games, has a calming effect on the mind and body which, after a long space flight, have to readjust to earthly conditions. During a visit to the Space Centre Pavilion, I was shown a number of photos of cosmonauts 'relaxing' in a game of croquet'.

Wales

Wales currently boasts two clubs. A small club, with two courts, has existed at Knighton in Powys for just over a decade, but in the summer of 1986 a new club was formed at Dyffryn Gardens, a council-owned estate and recreational facility, some four miles west of Cardiff city centre.

Dyffryn Croquet Club has two courts but has plenty of room for expansion and the potential for development was proved when over fifty-five people joined as members in its first season. As a result of this success, and with an eye to future developments in South Wales in the short term, and throughout the country in the long term, a meeting was held at the National Sports centre in Cardiff in December 1986, to form a Welsh Croquet Association.

Wales has, in fact, boasted a National team for some years, but these players have all been members of English clubs.

20 Stars of the Modern Game

Every sport spawns its stars – men and women who, through their deeds, create legends. Donald Bradman, Bobby Charlton, Billie-Jean King, Arnold Palmer – names to conjure with, names that evoke a thousand memories, their feats growing each time in the telling.

Croquet is no exception. Cyril Corbally, Humphrey Hicks, Cyril Miller, Arthur Ross, John Solomon and Dorothy (D.D.) Steel are some of the names that evoke awe and reverence in croquet circles, and will continue to do so as long as such circles exist. But what of the present? Who are the players who are still competing and winning at the highest level, yet have already secured their places on that scroll of legend?

In England, Nigel Aspinall still bestrides the sport like a colossus. He has fulfilled the promise spotted by Ian Baillieu at Cheltenham in the spring of 1965, who, writing in the *Croquet Gazette* that July (No. 81), described the young man playing in his first tournament as 'a potential grand master of the game'. By 1966 he had bagged his first major domestic title, the Open Doubles with John Simon, and by 1986 his haul was thirty-four, just six short of John Solomon's all-time record (excluding the Champion of Champions, which is no longer played).

Dubbed the 'Happy Warrior' in a *Croquet Gazette* editorial in September 1968 (No. 102), he was described as follows: 'There is something panther-like about him. Lean, swift and with a long shot unbettered in a period of brilliant marksmanship, Nigel Aspinall has the air of a conqueror, even when conquest does not prove to be his lot. Today he is at, or very near, the top, as he well deserves to be, and will remain there as long as he cares to play'.

Nigel reached the top in the 1969 test series in Australia, winning all of his matches and rightly being acclaimed the world's best player. Though that crown may no longer be his, there are many that would still support his claim to it.

A bachelor, whose private means have afforded him the time necessary to devote himself to croquet, Nigel has put back a lot into the sport that has afforded him so much glory. Many clubs and individuals, both in England and the USA, have benefited from his coaching and demonstrations, and his victory in the spring of 1986 in the first ever television croquet tournament, the Royal Bank of Scotland Nations Trophy (*see* Fig 196), televised by Granada TV in Manchester, means his is the first croquet name of legend that will be more than just a name for future generations of croquet enthusiasts. Will 'celluloid' add to or detract from the legend? Only time will tell.

In a hundred years time the name of John Prince will probably stand at the top of croquet's roll of honour, even above those of Aspinall and Solomon. On 31 January 1963, John made his test debut for New Zealand, against England at Napier in the second test, at the age of seventeen years and six months, thereby becoming the youngest player to have appeared in the MacRobertson Shield since its inception, a record that he still holds. In 1986, John created another record, playing in his sixth series. His appearance in the third test v. Great Britain at Hunstanton on 10 July may have been his swan-song, but in making it he created a third world record with his thirty-third consecutive test appearance.

Fig 196   Familiar poses: Nigel Aspinall –
silverware collector . . .

Fig 197   . . . John Prince – the master at work . . .

Fig 198   . . . Neil Spooner – another power-play.

At home in New Zealand he won his first major domestic title, the Men's Championship, in 1963. To date he has accumulated thirty-one. From those early days he was committed to enterprising play that would stretch his talent to the limit. Triples became commonplace, and on 30 March 1970 he became the first player to scale croquet's Everest by completing a sextuple peel in competition, the occasion being the final of the Hawkes Bay Easter invitation tournament at Hastings. On 8 November 1983, during the President's Cup at Gisborne, he completed two sextuple peels in one day, another world first.

He reached the peak of his croquet career, however, during the 1974 test series in England. Playing at number one for New Zealand, he won all of his three singles matches against Aspinall, thereby wresting from Nigel the crown of acclamation as the world's best player.

Multiple title holder and world record holder that he is, John also fills the roles of husband and artist (see Fig 210). Married, with two young sons, his Saturday and Sunday mornings in summer are these days taken up with watching his eldest boy play cricket. His paintings have been displayed at a number of commercial and group exhibitions, but he does not anticipate turning professional, preferring to get pleasure and some pocket money from his hobby, rather than being committed to produce for a living.

Captain of his country for four test series, and having led it to victory in two of the last three series, John Prince has been an inspiration to a generation of croquet players in New Zealand.

Australian croquet had been in the doldrums, internationally, for many years. The country that inaugurated the MacRobertson Shield test series won three of those first four series but its last success was in 1935. Then, in the 1970s, a man arrived on the scene who was committed to putting things right.

Neil Spooner appeared on the international scene in 1974 in England, and immediately made his mark in two ways. Firstly, he rose to number one in the Australian team and defeated John Prince, and then he withdrew from the team before the third test against New Zealand, due to the first of what were to be a series of clashes with the Australian croquet administrators.

He was selected for the series in 1979, but again withdrew, this time before the series, as a protest against the fact that the selectors had clearly not selected the strongest available team. His campaign eventually bore fruit, and in 1982 Australia selected its strongest post-war team for the series that was to be played on home soil.

Neil led from the front and, playing at number one, won five out of his six singles matches, including one of the all-time great MacRobertson Shield performances when defeating John Prince in three games at Sydney. Keith Wylie, in the *Croquet Gazette* the following spring (No. 169), commented: 'Spooner's bearing when game and break down was particularly impressive'. Australia went on to win the series against New Zealand 3–0.

On 22 November 1982, in his home town of Adelaide, Neil led Australia to its first victory in a test match against Great Britain (formerly England) since 1937, to square that series 1–1. David Openshaw, the British captain, writing in *Croquet Gazette* (No. 169) observed: 'Of our opponents, the play of Neil Spooner stands out. His shooting and roll strokes were exceptional and at Sydney, when he was really on song, he seemed unbeatable. I'm sure his performance put a lot of heart into the Australian team'.

The series was to hold a sting in the tail for Neil though. The deciding test against Great Britain in Melbourne went to 4–4 and game all in the deciding match between Neil and Britain's number one, Keith Wylie. For once Neil could not find his best form, and a great performance by Keith secured the Shield for Britain. The dream, that looked like becoming a reality, had once again become a dream.

Nevertheless, his achievement in leading the Australian team to some success against Britain after a forty-five year wait, and to victory against New Zealand, was no small feat. He also helped to produce the most exciting series in the history of the competition for his home crowd to enjoy.

He won his first major domestic title in 1975 and has now accumulated ten. Because competing for the major titles in Australia requires more time and a great deal more travelling than in Britain or New Zealand, Neil has not competed for them on a regular basis, unlike Nigel and John. If he had, his tally would probably have been much higher.

Married for a second time, Neil and his wife have now moved to California, where Neil has become the Director of Croquet at the Sonoma-Cutrer winery, becoming the second Australian international to accept a professional status in the USA. Australia's loss is America's gain.

PORTRAITS

The stories that follow are based on interviews made before and after the 1986 test series. Nigel and Neil were interviewed before the series, Nigel at Manchester in May and Neil in Ireland in June. John was interviewed after the series, at Hurlingham in July. These stories are croquet lessons on their own. If you can spot the similarities, perhaps you have discovered part of the secret that distinguishes the great player from the merely good.

Nigel Aspinall

Date of birth: 29 July 1946
Place of birth: Reading, Berkshire, England
Now resident in: Walton-on-Thames, Surrey, England
Occupation: Freelance computer programmer
Current club: Roehampton
Previous clubs: Bristol, Caversham
Major titles: Eight times British Open Cham-

pion, Eleven times British Open Doubles Champion, twice British Men's Champion, twice British Mixed Doubles' Champion, eleven times President's Cup winner.
International honours: Represented Great Britain (formerly England) in the MacRobertson Shield test series of 1969, 1974, 1979 and 1986; also played for Great Britain against the USA in 1985 and 1987.

Nigel is a retiring, extremely modest man, but his story nevertheless reveals an intense passion for the game of croquet, on which he speaks with confidence and authority.

'I was introduced to croquet purely by chance. When I was about twelve years old my father, a Professor of Modern History at Reading University, brought home a croquet set that he had bought on the spur of the moment at an auction, and we started playing at our Reading home.

When, on leaving Charterhouse, I learned that I had secured a place at Bristol University to read Physics and General Science, I went to a Citizens' Advice Bureau in Reading and through them, and the Croquet Association, I learned of the existence of Bristol Croquet Club. I started playing at Bristol in autumn 1964. The handicapper there watched me play a round and gave me a handicap of 6 from which to start. I soon beat Miss Ault level and was reduced to 3. By the time I played in my first tournament, the Whit weekend tournament at Cheltenham in 1965, I was playing off 2.

I practised a lot in my early days at Bristol; you might say I studied too much croquet. Practice then consisted of playing games, both friendlies against opponents and games against myself. I don't recall taking out a rack of balls to practise strokes. Nowadays I find I don't need to practise very much, maybe once a fortnight shooting balls at the peg. I try to make sure that I am hitting straight and the rest follows.

It was extremely beneficial for me that there were two better players at Bristol at that time,

William Ormerod and John Simon. I learned a lot from John, who was a schoolboy then but no longer plays. William and Kay Ault also gave me some help.

I remember losing my very first game in that Cheltenham weekend to Giles Borrett, thereafter winning all my games. That September I went to the Parkstone tournament and did my first triple peel against one of the Beamishes. I was probably more adventurous then about trying triples than I am today. I don't think I've ever been nervous during a game, and if I have it has only been momentary. After that Parkstone tournament, I was brought down to scratch and by June 1966 I had become a minus player.

I have fond memories of my first match (best of three) in the Opens in 1966. I played Humphrey Hicks, who was then one of the top three players. I won the first game easily, +25. In the second game he got to 4-back and

peg, but I hit the last lift and pegged out his forward ball, when my other ball was for 1 or 2. He, however, soon hit what I thought was a wired ball and won. The third game had an identical start to the second. I again hit the last lift and pegged his forward ball out, saying to myself "I'll show you, Mr Hicks". I was more successful in this game, and made all the hoops with my backward ball, only becoming hampered after running rover. I elected to go into a neutral corner, but Humphrey, by now on rover, hit the lift and won.

It was at that Opens that I won my first major title, the Open Doubles with John Simon. The secret of good doubles play? I think you need to be patient and tolerant of your partner, for example the speed at which he plays. I felt that if I made a mistake with John Simon, he would hit in and rescue the situation. He said to me, when I once told him that, "funny, I had the same feeling about you". If it is to be a lasting

Fig 199   Games against Nigel can be so relaxing.

partnership, you should have an understanding of the game your partner plays, as far as tactics go. I think it is a good idea if you are both of similar ability. In handicap doubles you should always keep buttering up your partner.

The best British player I ever played against was, without question, John Solomon. The best overseas players I have played against are John Prince and Bob Jackson. It is difficult to say who is better because I played them at different times – John Prince in 1969 and Bob Jackson in 1979. I remember Bob Jackson as a terrific hitter of a single ball. He put in the best ever performance against me the first time out in Westport in the 1979 test series in New Zealand. I won the first game, and I perhaps should have won the second. I was rover and peg and he had just missed the last lift. I went off in a take-off. He was 3 and 4-back. He laid up, gave me a 12-yard shot with the rover ball, I missed, and he then played from the fourth hoop and did extraordinarily well to do a straight triple to win the game.

What I consider to be my own best ever performance was a turn I played in the Open Doubles Championship in 1983 at Cheltenham. The weather had been very unusual that week, the temperature was above 90 degrees Fahrenheit most of the time, the lawns were extremely fast and the hoops solid – all in all, very testing playing conditions. As time approached in the third game of our second round match against David Openshaw and Mark Avery, I had two minutes to set the court, make sure the enemy was far apart, that I had a sufficiently good rush and that I wasn't caught in play. I managed to finish with twenty seconds to spare and time was called in their turn. We were for 4 and 3-back and I had laid up by the side of hoop 4. They were on peg and penultimate, so I had to do two peels on William (Ormerod) and peg out to win. They played one of their balls into corner 3, leaving the other south-west of 1-back. I managed it and think I did well because the playing conditions were so difficult and I was under the greatest pressure possible – because it was

after time, a single mistake would have meant automatic defeat.

I won my first Open singles title in 1969, beating John Solomon in the final. I think these days it is slightly more difficult to win the Championship than it was then. I don't think I've improved since then and there are more people of good ability one can lose to now.

It was also in 1969 that I played in my first test series, in Australia. I managed to win all my matches. Possibly that was the best I ever played but I think my form has been reasonably stable over the years. It was in Australia that I played in front of the largest crowd I ever experienced – between two and three hundred people in Adelaide. I have no real preference for playing with or without a crowd, as I am only dimly aware of an audience.

The good team morale was an important factor in our success in 1969. When we played the next test series abroad, in New Zealand in 1979, there were morale problems on that tour. It may have had an effect on our poorer showing there, although that is difficult to measure. The problem was the team's relationship with its manager. The team as a whole got on well together, and we didn't argue among ourselves. One or two people might have let it affect them more than I did, and I'm not convinced that my play was affected. The main lesson of defeat in 1979 was that we needed some system where the better players could be encouraged to play more against each other – hence the birth of the Home Internationals.

I did not make myself available for the 1982 tour to Australia because I don't like flying and knew it would be extremely hot. I also felt that if I wasn't keen to go, I wouldn't play as well as someone who wanted to go.

I think the 1986 series will be very close between all three countries. I would not like to predict that another team will win when I am playing, so I won't forecast a winner. I think our strongest opposition will be New Zealand.

I think there have been three major changes in croquet in the past twenty years. There has been an increase in the number of people who play, and an increase in the number of good players, but the thing that stands out in my mind is the absence today of a 'circuit'. When I first started playing there were still people who would tour the country, mostly in the south of England, going from one tournament to the next. They stayed regularly in the same hotels, where they were always guaranteed amusement and conversation in the evening.

I became a member of the Council of the CA in 1970, having been encouraged to stand. I have put a certain amount back into the game. One or two ideas of mine have changed one or two things for the better, for example the conditions of play in the CA fixtures list. Council itself has also changed in the last twenty years. Twenty years ago there was not such a preponderance of good players on Council and there was more of a London bias to it than there is today. It is an advantage having the top players to administer the sport, because they know what they want, but they do not always see things from the lesser player's point of view. Ideally, Council should have a bigger spread of playing abilities and ages.

I hope to go on playing as long as I enjoy it. I was not aware until it was mentioned to me that I am only seven short of John Solomon's record of forty major domestic titles. I think the main reason for my continued success has been the fact that the other good players have not bothered to play. John Solomon has given up, and Keith Wylie has half given up. I don't think I play all that well actually. Generally I become more relaxed in a difficult situation. I think my reputation for hitting the last shot is mythical.

If croquet attracted substantial prize money, like bowls, then I might turn professional – I'd have to think carefully about it. I would be worried about being banned, but if that wasn't a danger, then there wouldn't be a problem for me.

I would agree that there is merit in changing the laws of the advanced game to make it more difficult, but only if the lawns are sufficiently easy. I would suggest a change of the boundary rule so that you can't rush a ball off the lawn, except on the first stroke of your turn.'

Nigel's Tip for Beginners Find a way of making practice interesting, for example try moving a ball from a corner to the peg by continuous rushing. Your first attempt at an exercise like this will give you a target that you can then try to beat.

Nigel's Tip for Ambitious Players If you're just entering the A Class, cut out silly mistakes. You win games not by brilliance, but by cutting out silly mistakes. It is largely a matter of concentration.

John Prince

Date of birth: 23 July 1945
Place of birth: Lower Hutt, near Wellington, North Island, New Zealand
Now resident in: Hastings, North Island
Occupation: Bank officer
Current club: Hastings
Previous clubs: Naenae, Waimarie
Major titles: seven times NZ Open Champion, seven times NZ Open Doubles Champion, nine times NZ Men's Champion, eight times NZ President's first eight winner.
International honours: Represented New Zealand in the MacRobertson Shield test series of 1963, 1969, 1974, 1979, 1982 and 1986.

John's story illustrates the many gifts that lie behind his placid and friendly demeanour. Like the artist he is, he embellishes his recollections with vivid points of fine detail. Like the sportsman he is, he acknowledges the part played by others, whether as coaches, team-mates or opponents, in helping to shape the rich canvas of his unrivalled croquet career. Like the leader he is, he offers, both directly and indirectly, clear markers to those who would aspire to match his achievements.

'I got interested in croquet by accident. There was a club (Naenae) not far from where I used to live and I wandered over one day and watched them play. One of the women there, Mrs Melba Miller, had actually started when she was quite young herself and she asked me if I would like to have a couple of hits round, which I did. I later got a book out of the library; it happened to be Maurice Reckitt's book, *Croquet Today*. I was intrigued by the photos in there of John Solomon, being a young player. Anyhow, one of the women from the club, Mrs Muriel Palmer, popped round to my home and asked me if I'd like to come back and have a few games because they'd get a well-known player to give me some coaching. As it turned out, it was Ashley Heenan. I was about fourteen at the time.

Ashley was a member of the neighbouring Waimarie club and he started to come out on Saturday and Sunday mornings to coach me, so I got hooked from then onwards. The lawn that we played on at Naenae was extremely fast, so I developed a fairly gentle style, touch being the most important thing.

In those early days I used to practise every day after school, probably for two and a half to three hours. At weekends I probably played just about all day Saturday and all day Sunday and sometimes I even used to go and play at six o'clock in the morning. Usually I used to play games, red and yellow against black and blue, and I can honestly say that I never used to give preference to either side, the object being to play games in which I made no error if possible. I think that playing a game against yourself is a good idea because, you know, after all, it takes the same format as a game against another opponent. You get used to playing, and trying to pick a break up off either the fourth shot or the fifth turn, and so on, having to take the lift shot. Later on, before a tournament, I would practise two-ball breaks, shooting at the peg, and things like that.

My first tournament was in 1961. I was a 12 bisquer (handicaps run from 12 to −4 in New Zealand). I got to the final of the handicap doubles with my partner, Monty Reitchesen, a half bisquer from Waimarie CC and a very keen player, with whom I played an awful lot. We lost the final, but I think I came down to 7.

I also played a lot with Ashley, I had the opportunity to play with Jean Jarden, one of New Zealand's greatest women players, and with a group of strong players in Wellington, including Herbert Ford, captain of the New Zealand team in 1963. I was lucky to be able to play with these people. It took me two and a half seasons to come down to minus, and I went to −2 in 1963. I did not actually play in another tournament until I got picked to play for New Zealand.

When I was seventeen I left my school, the Hutt Valley High School, and went straight into a job with the Bank of New Zealand, where I've been ever since.

When I started, there were very few juniors, only two that I knew of, Tony Stephens and Ralph Browne. Tony was picked to play in the New Zealand team for the 1963 test series and Ralph was picked for a North Island representative side to play a match against the Australian and British touring teams. Following illness in the New Zealand side, Ralph was promoted into the test team part way through the tour, and I was brought into the North Island side.

In the representative match against Australia I played with Edna Hight and won a doubles against Olive Lewis and Gwen Rumbelow. I then played a singles against Olive Lewis and I won that. I was then put into the New Zealand team for the last three test matches, two against Great Britain and one against Australia.

In my first test match we played against Great Britain. I played Brian Lloyd Pratt and David Curtis in the doubles, with my partner Les Middlemass. We won that, and I think it went to three. I played David Curtis in the singles – we were both the number sixes on the teams – and I won that match also.

In the next test, against Australia, I was promoted to number three and went up to the second doubles. I played with Herbert Ford and we beat Edna Rudder and Merle Day in the doubles. I also played Merle Day in the singles. There had been quite a bit of rain, the lawn was fairly heavy, and I think it gave me an advantage because I could hit harder than she could. I won in straight games.

My third test was against Great Britain and I was promoted to number two in the singles order, Jean Jarden being number one. The doubles were all completed very quickly in the morning of that first day, all going to Great Britain. Then two bus loads of people from Auckland arrived to watch and so, hurriedly, exhibition games were put on. I partnered John Solomon against Tony Stephens and Pat Cotter, and I did my first triple peel in that doubles game. In the singles I played against John Solomon, and Jean Jarden played against Patrick Cotter. I won in straight games and Jean also beat Pat Cotter. Although we lost the match 7–2, we thought we'd achieved something.

I was quite nervous in those matches. When I played in them, it was so exciting to play against these people that I had read so much about, that I didn't really go out with the attitude of trying to win, but simply enjoyed playing against them. However, I felt that, in respect to them, I should try to play as well as I could, probably a great attitude of mind to have. I think you become more nervous as the years pass. I probably don't practise as much as I ought to, and therefore, you know, from time to time my swing starts to go a bit off line. Then, I think, when you are aware that things are not going so well, you probably do feel more nervous, with the feeling 'what's going to go wrong next?'.

The first New Zealand Championships I played in were in 1963, following the test series. It is a long, two-week tournament that incorporates the Open Singles, Open Doubles and the Men's and Women's titles. I got through to the semi-finals of the Open Singles, where I was beaten by John Solomon. In the Men's I beat Humphrey Hicks in the semi-final and Brian Lloyd-Pratt in the final.

I've had a number of doubles partners over the years. Ashley Heenan was the first, then, later, Jean Jarden, Keith Woollett, Richard Clarke, Alan Anderson and Paul Skinley. It was simply circumstances that caused me to change partners – we swop around a bit in New Zealand. I think the secret of good doubles play is appreciating your partner's strengths and abilities and allowing him to get on to play the game the way he sees it. If you get a partner who looks at the game in the same light as you do, you are well on the way to having a successful doubles partnership.

Neil Spooner is the toughest overseas player I've had to tackle. I have played him twice and played well, but he won both times. The most complete player I have seen is John Solomon – to watch him play is like listening to a favourite piece of music; there is an artistic quality about his play.

Fig 200   Even the mighty are fallible!

175

Playing against Nigel Aspinall is quite something. I remember the match in Australia in 1969 in which I scored a total of one point in two games, Nigel finishing one game in the fifth turn with a triple. I also remember the first test match at Hurlingham in 1974. It looked like I was going to suffer the same fate, when Nigel became hoop-bound with a triple after 3-back. I managed to go round, he missed and I did a triple and then took the second game. We had a fairly close match at Budleigh, which I won, and another good one at Nottingham, where Nigel did a triple in the first game, I did a triple in the second game, and I won an exciting pegged out game in the third.

Paul Skinley is the best New Zealand player I've ever played against, although there are a number of them. Bob Jackson is probably one of the toughest to beat, but I prefer watching Paul Skinley playing.

The greatest match I've played in? Well, I've always had fond memories of winning the English Doubles Title in 1974 with Gordon Rowling. We played against Martin Murray and Andrew Hope. We were the first people outside Great Britain to win the Doubles title, it was a great match, there was some marvellous croquet, and there was a wonderful atmosphere which, frankly, you only get in Great Britain. Back home our tournaments, tending to run well into the second week, usually dwindle down to the finalists, the manager, a referee and a couple of locals watching. I think Martin and Andrew won the first game, we came back in the second, and I remember doing a triple in the third.

I think I've done five or six sextuples in competition, both the standard and the delayed ones. I remember doing two in one day in the President's Cup in New Zealand, so that was a day in 1983 when I remember playing particularly well. I did two sextuples and a TPO (triple peel on the opponent's ball), which I'd actually set up for a second sextuple, but took the option of the TPO. I remember playing a particularly good turn against Paul Skinley in the Opens, strangely enough a

match which I lost because the last stroke of the turn went awry. He'd gone to 4-back and I hit in and I did a 1-back leave in the third corner, with the intention of triple peeling him out. He fired and missed and I did the triple peel, followed by the peel through 1-back. I then missed the peg out from about four feet – unbelievable!

In the 1963 test series, when we played at home and it was my first series, I think we probably didn't have a good team in the sense that the team didn't really appear to me to get on too well together. There were lots of changes made during the series and I think people just didn't play up to their best form. England won quite easily really.

In 1969, when we went to Australia, again I think we had two extra players, with eight in the party, and I think it is far better to stick to the six. The Great Britain team that time had six fine players who got on very well and I could see from that the importance of not necessarily having the six best players but the six who would get on and make a team, doubles being very important.

So when it came to 1974 and we came over here, we felt reasonably confident. We knew it would be very difficult to beat Great Britain at home, but we had some of our up-and-coming new players in the team, plus some experience. Although we managed to beat Australia 2–1, we lost 3–0 to Great Britain, but in the matches against Great Britain, Alan Anderson and I won two of the three doubles at number one. I also won three singles at number one, so we could say that it was just a matter of getting a strong side together all the way through.

Before 1979 two new players emerged, Paul Skinley and Joe Hogan, and Bob Jackson became a much stronger player than he had been in 1974. So we felt that at home in New Zealand in 1979, we had it all going for us – experience, exciting new players and playing on our home grounds, which I think gave us the edge. We went from strength to strength, with a very narrow victory at Westport, 5–4 on

Then, in Hastings, we started off very well, won all three doubles, winning the test 6–3, and then won again at Wanganui 7–2. 1979 was my second time as captain, and I've been captain four times now. I was actually captain in 1969, but in 1974 I don't think I was popular back home, as I only just squeezed into the test team. There are likes and dislikes of players, perhaps a bit of jealousy somewhere along the line which always rears its head, but I wasn't really too worried.

In 1982, when we went to Australia, Bob Jackson wasn't available. Well now, one player may not necessarily make all the difference, but he is a very, very good match player, and was our Open Champion. We went over early in the season, and none of us had had enough practice. I didn't play particularly well myself as the tour progressed. I played reasonably well to start with, but I found it difficult to motivate myself, and therefore to motivate the team, and we lost four test matches 4–5, by the narrowest margin. I feel that if Bob Jackson had been there, his presence would probably have strengthened our doubles and singles, as the younger guys really look up to him, and it would perhaps have made that little bit of difference.

Reflecting on this series (1986), I think the critical game was the doubles match that Roger Murfitt and Joseph Hogan won, the third game at Cheltenham. It was extremely close and whichever side won that one obviously had a big psychological advantage, having two doubles, each side with one each at that point. That gave us a slight edge. After that, we kept control of the situation. I felt that in Bob Jackson, Paul Skinley and Roger Murfitt, who we had playing each time on the last day, we were playing to our strength as a team. If the match was square 3–3, we had a good chance of winning two of those. We even felt that if we were slightly down, we might even win all three. We felt we were fortunate in the matches against Australia. Several games went our way when we wouldn't have expected them to. There was a doubles where a player rushed a ball for the

peg on to the peg, one of those shots which ninety-nine times out of a hundred wouldn't happen. That would have probably given them another match, and therefore the chance to keep in it. There was also an excellent win by Graham Beale in his singles, in the Hurlingham test against Australia, so I really felt that in that test the score-line flattered us. At Parkstone, again having two doubles was important, and then we got two singles on the second day which just kept us ahead all the time. I think it makes it much harder for the other side to come back when they know they've got to pick up so many games.

In 1982 and 1986 I felt that I really had not played as well as I would have liked to, or as well as I probably should have. I think you've got to decide that you know you've had your turn and, as we've been picking teams for both those series, I've been looking around and hoping that another couple of Skinleys and Hogans would turn up. Well they haven't quite yet, but I think they will in 1990, and I will be only too pleased to sit back and relax on the sidelines.

I think I will keep playing, but it just really depends on how you play, whether you have a good season. I remember in 1982 being fairly dispirited after the test series. I didn't play early in 1983 and I went to the President's cup in Gisborne thinking 'well, if I don't play any decent croquet in this, that'll be it'. That was the time that I did the two sextuples and the TPO, so I thought '. . . well, you know, still a bit of life left!'

If I had to ascribe my success to one factor, I think it would be practice – practice, yes, and having such a beautiful lawn on which to practise.

If croquet started attracting big prize money, well, it would be interesting to play for money, as it would be something I haven't done. I think if I felt I was playing well enough, I wouldn't mind having a go. It would be interesting to see how people reacted under the lure of the dollars. To start with, I think games would be very much like test match games, where there is quite a lot of defensive and dry play because the outcome is so important, and you don't want to give too much away. I think initially that would probably be the case, but if players ever got into a position where they were comfortably placed, as some golfers are, I think then we would see it revert back to open, attacking and exciting play.

I don't really think a change in the advanced game is needed, especially in doubles. You don't get a lot of 26 triple peels in doubles. Perhaps in singles the only thing I would suggest would be that after the initial roquet of a turn, your turn would end if a ball was roqueted off the court. That would make picking up breaks more difficult, and also the playing of them. You would have to make sure that you rushed the ball sufficiently far to be able to croquet it forward to where you wished, without playing it off the court, so I think that would add to the touch game.

Looking back, the big change in New Zealand croquet in my time has been the change in the tournaments, where the majority of players used to be women. I can remember New Zealand Men's Championships, when I played in them in the early days, where there may have been only nine or ten entries. Now it's completely reversed, and the field in the Women's can be quite small, while the Men's is always larger.'

John's Tip for Beginners Practise! You know, all of the top players put in an enormous amount of practice, especially initially, to become completely familiar with all the shots. If there are any shots they don't play well, they practise at getting them right.

John's Tips for Ambitious Players
1. Play as often as you can against the top players.
2. Try, in every game, to play the game at the highest level. Don't play too cautiously, and endeavour to improve your game as you go along, by attempting peel finishes and so on. It is very important to be able to do these things in test match croquet.

Neil Spooner

Date of birth: 13 January 1953
Place of birth: Adelaide, South Australia
Now resident in: Windsor, California, USA
Occupation: Director of Croquet
Current club: Sonoma-Cutrer Vineyards
Previous clubs: Brighton and Prospect (Adelaide)
Major titles: Three time Australian Open Champion, five times Australian Open Doubles Champion, twice Australian Men's Champion
International honours: Represented Australia in the MacRobertson Shield test series of 1974, 1982 and 1986.

Neil is a quietly spoken man with a jovial personality, but his story exposes a single-minded determination to be successful, a trait which has sometimes brought him into conflict with the administrative heirarchy of Australian croquet. He pulls no punches in his criticism of their policies and actions, which he sees as having been detrimental to the hopes of success of successive national teams in their quest to win the MacRobertson Shield.

'My introduction to croquet came in 1969, when I was at school at Westminster College in Adelaide. One day I was sitting in a classroom overlooking a tennis court where croquet was being played – in fact it was Golf Croquet. I thought it was quite interesting, so in my activities period I changed to croquet, and that was what set me off. I only played Golf Croquet for the first eighteen months of my career. I owe a lot to Tom Armstrong, who brought the game to Westminster and coached me in the early stages.

My first club was Brighton, but when I started playing Association Croquet I joined the Prospect club, in order to use their floodlighting. In the winter of 1970 I went out every single night for six months under lights – there's a record of it at the club in the book – paying sixty cents a night for lights. That was six solid months through winter, when it was raining, and even with hail on the lawns.

I modelled myself on John Magor, who was the one player in Australia who was really excellent when I started playing. It was my aim to become as good as him and beat him, which I eventually did in 1977.

I played in my first tournament off a handicap of 15. It was a handicap doubles tournament which I and my partner, Mrs Olive Jenkin from the Prospect Club, won. Within nine months I was an A Class player, down to a handicap of 3. It took me another eight months to become a minus player.

When I first started practising I played games against myself. I found that was the best practice because I tended to try things I wouldn't otherwise try in a match, and by doing that I realised I could do them. These days I practise very rarely, not enough, and, when I do, I don't practise particular strokes – I haven't done that for years – but just basically play games, match practice.

I always suffered from nerves in my early tournaments and still always do, but being under pressure improves my play one hundred per cent. John Prince notices the pressure unfortunately – I feel sorry for the guy.

I first won a major title in 1975. That year I won the Open Singles and the Open Doubles (with Barrie Chambers). I beat Ron Sloane in the Singles final, it was a four-hour, drawn out game, on a very dark, dingy wet day. It was a single game final, as the event is a draw and process. You need three weeks holiday to play in the Opens, and after winning my third Singles title in 1979 I didn't play again until 1985, when it was held in Sydney. Even there I had to withdraw. I played eighteen games undefeated, but the tournament was delayed because of rain and went on for far too long for me, as I had to get back to Adelaide.

I've done sextuples in practice, I did them back in 1970, but in tournament play I don't bother setting up for them, too much hard work! The way to win is with a triple peel.

I have a good memory for important games. The best match I ever played in was against John Prince in Sydney in 1982. John won the first game 26–0 with a triple, I won the second 26–9 with a triple, and I won the third 26–0 with a triple, in the MacRobertson, so it was rather a good match. What was the best performance against me? I tend to forget them! No, the most recent I can remember was by Keith Wylie in Melbourne in 1982. In the third game in a best of three he changed his game slightly and became much more attacking. I think he'd had enough of me attacking and he thought it was time he did so. He did, and played rather a good game there. It was a bit of in and out croquet, but it was still a great performance by Keith. Keith is the foreign player who I've been most impressed by, although perhaps the best performing one is John Prince.

As it happens it was against Keith that I played what I consider to be my best turn ever, in Adelaide, the second test in 1982. I was on the peg and had just made 4-back. I hit the ball after 4-back, put it to rover, went to a ball waiting at penultimate and I then over-rolled penultimate. There was a ball in the first corner with a lift. Well I thought, I can't give anything more away, so I'll have a crack at it. So I roqueted the ball in the first corner, right in the middle, and then pass-rolled that back up to the second hoop, gaining position at penultimate and going out to finish the game from there.

As to the best Australian players that I've seen, I'd put Peter Olsen and John Magor on a par. They've different styles completely but they are definitely equal to me.

As far as our game is concerned, the main changes that I've seen over the past sixteen years are that there is more thought put into leaves generally, and into ball placement during breaks. In the past it was a standard ball in the centre and off you go – it was a pivot ball, what you might call a beginner's break, I suppose, a C grade break. Now people tend to think ahead in the game more and place the balls to advantage, rather than making the sort of dull drab breaks of the past. The main difference between British and Australian play at the top level is that we don't get enough of it in Australia, as distance is obviously a problem. Players such as myself get top competition once a year maybe. I think Australian players tend to be much more aggressive, which I don't think is a good thing. It's a pity we don't get more international competition.

The Australian test performance in 1982 was so much better than previous modern performances because the top players were chosen. In 1979 it was a second-rate team that went over to New Zealand, because Barrie Chambers and Spencer Buck were not chosen when they should have been, and Peter Buck and myself pulled out of the team when it was orginally chosen. They weren't chosen, because they were not liked by the administration. It's just

Fig 201 Taking careful aim.

one of those things – a personality clash occurs, and so they're just not chosen.

In 1980 I won a gold medal in Adelaide but because I spent six weeks of that year in Sydney, between jobs, the ACC told me I was ineligible to have played in the event and so the medal was taken away from me. When I was in Perth the following year, on a holiday during the championships over there, I was talking to the President of the ACC and, during the course of conversation, she was rude in many ways and refused to listen. I was trying to find out why I was ineligible when another player, Bruce Ford, had just won the Brisbane medal and was allowed to play after he had spent about six months out of state. I'd only been away for six weeks, it was a crazy situation and she was very rude, wouldn't listen, and turned her back on me. I told her what I thought of her, so she used her presidency to get a suspension put on me for two years, which was lifted the following year because I had the support of virtually everybody, anyway. That made me determined to get back into the team.

How long do I intend to go on for? Probably until the end of the month! No, I don't know – it really is a year to year proposition at the moment. Four years ago I didn't think I'd be interested enough to be over here, I took a couple of years off, but then something happened again to make me determined to come back. A team was chosen to go to America, a very sly, cagey method of choosing it was used, and no players from the last test series were invited to go.

Administratively Australian croquet has changed little in the past twenty years and is still pretty poor. One problem is that only two top players, myself and Colin Pickering, are involved in it at the national level. To improve things for the players there must be a general improvement in communication. There's a very bad sort of situation now where we don't get information. Coming on this tour, we've been left out in the cold on a number of things that we just haven't been told about. For example, the Croquet Association of Ireland arranged with Jury's Hotel to have some accommodation for us at half the price that the Montrose is offering. That just never got through to us. Another one was that they also offered to billet us, which was never mentioned to us. There's just a complete lack of communication, and quite often I think it is deliberate.

Historically Australia has never done any serious forward planning for international competitions. Until the national body gives some genuine support to the top players, Australia will continue to lag behind New Zealand and Great Britain. The elite players must be identified and given financial assistance to attend national and specially arranged competitions. It is unfortunate that in Australian croquet, there is an element that believes solely in social croquet, and consequently does not support international competitions, unlike other nations.

Australia does have enough players of the right standard to win the MacRobertson Shield, but ignorant administrators drive them into early retirement one way or another, while others never realise their true potential. In 1982 Alan Cleland was omitted from the national team because one selector didn't like his beard! There are other such cases.

As captain, I hope making the team independent on this tour, as the 1982 Great British team was when they came to Australia, will improve our chances of winning. We're our own bosses, we've actually cancelled the accommodation that was organised with the tour, we've organised our own accommodation, and we're finding our own way around.

My forecast for the outcome of the 1986 test series? Probably rain mostly, a few days of sunshine for Australia. We're quietly confident, and we've been playing very well. We've used, for the first time, a sports psychologist, so our preparation has included everything – practical, theory and psychology. With all of our preparation I seriously think we can win the MacRobertson Shield, none of us would be here if we didn't. Of the two opposing teams, I think Great Britain is going to be more difficult, definitely Great Britain. I think Great Britain overrates New Zealand.

Looking ahead, if croquet ever attracted big prize money, I think I would consider turning professional, yes. I'd probably even start practising again! I think with a professional circuit, tactics in particular would be improved. At the moment, Australians in particular, and I'm guilty of this myself, tend to take a shot at things where there is a long roquet.

I don't think there is a need for new laws for the advanced game, I just think there is a need to enforce the ones we have now. I don't think hoops are restrictive enough, particularly in Australia where they're three and three-quarter inches (9.5cm) plus. There is very rarely a regulation hoop over there.'

Neil's Tips for Beginners
1. Practise!
2. Try to master the basic strokes and try to put them together to improve.
3. Get as much practice as you can against the better players, and don't be afraid to ask a better player for a game.

Neil's Tip for Ambitious Players Pick out somebody who's at the top and try to be their doubles partner. Doubles is a great situation for learning.

21 The World Series 1986

Appendix III shows the history of results in series to contest the MacRobertson Shield, croquet's world team championships. With three teams competing, the contest is essentially made up of three separate rubbers: Australia v. New Zealand, Australia v. Great Britain and Great Britain v. New Zealand. Each rubber involves three test matches, giving a total of nine test matches in all. Any team winning two rubbers or four test matches (in the case of a tie on rubbers) wins the Shield and there is provision made for a play-off if each nation wins one rubber and three test matches.

Teams consist of six players and each test match involves three doubles matches played on day one, and six singles matches, three played on day two and three on day three. Teams must play in order of merit, based on current form (which can cause controversy!), with numbers 2, 4 and 6 playing singles matches on day two and numbers 1, 3 and 5 playing on day three. Each match is the best of three games.

Prior to the 1986 series, conventional wisdom decreed that the contest's results table illustrated two important facts. Firstly, that the host nation possesses a great advantage. Nine of the twelve series were won by the host nation. Their advantage is, of course, that they can pick their best team, whereas touring teams can only select from those available to tour. Great Britain was therefore denied the services of Hands and Wylie in 1979, and Aspinall in 1982, New Zealand missed Jackson in 1982 and Australia were severely depleted in 1979. The second fact is the edge Great Britain (formerly England) has over the other nations. They had won seven of the twelve series, were unbeaten at home, had notched up the only three away wins, and were the only team never to have finished third. Statistically Great Britain were firm favourites for the 1986 series.

The two most recent series suggested things were not as clear cut. In 1979, a talented New Zealand team overpowered Great Britain in what, due to Australia's political problems, was essentially a two-sided series. The emergence of new stars Joseph Hogan and Paul Skinley, added to the tremendous progress made by Bob Jackson, had given the Kiwis an extremely strong squad, five members of which went on to play in the 1982 series, with five members of that team playing in the 1986 series. Only having to field one 'rookie' would surely be to their benefit.

In 1982 that did not appear to be the case, as New Zealand slipped to third place. In fact this was unquestionably the closest series since the contest became a regular three-way affair. New Zealand lost their first test to Australia 5–4, and each one of their three tests against Britain 5–4. Meanwhile, two of the Australia v. Great Britain tests had 5–4 scorelines and, for the first time since 1935, the issue was still in doubt going into the third round.

The script for that historic third test in Melbourne could have been written for Hitchcock. 2–1 to Britain after day one, 3–3 after day two, going to 4–4 and game all in the match between the number ones Neil Spooner (Australia) and Keith Wylie (Great Britain) before Keith clinched it for Britain. On the evidence of that series, there was every likelihood that the 1986 series would be equally close, with Australia, at full strength, being a team very much to fear.

PROGNOSTICATIONS

After the teams had been announced, the general view was that Great Britain and New Zealand were well matched, but that Australia, without Peter Olsen, and with three new-comers in their squad, were not strong enough to win.

Martin Murray, a veteran of the three previous series for Great Britain, writing in *Croquet* (July 1986), before the start of the series, stressed the psychological nature of test match croquet and suggested that the outcome might depend on how the 'new boys', Mark Avery and Colin Irwin for Great Britain and Graham Beale for New Zealand, reacted to the pressure. He concluded: 'Pressed for a forecast, I would choose New Zealand as winners'.

John Prince, the New Zealand captain, expressed a common belief when he said, 'We left New Zealand certain that the doubles would be a deciding factor'. Britain's dominance in the doubles had been widely acknowledged as the deciding factor in their favour in the 1982 series, and most experts agreed that a 2–1 lead after the doubles could be decisive where two teams were very evenly matched. After the series John revealed that New Zealand's plan was for 'a minimum 2–1–2 pattern', and that to give them every chance of achieving the two wins on the third day, they would play their more match-hardened players in spots one, three and five.

Given the even matching of these two teams and an acceptance that victory in their first meeting at Cheltenham would give the winners a tremendous psychological advantage in their second encounter at Parkstone, some pundits went so far as to suggest that the first day's play at Cheltenham would be critical in deciding the outcome of the series. Certainly Australia in 1982 was an exception to the general rule that the team that won two tests in the first round usually won the series by the end of the second round. In that context, the comments of New Zealand's Roger Murfitt after the series

were illuminating. He revealed that New Zealand had convinced themselves that, even if they were to lose at Cheltenham, they could win the next two tests in the rubber. Their reasoning was that Cheltenham was the most familiar venue to the British team, at which their home advantage would be at its greatest. The very fact of this mental preparation suggests to us that they realised how crucial the Cheltenham test would be.

Psychology and mental preparation were very much the fashion of the 1986 series. The Australian team had actually employed the services of a sports psychologist, most noticeably manifested in George Latham's preparation before taking crucial shots (*see* Fig 202). George certainly seemed to benefit at times, but maybe the team did not really share their captain Neil Spooner's pre-tour confidence.

What the pundits should have noted was that,

Fig 202 George Latham, with the will to win.

Fig 203   New Zealand in control: Bob Jackson . . .   Fig 204   . . . Joe Hogan . . .

Fig 205   . . . Paul Skinley.

whereas the Australians and New Zealanders openly stated their belief that the right result was going to come, no such confident predictions were heard from the British camp. Was it just British reticence which led team members to state that they expected it to be a close-run affair against New Zealand? Perhaps, as Neil Spooner suggests, they did overrate the New Zealanders, with the result that the New Zealanders proved them right.

AUSTRALIA v. NEW ZEALAND

The series opened at Bowdon with a crushing 7½–1½ victory to New Zealand, a result that seemed to confirm the pundits' predictions. It was a result from which Australia were not able to recover in this rubber. Defeats of 2–7 at Hurlingham and 1½–7½ at Southwick followed.

The dominance of the top three in the New Zealand order, Jackson, Hogan and Skinley, was particularly noticeable. Between them they won all of their matches against Spooner, Chambers and the various Australian number threes, culminating in their performances at Southwick, where each achieved a triple peel as they underlined their superiority.

AUSTRALIA v. GREAT BRITAIN

Australia certainly performed better against Great Britain. In view of their heavy defeat by New Zealand at Bowdon, they caused something of a surprise by tying up the first test at Budleigh 3–3, at the end of day two. The two Australian newcomers, Damon Bidencope and Alan Cleland, performed particularly well to defeat Steve Mulliner and Mark Avery (with a triple) respectively. An excellent performance by Colin Irwin on day three, however, enabled Britain to scrape home on the back of the ever-reliable Nigel Aspinall.

Britain won handsomely at Compton, a 7–2 margin of victory giving them the rubber and

Fig 206   Problems for Australia: Damon Bidencope and Barrie Chambers.

condemning Australia to the wooden spoon. Their margin of superiority certainly was not as great as the score suggests – it is interesting that ten games in that match were won by five points or less, a truer reflection of the closeness of the contest.

In fact, Australia left it to the last day of the 1986 series to show what they were capable of. At Colchester, 4–2 down after day two, they won all three matches on the final day to become the only team to overturn a doubles deficit to win a test match. Neil Spooner and Barry Chambers must have been particularly relieved to record their first singles wins.

Fig 207   A tight squeeze at Budleigh: William Prichard investigates.

GREAT BRITAIN
v. NEW ZEALAND

As forecast, the show-down for the world title was between Great Britain and New Zealand.

New Zealand arrived at Cheltenham hoping that the advantage of having a win under their belts and having got into the rhythm of a test match would counterbalance the advantage to the British team of playing on such familiar territory in front of a partisan crowd.

Many of the prognostications were to be substantiated. The singles split 3–3, New Zealand winning two games on day three, with Jackson staking his claim to recognition as the world number one by establishing superiority over Aspinall, just as he had over Spooner. Beale won the battle of the rookies against Irwin, but only just, in a nervy match in which he scraped home +4, +5. Avery balanced this for Britain by a fine performance against the vastly more experienced Murfitt. David Openshaw played a real Captain's role by doing a splendid delayed triple against Hogan when one game down, before winning the third. Mulliner presented Prince with game two by playing a wrong ball, with four balls in the middle of the court and Prince for peg and 4-back, but redeemed himself with a quick

win in the third game. Paul Skinley won the battle of the stylists against William Prichard.

And so it was, after all, the doubles on day one that decided this test. Jackson and Skinley made it 1–0 to New Zealand, establishing a series dominance over Mulliner and Prichard. Avery and Openshaw, the reigning British Open Doubles Champions, proved too strong for Beale and Prince, with John Prince looking surprisingly out of form.

It was 1–1, and so to the Aspinall/Irwin v. Hogan/Murfitt match. Some experts, as we have seen, fancied New Zealand to have a slight edge. What we did not know was how small that crucial edge would prove and what excitement was in store for us before it revealed itself. A croquet classic was about to emerge. The story of that match, concentrating on the titanic struggle at the end of the third game, is described in Chapter 22. It resulted in a 5–4 win for New Zealand.

The vital psychological advantage they gained proved too much for Great Britain at Parkstone. By day two of the second test they had gained a 4–2 lead. A quick win for Mulliner against Skinley put heart back into the British team and, for a while, Aspinall and Avery offered hope of snatching victory. It was too much to expect, however, that the experienced trio of Jackson, Skinley and

Fig 208   An enthralled audience at Cheltenham.

Fig 209   A confident rookie. Graham Beale makes a point to his captain.

Murfitt would allow themselves to be white-washed and, sure enough, they produced the two wins their captain was depending on. New Zealand thus took the test, rubber, series and Shield with this 6–3 win.

Easing up at Hunstanton, they were beaten 6–3 by Britain, which perhaps suggests that discipline and the will to win were more important in their crucial matches than any clear superiority in technical ability.

CONCLUSION

New Zealand won because they wanted to win, believed they would win, and approached their goal in a single-minded way. Externally this was exemplified by their smart appearance. With their striking black and white kit, they looked more like a team than the other two. Whenever one member was not playing, he would watch and support his colleague. To some they appeared to stick together too much, never relaxing completely after the early tests. They knew that their dedication to the task must border on obsession if they were to repay the support at home and bring back the World title. Well done you Kiwis!

The Australian team was clearly not as strong as the other two. Their lack of experience showed. At present the top Australian players are starved of regular competitive experience using the 'best of three' format on which test match play is based. The geographic factor mitigates against regular contact between the top players in Australia, but if Australia really wants success in this competition in the future, the ACC will have to answer Neil Spooner's plea from the heart, voiced in Chapter 20.

Now we suggest that you look again at Appendix III and join with us in discarding the two old theories, replacing them with a new one, namely that, in these days of air travel, the advantage now lies with touring sides. It is surely no coincidence that England, in 1963, became the first victorious touring team, as they were also the first touring team to be able to take advantage of air travel. This naturally slashed the amount of time required to participate in series overseas and allowed virtually full strength teams to be sent abroad.

Since 1963, four of the six series have been won by touring teams. Provided a strong team spirit, such as that exhibited by the British team in 1982, and New Zealand in 1986, is fostered by the touring team, it gives them a significant edge, as they are untroubled by domestic concerns and are free to concentrate on their croquet. It was noticeable in 1986 that some members of the British team were absent from matches on days when they were not playing, perhaps trying to pare leave requirements to a minimum, under pressure from employers. The same employers would probably not balk at giving special leave for 'once in a lifetime' overseas tours.

Elsewhere John Prince suggests that you should not pick the best six players for a touring side, but rather the six who would gel together best to make a team. Perhaps home nations should not pick their six best players, rather the six best who can free themselves of all commitments for the series at home.

We have no hesitation in predicting a British victory in New Zealand in the next series.

Fig 210   Kiwi cock-a-hoop.

22 Tension in the Twilight

BACKGROUND

Date: Saturday 14th June 1986.
Location: Lawn 8 at Cheltenham Croquet Club.
Test series: Great Britain v. New Zealand.
Occasion: First test, first day.
Match: Number two doubles.
Sides: Nigel Aspinall (blue), and Colin Irwin (black) for Great Britain, v. Joseph Hogan (yellow), and Roger Murfitt (red) for New Zealand.
Weather: The end of a hot and sunny day.
Court condition: Slowing to medium pace as the evening dew formed.

Hoop setting: Accurately set and very firm in the hard ground. Very testing.
Score in game 1: 26–10 (+16) to Hogan and Murfitt.
Score in game 2: 26–17 (+9) to Aspinall and Irwin.

INTRODUCTION *(Figs 214 to 217)*

What made this game a classic was the end-game. There was certainly nothing surprising about Nigel getting the first break, although an error after 2-back was the first hint of the unusual events to come. The significance of

Fig 211   Roger (left) and Joe (right) at Cheltenham, during the match.

Fig 212   Colin (left) and Nigel (right) at Cheltenham, during the match.

Nigel's clip being on 3-back and not 4-back was not to emerge for some time.

Roger punished Nigel's mistake and took red to 4-back. However, Colin hit the lift and, in his next turn, replied by playing an all-round break with black, making the leave shown in Fig 214.

A miss by Joe would have made Nigel's task of finishing a lot easier, so Roger took the lift shot and hit yellow. He then laid up for Joe, as shown in Fig 215.

After some deliberation, Nigel shot at black, but missed. From that position, Joe constructed a four-ball break. An early attempt to peel red through 4-back failed, but eventually he peeled red through 4-back, reached the peg with yellow and pegged black out (see Fig 216). He laid up as shown in Fig 217.

At this stage, the clip positions were as follows: Nigel, 3-back; Joe, peg; Roger, penultimate.

Fig 213   Nigel during an early break, at the scene of the drama to come – hoop 3-back.

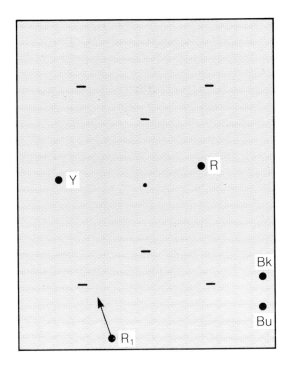

Fig 214

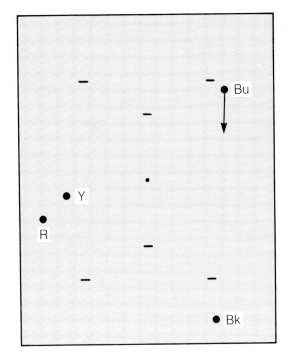

Fig 215

Fig 216   Joe pegs out Colin's ball under scrutiny from referee Ian Vincent.

191

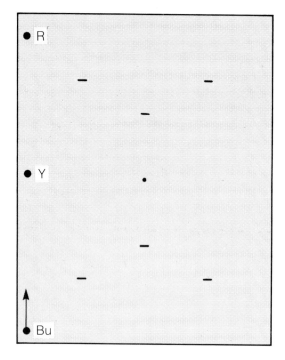

Fig 217

THE ENDGAME

Many beginners mistakenly assume that once one side manages to peg out one of the opponent's balls, the result, namely a win for the side with two balls, is a foregone conclusion. Certainly it conveys a powerful advantage, in that the one-ball side never has an easy roquet because it no longer has its partner ball to lay up beside. At the beginners' level, where the standard of roqueting, rushing and hoop approaches is generally so poor that it makes two or three-ball breaks rare, that advantage is usually a conclusive one. A Class and test players are another breed, however, and the single-ball player becomes the attacker, often winning from such a situation.

Let us imagine what the two sides might have been thinking at this stage of the match . . .

Nigel: 'I just need one rush . . . I think you might be sorry you did this, Joe, you should have made a tight leave and forced the peg ball to take the lift'.

Colin: 'It gives them the advantage, but Nigel is playing well and shooting well; if he hits, he'll probably go out . . . there's no one in the British team I'd rather have playing for us in this situation'.

Joe: 'All we need to do now is be patient and careful, don't let's give him a chance of a break'.

Roger: 'Come on Roger, 2–1 in the doubles and we'll win this test, that's what we came over for'.

The Turns *(Figs 217 to 231)*

Let us now study that remarkable endgame turn by turn:

Turn 1: Fig 217 shows the position after Nigel had lifted his ball from the middle of the court. Because advanced play is the form of play used in test matches, Nigel was entitled to a lift under law 36(a)(ii). For this reason, Joe could not lay up with his balls near either baulk-line, nor did he want to leave either ball near Nigel's hoop (3-back). Thus, the second corner was the obvious choice for one ball (red was in fact just south of the corner), with the other ball well down the west boundary. With Nigel having a relatively short shot (less than twenty yards (18m)), Joe left his balls well separated in case Nigel hit it, so that even then it would be difficult for Nigel to get a rush.

Nigel could have tried for position at 3-back, but that could enable his opponents to join up a safe distance away from him, and possibly even wired from him. These opponents were not about to let him make a hoop at a time, and he knew he had to create a two or three-ball break to win. The shortest available shot was from B-baulk at red, but a miss on the left would have given red a rush to yellow and a chance to finish. Nigel decided to shoot from the first corner at yellow. This had two advantages. First, if he were really lucky, he might rush yellow close to red, and second, if he missed, blue should end up on the north boundary, giving red the innings, but denying it a rush to yellow.

Nigel shot and roqueted yellow, which went off the west boundary, a few feet north of the position shown in Fig 217. He then played a croquet stroke, sending yellow near 4-back and blue close to red. In his continuation stroke, he roqueted red, giving the position shown in Fig 218.

He now played a take-off from red, hoping to get position at 3-back, so that he could run the hoop and roquet yellow near 4-back. Although the court was fairly fast, it was to everybody's astonishment that he sent blue off-court, thereby ending his turn.

Turn 2: Yellow shot at red, narrowly missing. This was certainly a good time to join, being forty yards (36m) from Nigel's ball.

Turn 3: Nigel shot at red and yellow in corner 2, but missed.

Turn 4: Roger roqueted blue with red and took off to behind yellow, to get a rush to his hoop. He rushed yellow close to penultimate and made the hoop, but did not get a useful rush after the hoop. He therefore roqueted yellow gently and played a roll stroke, trying to get position for rover. Both his balls ended at the side of rover, however, so, with his last stroke, he hit red off the south boundary. Fig 219 shows us the position at this stage.

Roger could not leave red by yellow, because a hit in by Nigel would give him an easy chance of getting a rush to 3-back. He could, and did, make any shot by Nigel very dangerous, however. Note that if Nigel shot at yellow and missed, his ball would end up near red, giving Roger an easy chance to finish. This is a good example of a *guard*.

Turn 5: As shown in Fig 219, Nigel hit blue off the south boundary, *triangulating*, that is, placing his ball at equal distances from his opponents' two balls. Notice that blue is close enough to corner 1 to guard against the shot red at blue.

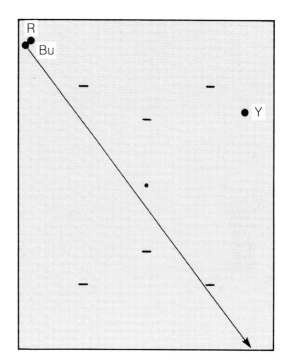

Fig 218

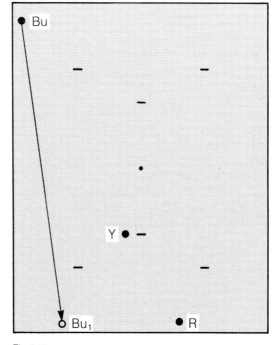

Fig 219

Turn 6: Red had to move, as it was too close to 3-back for comfort. Roger shot at yellow, but missed.

Turn 7: Nigel shot at, and roqueted, yellow. He then played a split roll from the position shown in Fig 220.

He got blue three feet (90cm) dead in front of his hoop. A controlled hoop at this stage could have given him the winning break. His hoop stroke failed, blue landing hard on the right hand wire.

Turn 8: by chance, yellow had a wiring lift under law 13, because it was wired from blue by hoop 3-back, and it was wired from red by the peg. Joe took the lift from B-baulk and just missed, leaving red the rush down the west boundary shown in Fig 221.

Turn 9: There was little Nigel could do. He tried to tap blue into the jaws of 3-back but, because of a slight slope, it rolled back, a couple of inches clear of the hoop.

Turn 10: As shown in Fig 221, Roger rushed yellow down to corner 1 and then took off to

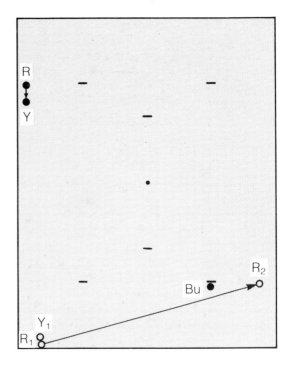

Fig 221

try and get a rush on blue towards rover (also, thereby, denying it its hoop). He played the stroke much too hard and red ended close to the east boundary. He just snicked blue, in trying to roquet it, and blue ended up in the position shown in Fig 222.

Needing to get blue well away from yellow, but seeing an opportunity to make rover, Roger played a great split shot, sending blue near corner 3 and getting position about eighteen inches (45cm) in front of rover, at a slight angle. His hoop stroke was not so good, however, and red stuck plum in the jaws of the rover hoop (*see* Fig 223).

Turn 11: To tumultuous applause from the home crowd, Nigel hit the thirty-five-yard (31.5m) shot, blue at yellow. Taking croquet from the position shown in Fig 224, he played a good split shot, sending yellow to 4-back and getting blue a few feet south of red. With his continuation stroke, he roqueted red back out of the jaws of rover. He then played a split shot from the position shown in Fig 225.

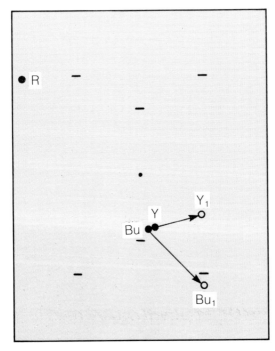

Fig 220

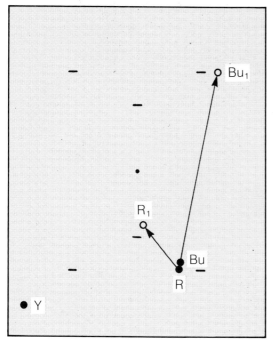

Fig 222

Fig 223   Roger blobs rover as the evening draws in.

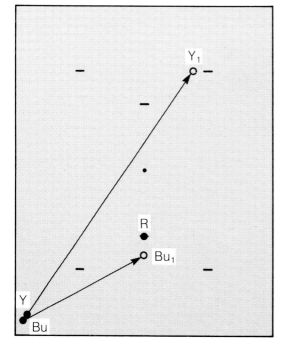

Fig 224

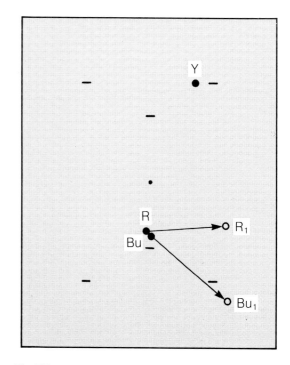

Fig 225

He failed to get blue in front of 3-back. With his last stroke he knocked blue sideways to a position wired from red, but in front of 3-back, some one and a half to two feet (45–60cm) away. This was a very powerful position. Yellow dare not shoot at red because, if it missed, blue could turn round and would have only a seven or eight-yard (6.3–7.2m) shot to hit for a three-ball break. Similarly, a miss after red at yellow would give Nigel an easy chance of a three-ball break if he could run his hoop hard to the north boundary. Red had no shot at blue, and yellow's partial target was more difficult and as dangerous as the shot at red.

Turn 12: Because yellow was such a good pioneer at 4-back, the New Zealand pair decided to move it, sending it to the middle of the west boundary, as shown in Fig 226. They hoped that Nigel would not get a rush to 4-back on red, which was lying slightly east of the line between 3-back and 4-back.

Turn 13: To the disbelief of the crowd, many

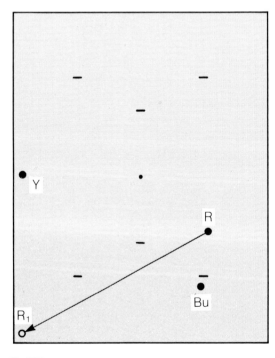

Fig 226

of whom rated Nigel as the world's number one, he proved he is only human by sticking in the hoop. As was to become even clearer later, the vital importance of this game, and the agitation of the crowd, was having an effect on the players.

Turn 14: Roger's red was four or five yards (3.6–4.5m) from 3-back, and a miss at less than a full target could give Nigel the chance to make two or even three hoops. He therefore hit it off into corner 1. Why didn't he join up with yellow? That would allow Nigel a twenty-yard (18m) shot for a rush after running 3-back, and Roger correctly recognised that whilst the pressure was having a detrimental effect on Nigel's hoop running, it was having the opposite effect on his shooting, which was becoming inspired. He would bide his time to join up.

Turn 15: Nigel ran 3-back hard, but did not end too close to 4-back. He used his continuation stroke to try to hit blue in position in front of 4-back, but ended in a seemingly unrunnable position, about two feet (60cm) away at a forty-degree angle to the hoop, as shown in Fig 227.

Turn 16: Now was the time to join, with Nigel nearly forty yards (36m) away, having an apparently unrunnable hoop and having a hampered backswing if he wanted to shoot towards corner 1. Joe in fact roqueted red with his yellow and laid up as shown in Fig 227, leaving Roger an easy rush to rover and, for good measure, wiring both balls from Nigel's blue.

Turn 17: With no shot, Nigel had no option but to try the impossible hoop. Yes, you've guessed it, having previously missed two easy hoops, he played a fantastic jump shot and ran 4-back to the position shown in Fig 227, from which he was no longer wired from red and yellow. Despite the fact that it was a forty-yard (36m) shot, I think everyone, including Joe and Roger, expected him to hit – this saga would surely not end limply. He missed.

Turn 18: Ignoring Nigel's ball (he had a good rush anyway and doing so gave him the option of wiring his balls from Nigel if things went

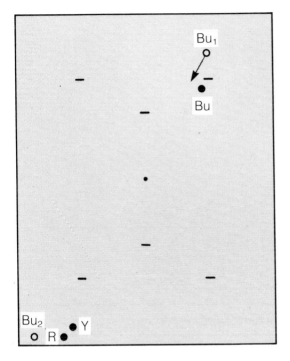

Fig 227

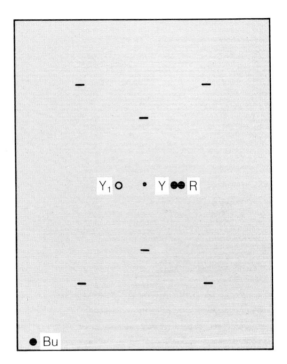

Fig 228

wrong), Roger rushed yellow to rover, played a reasonable approach stroke, ran the hoop and rushed yellow to a position eight feet (2.4m) east of the peg, as shown in Fig 228.

We were now about to witness the most remarkable demonstration of the toll three long games on a hot day, under the most intense pressure, can take on even the greatest players. Any A Class player worth his salt knows that the way to peg out is with a firm stop shot, and that, on a reasonable lawn, from that situation, you would expect to peg out successfully nine times out of ten. With Roger lining the balls up for the peg out, Joe walked on to the lawn and to our surprise started making some point about a spot some two feet (60cm) west of the peg. When Roger came over to look and they both started looking at blue, it became obvious that Joe was pointing to a spot wired from blue. With the New Zealand followers looking on in horror, Roger proceeded to play a soft roll, apparently more concerned to make sure that yellow ended up

wired from blue if it missed the peg, rather than concentrating on the pegging out of yellow itself. Of course, yellow missed the peg, and the wired spot. Roger pegged out red, leaving yellow in the position shown in Fig 228, some four to five feet (1.2–1.5m) west of the peg. If Nigel missed, the game was over, but a shell-shocked New Zealand pair were just realising the enormity of their mistake – they had just left him a potential rush to his hoop.

Turn 19: With the crowd at fever pitch, Nigel showed the quality of a champion and hit the twenty-yarder (18m), yellow being rushed to a position some three yards (2.7m) south-west of penultimate, as shown in Fig 229. At that moment, I don't think a single spectator would have backed New Zealand to win. Nigel played a slightly thick backward take-off, nudging yellow to a position between penultimate and the peg, so that he had the best chance of a rush after the hoop. Maybe he relaxed a little after the pressure of the last

197

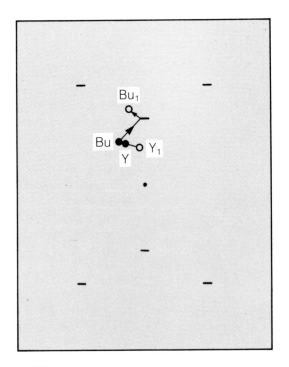

Fig 229

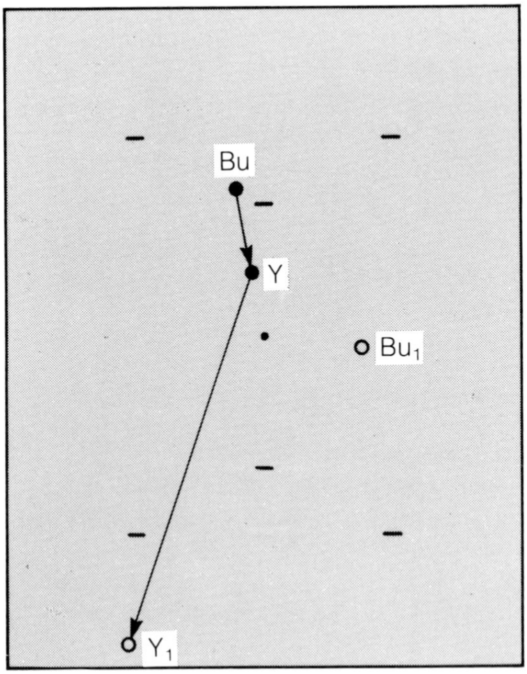

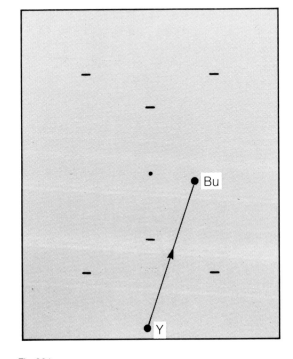

Fig 230

shot, but a stunned silence greeted the vision of blue bouncing off the side of penultimate into an absolutely unrunnable position: a bad mistake that would even disappoint a C Class player. I will never forget immediately turning round to view Colin's reaction – he seemed to be gazing into an infinite void, as if he was waiting for blue to start moving again, so great was his incomprehension of what had just occurred. Nigel still had one more shot though, and yellow was so close to the peg that Joe would be bound to peg out if Nigel did not move it. No one should have been surprised when Nigel once more delved into his store of brilliance, playing a scatter shot that not only sent yellow to the south boundary, but left blue sufficently close to the peg to stop Joe trickling up to it, as shown in Fig 230.

Turn 20: By a quirk of fate, however, Joe had a wiring lift, as yellow was denied a shot at blue by hoop 5. Joe was thus able to lift blue to the right-hand end of A-baulk, as shown in Fig 231. This gave him a seventeen-yard (15.3m)

Fig 231

shot at blue (he had a shot of a similar distance to the peg, but a ball is half as wide again as the peg, so is a better target at the same range). He now completed the sequence of remarkable shooting by roqueting blue and, to great cheers from his team-mates, he took off to the peg and pegged out to win, +3.

CONCLUSION

New Zealand had got the vital 2–1 lead after the doubles. As so many experts were predicting, these two well-matched teams shared the singles 3–3, for a final score of 5–4 to New Zealand. Not only did New Zealand now only require one more victory from the remaining two tests against Great Britain, but they had achieved that psychological edge, so vital at the highest level of any competitive sport.

Colin and Roger later reflected on that ending:

Colin: 'I didn't really get worried until the second time he blobbed 3-back. It seemed strange that Nigel seemed to be able to hit anything at any distance, but just didn't seem to be able to make that hoop'.

Roger: 'My memories are of Nigel's great shooting, getting positions and failing hoops. The ending was very nerve-racking; if Nigel had run 3-back, that would have been the end. The silly peg out we tried? Mentally the whole way round we had been going for wiring positions. Joe walked out and I said "hey, there's a wired position". I was only trying to peg one ball out and go for a wired position . . . just one of those mental blocks'.

We all remember those great sporting occasions where, as the tension rises, the competitors become sucked into it and unleash the dramatic punch and counter-punch that television immortalises – the late night World snooker final between Steve Davis and Dennis Taylor, Italy v. West Germany in the semi-final of the 1970 World Cup, England v. Australia in the Headingley test – we had been privileged to be part of such excitement at Cheltenham, in the twilight of that June evening. Not millions of us by way of our television screens, but maybe a hundred and fifty of us, for that is the way of croquet. However, that excitement wasn't any the less, so if, in the years to come, you hear someone say 'I remember, back at Cheltenham, in '86 . . .', sit a while and you will hear a first-hand account of a sporting legend.

Appendix I

Equipment Manufacturers

Australia
The Australian Croquet Company,
1349 South Road,
Bedford Park,
South Australia

Scott Croquet Equipment,
Bruce W. Scott,
14 Monie Street,
Woonona,
New South Wales 2517

Canada
Fleming Croquet Equipment,
Reid Fleming,
7691 Eperson Road,
Richmond,
British Columbia V7C 2K5

England
John Jaques & Son Ltd,
361 Whitehorse Road,
Thornton Heath,
Surrey CR4 8XP

Bernard Neal Croquet Mallets,
Moat Cottage,
Kidnapper's Lane,
Cheltenham,
Gloucestershire GL53 0NR

Townsend Croquet Ltd,
Claire Road,
Kirby Cross,
Frinton-on-Sea,
Essex CO13 0LX

Walker Croquet Equipment,
82 Queens Crescent,
Chippenham,
Wiltshire SN14 0NP

New Zealand
Jackson Croquet Mallets,
18 Caspar Road,
Papatoetoe,
Auckland

USA
Forster Croquet Equipment,
c/o Croquet International Ltd,
100 Devonshire Way,
Palm Beach Gardens,
Florida 33418

Pendulum Precision Mallets
Garth Eliassen,
PO Box 5,
Sonoma,
California 95476

Appendix II

Modern Champions

Here you will find listed the winners of all the major croquet championships in the world during this decade. The British section supplements the exhaustive list of British champions from 1867–1980 provided by D.M.C. Prichard in the appendices to his book *The History of Croquet* (Cassell Ltd, 1981). Note that NZ denotes a visiting player from New Zealand. SA denotes a visiting player from South Africa.

Australia

Open Singles

1980	S.A.Buck
1981	B.Chambers
1982	S.A.Buck
1983	G.Thorburn
1984	G.Latham
1985	G.Latham
1986	R.V.Jackson (NZ)
1987	J.Tyrrell

Open Doubles

1980	P.Buck and S.A.Buck
1981	B.Chambers and T.Cresswell
1982	P.Buck and S.A.Buck
1983	Mrs V.Crane and G.Thorburn
1984	D.Bidencope and G.Thorburn
1985	B.Ford and A.Read
1986	G.Latham and N.Spooner
1987	G.Latham and J.Tyrrell

Men's Singles

1980	S.A.Buck
1981	R.Sloane
1982	S.A.Buck
1983	G.Latham
1984	G.Latham
1985	B.Ford
1986	R.V.Jackson (NZ)
1987	G.Latham

Ladies' Singles

1980	Miss C.Dawson
1981	Mrs L.Bray
1982	Miss C.Dawson
1983	Mrs S.McDonald
1984	Miss C.Dawson
1985	Mrs M.Grieve
1986	Mrs M.Grieve
1987	Mrs M.Grieve

Great Britain

Open Singles

1980   W.de B.Prichard
1981   D.K.Openshaw
1982   G.N.Aspinall
1983   G.N.Aspinall
1984   G.N.Aspinall
1985   D.K.Openshaw
1986   J.K.Hogan (NZ)

Men's Singles

1980   M.Murray
1981   D.K.Openshaw
1982   M.Murray
1983   G.N.Aspinall
1984   S.N.Mulliner
1985   S.N.Mulliner
1986   D.R.Foulser

President's Cup

1980   G.N.Aspinall
1981   S.N.Mulliner
1982   G.N.Aspinall
1983   S.N.Mulliner
1984   G.N.Aspinall
1985   G.N.Aspinall
1986   S.N.Mulliner

Ireland

Open Singles

1980   T.O.Read
1981   R.J.Murfitt (NZ)
1982   T.O.Read
1983   C.M.von Schmieder
1984   G.P.N.Healey
1985   T.O.Read
1986   G.P.N.Healy

Open Doubles

1980   S.N.Mulliner and W.de B.Prichard
1981   S.N.Mulliner and M.Ormerod
1982   A.B.Hope and M.Murray
1983   P.Cordingley and J.R.McCullough
1984   G.N.Aspinall and S.N.Mulliner
1985   D.K.Openshaw and M.N.Avery
1986   G.N.Aspinall and S.N.Mulliner

Ladies' Singles

1980   Mrs B.Meacham
1981   Mrs V.Carlisle
1982   Mrs S.Wiggins
1983   Mrs S.Wiggins
1984   Mrs V.Carlisle
1985   Mrs M.Collin
1986   Mrs S.Wiggins

Mixed Doubles

1980   B.C.Sykes and Mrs S.Sykes
1981   M.Murray and Mrs B.Meacham
1982   G.N.Aspinall and Mrs C.Knox(SA)
1983   M.Murray and Mrs K.Yeoman
1984   I.D.Bond and Mrs V.Carlisle
1985   K.M.H.Aiton and Mrs M.Collin
1986   T.Griffiths and Miss J.MacLoed

Japan

Open Singles

1984   T.Takano
1985   K.Kagawa
1986   T.Takano

Open Doubles

1984   A.Nemeto and T.Takano
1985   A.Mitsui and A.Tanaka
1986   K.Kagawa and T.Yamada

New Zealand

Open Singles

1980   P.J.Skinley
1981   P.J.Skinley
1982   R.V.Jackson
1983   R.V.Jackson
1984   R.V.Jackson
1985   P.J.Skinley
1986   J.K.Hogan
1987   J.G.Prince

Open Doubles

1980   J.K.Hogan and R.V.Jackson
1981   J.K.Hogan and R.V.Jackson
1982   J.K.Hogan and R.V.Jackson
1983   R.J.Murfitt and B.Wislang
1984   R.J.Clarke and G.J.Roberts
1985   J.K.Hogan and R.V.Jackson
1986   J.K.Hogan and R.V.Jackson
1987   J.K.Hogan and R.V.Jackson

Men's Singles

1980   P.J.Skinley
1981   J.K.Hogan
1982   G.J.Roberts
1983   P.J.Skinley
1984   G.J.Roberts
1985   R.V.Jackson
1986   R.V.Jackson
1987   R.V.Jackson

Ladies Singles

1980   Mrs R.A.Johnstone
1981   Mrs R.A.Johnstone
1982   Mrs M.Ward
1983   Mrs M.Hadwin
1984   Mrs M.Hadwin
1985   Mrs M.Hadwin
1986   Mrs M.Hadwin
1987   Mrs M.Hadwin

President's Cup

1980   R.V.Jackson
1981   P.J.Skinley
1982   P.J.Skinley
1983   P.J.Skinley
1984   J.G.Prince
1985   P.J.Skinley
1986   J.G.Prince
1987   G.W.Beale

Mixed Doubles

1980   P.Couch and Mrs S.M.Grigg
1981   P.J.Skinley and Mrs R.A.Johnstone
1982   D.Bulloch and Mrs M.Hadwin
1983   S.Wardle and Mrs H.Woollett
1984   P.J.Skinley and Mrs C.Ross
1985   not held
1986   not held
1987   R.V.Jackson and Mrs M.Jackson

South Africa

Open Singles

1980	T.Barlow
1981	T.Barlow
1982	T.Barlow
1983	C.Barlow
1984	C.Barlow
1985	C.Barlow
1986	R.Bamford

Open Doubles

1980	R.Bamford and C.Coulson
1981	T.Barlow and Mrs C.Knox
1982	T.Barlow and R.Le Maitre
1983	R.Bamford and C.Barlow
1984	R.Bamford and C.Barlow
1985	C.Barlow and T.Barlow
1986	T.Barlow and R.Le Maitre

USA

Open Singles

1980	J.A.Peck
1981	R.Pearman
1982	J.A.Peck
1983	E.A.Prentis IV
1984	J.Bast
1985	R.Bell
1986	R.Fleming

Open Doubles

1980	N.Prentis III and E.A.Prentis IV
1981	N.Prentis III and E.A.Prentis IV
1982	A.Burchfield and M.Burchfield
1983	R.Illingworth and K.Jones
1984	J.Bast and R.Bell
1985	R.Bell and D.Dribben
1986	R.Bell and D.Dribben

National Club Team

1980	J.R.Osborn and E.A.Prentis IV (New York CC)
1981	J.R.Osborn and E.A.Prentis IV (New York CC)
1982	J.R.Osborn and E.A.Prentis IV (New York CC)
1983	J.C.Osborn and J.R.Osborn (New York CC)
1984	R.Bell and E.Cline (Arizona CC)
1985	R.Kraft and D.Stallings (Arizona CC)
1986	J.C.Osborn and J.R.Osborn (New York CC)
1987	A.Burchfield and R.Kraft (Stamping Ground CC, Kentucky)

Appendix III

The MacRobertson Shield, 1925 – 1986

Year	Venue	Winners	Second	Third
1925	England	England (3)	Australia (0)	
1927/8	Australia	Australia (1½)	England (1½)[1]	
1930	Australia	Australia (3)	New Zealand (0)	
1935	Australia	Australia (5)	England (4)	New Zealand (0)
1937	England	England (5)	Australia (0)	
1950/1	New Zealand	New Zealand (2)	England (1)	
1956	England	England (5)	New Zealand (0)	
1963	New Zealand	England (6)	Australia (2)	New Zealand (1)
1969	Australia	England (6)	New Zealand (3)	Australia (0)
1974	England	Great Britain (6)	New Zealand (2)	Australia (1)
1979	New Zealand	New Zealand (6)	Great Britain (3)	Australia (0)
1982	Australia	Great Britain (5)	Australia (4)	New Zealand (0)
1986	England	New Zealand (5)	Great Britain (3)	Australia (1)[2]

Notes
The numbers in brackets indicate the number of test matches won.
1. Australia were declared the series winners as they had won twenty games to England's nineteen.
2. Full results of 1986 series in Appendix IV.

Appendix IV

The MacRobertson Shield 1986 Series
First Test, Bowdon CC, 10 – 12 June.

AUSTRALIA v. NEW ZEALAND

Doubles

G.Latham and N.E.Spooner lost to R.V.Jackson and P.J.Skinley, −26tp,−17
D.Bidencope and B.Chambers beat J.K.Hogan and R.J.Murfitt, −21,+14,+3
S.A.Buck and A.Cleland lost to G.Beale and J.G.Prince, −3,−3

Singles

Spooner lost to Jackson, −17tp,−13
Chambers lost to Hogan, −26,−11
Latham lost to Skinley, −24,−9tp
Buck lost to Beale, −26,−18
Bidencope v. Murfitt, −11,+25tp, unfinished
Cleland lost to Prince, −5,−17tp

Result: AUSTRALIA 1½   NEW ZEALAND 7½

Second Test, Cheltenham CC, 14 – 16 June.

GREAT BRITAIN v. NEW ZEALAND

Doubles

S.N.Mulliner and W.de B.Prichard lost to Jackson and Skinley, −17,+17,−25
G.N.Aspinall and C.J.Irwin lost to Hogan and Murfitt, −16,+9,−3
M.N.Avery and D.K.Openshaw beat Beale and Prince, +7,+26

Singles

Aspinall lost to Jackson, −10,−13
Openshaw beat Hogan, −26,+24tp,+25
Prichard lost to Skinley, −25,−3
Mulliner beat Prince, +16,−11,+25
Avery beat Murfitt, +11,+13
Irwin lost to Beale, −4,−5

Result: Great Britain 4   New Zealand 5

Third Test, Budleigh Salterton CC, 18 – 20 June.

AUSTRALIA v. GREAT BRITAIN

Doubles

Latham and Spooner beat Mulliner and Prichard, −11, +14, +10
Bidencope and Chambers lost to Avery and Openshaw, −21, −26
Buck and Cleland lost to Aspinall and Irwin, +3, −17tp, −25

Singles

Spooner lost to Aspinall, −8, −13tp
Chambers lost to Openshaw, −4, −6
Latham beat Prichard, +16, −16, +16
Bidencope beat Mulliner, +2, +5
Buck lost to Irwin, −26, −26
Cleland beat Avery, +3, +26tp

Result: Australia 4   Great Britain 5

Fourth Test, Hurlingham, 23 – 25 June.

AUSTRALIA v. NEW ZEALAND

Doubles

Latham and Spooner lost to Jackson and Skinley, −10, −14
Buck and Cleland lost to Hogan and Murfitt, −23, +26, −2
Bidencope and Chambers lost to Beale and Prince, +5, −11, −15

Singles

Spooner lost to Jackson, −9tpo, −10
Chambers lost to Hogan, +14, −20tp, −15
Buck lost to Skinley, −6, −13
Latham beat Prince, +16, −26, +6
Bidencope beat Murfitt, +25, −5, +14
Cleland lost to Beale, −23, +26, −2

Result: Australia 2   New Zealand 7

Fifth Test, Parkstone CC, 27 – 29 June.

GREAT BRITAIN v. NEW ZEALAND

Doubles

Mulliner and Prichard lost to Jackson and Skinley, −14, −16tp
Avery and Openshaw lost to Hogan and Murfitt, −10, +4, −16
Aspinall and Irwin beat Beale and Prince, +21, +17

Singles

Aspinall lost to Jackson, −24tp, +7tp, −8
Openshaw lost to Hogan, +22tp, −12, −8
Mulliner beat Skinley, +7, +3tp
Prichard beat Beale, +16, +5
Avery lost to Murfitt, −23, −13
Irwin lost to Prince, −26, −13

Result: Great Britain 3   New Zealand 6

Sixth Test, Compton CC, 1 – 3 July.

AUSTRALIA v. GREAT BRITAIN

Doubles

Bidencope and Cleland lost to Avery and Openshaw, +5, −3, −21
Chambers and Spooner beat Aspinall and Irwin, +9, −12, +4
Buck and Latham lost to J.R.McCullough and Prichard, +17, −11, −21

Singles

Spooner lost to Aspinall, −26tp, −22
Chambers lost to Openshaw, −4, +24, −23
Latham lost to Prichard, −11, −5
Bidencope lost to Irwin, −1, −25
Buck lost to Avery, +5, −3, −26
Cleland beat McCullough, +2, −1, +5

Result: Australia 2   Great Britain 7

Seventh Test, Southwick CC, 5 – 7 July.

AUSTRALIA v. NEW ZEALAND

Doubles

Bidencope and Cleland lost to Jackson and Skinley, −19,−6
Chambers and Spooner lost to Hogan and Murfitt, −6,−5
Buck and Latham v Beale and Prince, −13,+7 unfinished

Singles

Spooner lost to Jackson, −2,−17tp
Chambers lost to Hogan, −22,+22,−19tp
Cleland lost to Skinley, −26tp,+3,−9
Bidencope lost to Beale, −4,−14
Latham lost to Murfitt, −3,−20tp
Buck beat Prince, +17,+17tp

Result: Australia 1½   New Zealand 7½

Eighth Test, Hunstanton CC, 10 – 12 July.

GREAT BRITAIN v. NEW ZEALAND

Doubles

Avery and Openshaw beat Hogan and Jackson, +26tp,−17,+3
Aspinall and Irwin beat Prince and Skinley, +11,+22
A.B.Hope and Prichard lost to Beale and Murfitt, −3,−10

Singles

Openshaw beat Jackson, +15,+3
Aspinall beat Hogan, +9,−26,+25tp
Prichard lost to Skinley, +5,−25,−25tp
Irwin beat Beale, +4tp,+5
Hope lost to Murfitt, +9,−15,−21
Avery beat A.D.Heenan, +17,+21

Result: Great Britain 6   New Zealand 3

Ninth Test, Colchester CC, 14 – 16 July.

AUSTRALIA v. GREAT BRITAIN

Doubles

Chambers and Spooner beat Avery and Openshaw, +4, +26
Bidencope and Cleland lost to Aspinall and Irwin, −13, +4, −10
Buck and Latham lost to McCullough and Prichard, −12, −23

Singles

Spooner beat Openshaw, −8, +4, +18
Cleland lost to Aspinall, −13, +3, −19
Latham beat Prichard, −16, +14, +26
Chambers beat Irwin, +5, +17
Bidencope beat Avery, +3, +1
Buck lost to McCullough, +3, −24, −7

Result: Australia 5   Great Britain 4

Key   tp = triple peel to win game; tpo = triple peel on opponent's ball to win game.

Series Results
New Zealand beat Great Britain, 2 – 1
New Zealand beat Australia, 3 – 0
Great Britain beat Australia, 2 – 1

1st   New Zealand (5 test wins)
2nd   Great Britain (3 test wins)
3rd   Australia (1 test win)

Individual Statistics

	Singles	Doubles	Total
NEW ZEALAND			
R.V.Jackson	5/6	5/6	10/12
P.J.Skinley	5/6	5/6	10/12
R.J.Murfitt	3½/6	5/6	8½/12
J.K.Hogan	4/6	4/6	8/12
G.Beale	4/6	3½/6	7½/12
J.G.Prince	2/5	2½/6	4½/11
A.D.Heenan	0/1		0/1
GREAT BRITAIN			
G.N.Aspinall	4/6	4/6	8/12
D.K.Openshaw	4/6	4/6	8/12
M.N.Avery	3/6	4/6	7/12
C.J.Irwin	3/6	4/6	7/12
W.de B.Prichard	2/6	2/6	4/12
J.R.McCullough	1/2	2/2	3/4
S.N.Mulliner	2/3	0/3	2/6
A.B.Hope	0/1	0/1	0/2
AUSTRALIA			
G.Latham	3/6	1½/6	4½/12
B.Chambers	1/6	3/6	4/12
N.E.Spooner	1/6	3/6	4/12
D.Bidencope	3½/6	0/6	3½/12
S.A.Buck	1/6	1½/6	2½/12
A.Cleland	2/6	0/6	2/12

Appendix V

Useful Addresses

Australia

Dr Valerie Payne
President, the Australian Croquet
Association
6 Beddome Street,
Sandy Bay,
7005 Tasmania, Australia

Dr J.M. Sanz-Tonnelier
Secretary, the Australian Croquet
Association
95 Westmoreland Road,
Leumeah,
New South Wales 2560, Australia

Bermuda

Mr R.S.L. Pearman
'Calithea',
Paget,
Bermuda

Canada

Mr W. Langstroth
President, the Canada section, USCA
10 Thornbank Road,
Thornhill,
Ontario L4J 2A2,
Canada

England

The Secretary
The Croquet Association
The Hurlingham Club,
Ranelagh Gardens,
London SW6 3PR,
England

Finland

Jukka Kujansuu
Hakakuja 3,
33470 Ylöjärvi,
Finland

Holland

Johan Vunderink
Deventerstraatweg 100,
8171 AG Vaassen,
Holland

Indonesia

Jerry Brown
President, the Indonesian Croquet
Association
J.L. Bunyu 7,
Cilandak,
Jakarta,
Indonesia

Ireland

The Secretary
The Croquet Association of Ireland
Carrickmines Croquet and Lawn Tennis Club,
Carrickmines,
County Dublin,
Ireland

Japan

Masura Ikeda
Executive Director, the Croquet Association
of Japan
Isebu, Bld 1F, 2-11-20, Amakubo,
Sakuramura,
Niiharigun,
Ibaraki,
Japan 305

Kenya

Mr Arnold Curtis
PO Box 10,
Limuru,
Kenya

New Zealand

Mr A.D.J. Heenan
President, the New Zealand Croquet Council
11 Kiwi Street,
Alicetown,
Lower Hutt,
North Island,
New Zealand

Mrs G.H.L. Baker
Honorary Secretary, the New Zealand
Croquet Council
21 Egmont Street,
Hawera,
North Island,
New Zealand

Portugal

The Golf Director
Vale do Lobo Golf Club

Scotland

Mr I.H. Wright
Secretary, the Scottish Croquet Association
17 Greygoran,
Sauchie,
Clackmannanshire,
Scotland

South Africa

Mrs Carole Knox
Secretary, the South African Croquet
Association,
Late Vintage,
Rust en Vrede Avenue,
Constantia 7800,
Cape Town,
South Africa

Spain

Enrique F. De Bobadilla
Por-Vera 6
Jerez de la Frontera,
Spain

Sweden

Thor Kaijser
Sodra Ringgatan 39,
441 33 Alingsås,
Sweden

Niclas Behre
Ostrabanvagen 69A,
18462 Osterskar,
Sweden

Switzerland

Mr N. Eatough
La Forge,
Fenieres-Thoiry,
F-01630 St Genis-Pouilly,
France

USA

The United States Croquet Association
500 Avenue of Champions,
Palm Beach Gardens,
Florida 33418,
USA

Wales

Mr W. de B. Prichard
Gobion Manor,
Abergavenny,
Gwent NP7 9AY,
Wales

Glossary

The references in brackets at the end of certain definitions refer to the fourth edition of the Association Croquet laws book.

A-baulk   The start line between corner 1 and the middle of the south boundary (1.e.).

A Class player   One who regularly plays advanced play and has a handicap below 2.

Address   The act of placing the mallet head behind the striker's ball prior to playing the stroke.

Advanced play   A variation of level play with special laws to give the outplayer more chance of regaining the innings. Widely used in internationals, major championships and play between A Class players (36).

Advanced play with bisques   A variation of advanced play used in friendly games between A Class and B Class players.

Air shot   Stroke in which the mallet does not make contact with the ball, thus ending the turn (31.d.i.).

All-round break   A break of 12 hoops.

Alternate stroke handicap doubles   A variation of handicap doubles to ensure the high-bisqued partners get their fair share of play (Appendix 4).

Angle of swing   In a croquet stroke, the angle between the line of centres and the line of swing.

Approach stroke   A croquet stroke played with the prime objective of getting the striker's ball into a good position in front of its hoop.

Association Croquet   A term to describe those forms of croquet regularly used in club play, tournaments and international matches (except in North America).

Aunt Emma   A player who makes little attempt to set up breaks, usually scoring hoops off the partner ball and keeping the enemy balls split up.

ACC   Australian Croquet Council.

B-baulk   The start line between corner 3 and the middle of the north boundary (1.e.).

B Class player   A player with a handicap in the range 2 – 6½.

Backward ball   A side's ball that has the most hoops to make.

Backward take-off   A special type of approach stroke. A take-off from the non-playing side of a hoop to get position to run the hoop.

Baillieu Double   A two-ball target at long range, in which the gap between the balls is greater than one ball's width, but which nevertheless significantly improves a player's chances of making a roquet.

Ball in hand   A ball which has, or is deemed to have made a roquet, and which the striker is entitled to pick up (9).

Baulk-line   That part of the yard-line from which balls are played on to the court at the start of the game or following a lift (1.e.).

Big split   A split shot in which both balls are to be sent long distances.

Bisque   An extra turn in handicap play. It can only be played by the striker with the striker's ball of the previous turn. Each extra turn that the higher-handicapped player is entitled to is usually represented by a short white stick (38).

Blob   To fail to run a hoop.

Bonus stroke   An extra stroke gained by running a hoop or making a roquet (4.d.).

Break   A turn or unbroken sequence of turns (when bisques have been used) in which the striker's ball runs more than one hoop.

Break down   To make a mistake during a break which causes your turn to end.

C Class player   A player with a handicap in the

range 7 – 11.

Cannon 1. The act of moving a third or fourth ball in any stroke.
2. A croquet stroke in which the croqueted ball is in contact with a third ball (16.d.ii. and 19.b.).

Carrot The thicker part of an upright of a hoop that is sunk into the ground.

Centre style Style in which the mallet is swung between the legs.

Chop roll A roll stroke played without follow through.

Class system A system to indicate players' abilities by labelling them according to the handicap range in which their handicap falls.

Clips Coloured markers used to show which hoop a ball next requires. For hoops 1 to 6 the clip is attached to the crown of the hoop, for hoops 1-back to rover it is attached to the upright (2.d.).

Condoning Failing to discover an adversary's error before the limit of claims (26.c.).

Contact 1. To pick up the striker's ball and place it next to another ball to take croquet from it.
2. A special entitlement to the above under the rules of advanced play (36.b.).

Continuation stroke The bonus stroke played after running a hoop or playing a croquet stroke (4.g. and 21).

Control To be in command of the balls; to have a secure break; to run a hoop to a predetermined position.

Corner To deliberately play a single ball into a corner, usually for defensive purposes.

Corner ball A ball resting on a corner spot or which should be replaced on to a corner spot (12.a.ii.).

Corner cannon Three or more balls in contact, one of which is a corner-ball (16.d.ii. and 19.b.).

Corner spot The point where two yard-lines meet near a corner of the court (1.d.).

Croquet To place the striker's ball in contact with the ball it has roqueted and play a stroke so as to move both balls (4.d.iii. and 19).

CA The Croquet Association of England.

CAI The Croquet Association of Ireland.

CAJ The Croquet Association of Japan.

Croquet stroke A two-ball stroke subsequent to a roquet, in which the striker's ball is hit so as to impel the second (croqueted) ball to move (4.f. and 20).

Croqueted ball The ball which the striker's ball moves in a croquet stroke (20.a.).

Cross-peg The positioning of two balls, one either side of the peg, so that neither ball can hit the other.

Cross-wire The positioning of two balls, one either side of a hoop, so that neither ball can hit the other.

Crown The cross-piece on top of a hoop (2.b.).

Crush (stroke) A fault in which the striker's ball is squeezed between the mallet and hoop or peg, except if pegging out (32.a.xi. and xii.).

Cut rush A rush played so that the object ball is rushed at an angle to the line along which the mallet is swung.

D Class A player with a handicap of 12 or above.

Deadness A US Croquet description of a side's inability to roquet balls previously roqueted until they run the next wicket with the ball whose deadness is being referred to. For example, blue might be 'dead' on black and yellow.

Deadness board A board placed off-court that is used to help players and spectators remember which balls are 'dead' on what.

Deem Forfeit a stroke. This usually occurs when a player cannot improve on a leave by using a continuation stroke, or in defensive situations, when a side has no wish to move either of its balls (31.d.ii.).

Delayed triple A triple peel in which the 4-back peel is made after the striker's ball has run hoop 4.

Diagonal spread A special lift leave in advanced play.

Dolly rush A rush in which the two balls are very close together, say twelve inches (30cm) or less.

Double (target)   Two balls positioned so that the target area is effectively doubled.

Double-banking   Playing two separate games simultaneously on the same court (4.h. and Appendix 2).

Double peel   A break in which a ball is peeled through the last two hoops it requires and is pegged out.

Double tap   A stroke in which the striker's ball is hit twice or remains in contact with the mallet after it has hit another ball. This is a fault, except if caused due to the making of a roquet (32.a.ix.).

Draw and process   A two-life format for competition, commonly used in tournaments. The names are drawn for one half and are then rearranged in a predetermined way (the process) for the other half. The winners of the two halves play off (reg. 14.d.).

Drive   A croquet stroke in which the base of the mallet is parallel to the ground at the moment of impact, giving a ratio of about 3:1 when played straight.

Enemy ball   A ball belonging to the opposing side.

Far wire   The upright furthest from the striker's ball.

Fault   An illegality committed during the striking period that results in a penalty (32).

Finesse   To forego a shot and hit your ball off-court, usually into a corner, for defensive purposes.

First colours   The traditional colours of the four balls, namely blue, red, black and yellow (2.c. and 4.h.).

Follow through   To continue the mallet swing after it has hit the striker's ball.

Forestalling   Requesting your opponent to cease play so that a questionable stroke can be watched or, if it has already been played, be investigated or corrected. Also so that the position of a misplaced ball or clip can be corrected (26.a.).

Forward ball   A side's ball that has the least number of hoops to make.

Four-ball break   A break in which all four balls are used.

Four-ball cannon   A cannon in which the third ball is in contact with the fourth ball (16.d.ii. and 19.b.).

Free shot   A shot which gives little away if taken and missed.

Full-bisque game   A form of handicap play in which players receive bisques according to their handicaps, and not the difference between their handicaps (Appendix 3).

Full jump   A jump stroke in which the striker's ball jumps over another ball without hitting it.

Furniture   A term applied to the court equipment that cannot be temporarily removed when playing a stroke and thus provides potential obstacles.

Golf Croquet   A fun game, generally used as an introduction to Association Croquet.

Grip   The way in which a mallet is held by the hands.

Guarding a boundary   Leaving your two balls a few yards in court from the yard-line, so that any missed shot by your opponent at them gives you the chance of constructing a break.

Half bisque   A restricted bisque in which no point can be scored for any ball (38.a.).

Half jump   A stroke in which the striker's ball is made to jump slightly, so as to clip the top of another ball and move it forward but also to jump over it.

Half roll   A croquet stroke in which you hit down slightly on to the striker's ball and which gives a ratio of 2:1 when played straight.

Hammer shot   A shot played backwards, that is, by swinging the mallet towards you, and in which you hit down on the striker's ball. Used for angled hoops or where your backswing is hampered by furniture or another ball.

Handicap   A number given to a player to indicate his standard of play. The range of handicaps can vary from time to time and between different countries (reg. 10).

Handicap play   A form of play in which the

side with the highest handicap is given a number of bisques and/or a half bisque that represent the difference between the handicaps of the two sides, modified in cases where a shortened form of game is to be played (38, 39 and 43).

Heel The end of the mallet head not used for striking in a particular stroke.

Hit A shot in which a roquet is made, or a scatter shot is successfully played.

Hoop and roquet A special situation involving an object ball clear of a hoop on the non-playing side, in which it is deemed that a hoop is run and then a roquet is made, even though the object ball is struck before the striker's ball completes the running of the hoop (17).

Hoop-bound Cases where the striker cannot play the desired stroke because a hoop is an obstacle to the necessary mallet swing.

Hoop (running) stroke A stroke in which the striker tries to or succeeds in running a hoop.

Inner rectangle The rectangle formed by connecting up the four outer hoops.

Innings You are said to 'have the innings' if the balls are so positioned that you, and not your opponent, can make an easy roquet.

International Game (or rules) The name given to Association Croquet in North America.

Irish grip A grip in which both palms face outwards.

Irish peel A croquet stroke in which both balls are sent through a hoop.

Is for An expression used to indicate which hoop a ball must next run.

Jaws The area between the uprights of a hoop (2.b.ii.).

Join up To play the striker's ball so that it ends close to its partner ball.

Jump shot Any stroke in which the striker's ball is made to jump clear of the ground immediately after impact.

Lay up The act of preparing a leave.

Leave How the balls are left at the end of a turn. Thus, referring to the play of the player who left the leave, we say a 'good leave' or a 'bad leave', or describe one of a number of well-known leaves.

Level play The standard form of competition in which no special rules are used and in which the players compete on equal terms, that is, handicaps and bisques are not used.

Lift To have the right to, or actually to pick up your ball from where it lies on court and play it from either baulk-line (13 and 36).

Limit of claims The end of the period within which a particular error can be rectified according to the laws of the game (26.b.).

Line of centres The line, and its extension in either direction, between the centres of two balls placed for a croquet stroke.

Long bisquer A player with a high handicap.

Mandatory peel A peel or peels that certain low-handicapped players must do when playing Short Croquet.

Minus player A player with a handicap below zero.

Modified game A shortened form of game, sometimes involving rearranging the hoops. (52-55).

Near wire The upright nearest to the striker's ball.

New standard leave (NSL) A special lift leave in advanced play.

NZCC New Zealand Croquet Council.

Non-playing side The side opposite to that from which the hoop must be run (14.b.).

Object ball The ball aimed for in a particular stroke.

Old Standard Leave (OSL) A special lift leave in advanced play.

Open (shot) Blue has an open shot on red if it can hit any part of the front of red and either side of red (13.b.).

Opening The playing of the four balls on to the court and the few strokes thereafter (6).

Ordinary singles play The standard form of play as laid down in the laws, commonly

Outplayer The player not in play.

Pass roll A croquet stroke played in such a manner that, if it is played with a very small angle of split, the striker's ball travels further than the croqueted ball.

Peel The projection of a ball through its hoop by one of the other balls, usually by the striker's ball in a croquet stroke (14.e.).

Peelee A ball that is being or has been peeled in the current turn.

Peg down To stop a game and mark the positions of balls and clips, with the intention of restarting it later (reg. 12.K.).

Peg out To cause a ball to score the peg point and thus be removed from the game (15).

Pegged-out game A game in which one or two balls have been pegged out.

Penultimate The last but one hoop (1.b.).

Pilot ball A term sometimes used to describe the ball off which a hoop is about to be made.

Pioneer In a 3-ball or 4-ball break, a ball sent to the next but one hoop to be made.

Pirates A popular fun game.

Pivot In a 4-ball break, the ball left in the centre of the court.

Playing side The side from which a hoop must be run (14.b.).

Polarity (of leave) Tendency of a leave to influence your opponent to play one particular ball.

Positional stroke Single ball stroke played to send the striker's ball to a particular position on the court.

Progressive Handicap Doubles A variation of handicap doubles play, designed to give long bisquers more play and the experience of playing with several lower bisquers.

Pull 1. The tendency of the two balls in a split croquet stroke to diverge from their theoretical paths.

2. The fault in a hammer shot whereby contact between mallet and ball is maintained for an appreciable period, or whereby the mallet head is accelerated after initial contact with the ball (32.a.vii. and viii.).

Push The opposite of pull, as described in 2 above, but when committed during a normal stroke (32.a.vii. and viii.).

Ratio In a croquet stroke, how many times further the croqueted ball travels than the striker's ball.

Roll 1. Topspin

2. A croquet stroke played so that, when straight, both balls travel approximately the same distance.

Roquet To hit another ball with the striker's ball and gain bonus strokes (4.d.iii. and iv. and 16).

Rover 1. The last hoop (1.b.).

2. A ball which has run the rover hoop (15).

Run a hoop To hit a ball through its hoop so as to score a point (14).

Rush A roquet in which the object ball is projected towards a predetermined position.

Rush line The extension, in both directions, of the line of the proposed rush.

Rush peel A peel achieved in a rush stroke.

Scatter shot At the end of a turn, an attempt by the striker's ball to project a ball previously roqueted to a position more unfavourable for the next striker.

Score (a hoop or the peg) To run a hoop in order or hit the peg and thereby score a point (14 and 15).

SCA Scottish Croquet Association.

Scratch player A player with a handicap of zero.

Second colours The set of balls coloured brown, green, pink and white, used for double-banking (2.c. and 4.h.).

Semi-advanced play A variation of advanced play, in which no lifts are given when 4-back is run (37 and 42).

Sequence game Any form of croquet in which the turns are played in a strict sequence according to the colours of the balls, usually blue, red, black, yellow, blue, etc.

Shepherding A fault in a croquet stroke whereby, after the two balls have parted contact, the mallet remains in contact with the striker's ball (32.a.vii.).

Shoot To attempt to make a roquet.

Short croquet A variation of small-lawn croquet.

Short lift The term in advanced play for the lift shot from the east end of A-baulk or the west end of B-baulk at a ball near corner 4 or near corner 2 respectively.

Side The individual or pair playing two partner balls.

Side style Style in which the mallet is swung to the side of the body.

Single-ball stroke Stroke in which the mallet swing only causes one ball to move.

Single peel Break in which a ball is peeled through the last hoop it requires and is pegged out.

Small-lawn croquet Croquet played on lawns of less than full size, usually half size or smaller (56).

Solomon grip Grip in which both palms face inwards.

SACA South African Croquet Association.

Split roll A split shot played with topspin.

Split shot A croquet stroke in which the two balls are sent in different directions.

Stake Term for the peg in US croquet.

Stalking Lining up a shot by walking along an extension of the line between the striker's ball and its target.

Stance The positioning of the feet and body in relation to the line of mallet swing.

Standard grip Grip in which one palm faces inwards and the other outwards.

Standard triple Triple peel in which the first two peels are done as the striker's ball runs the corresponding hoops in the opposite direction.

Stop shot Croquet stroke played with no follow through or topspin, so that, when played straight, it produces a ratio of 5:1 or more.

Stop shot rush A rush played using a stop shot action, often used for dolly rushes.

Straight drive A drive played so that both balls travel in the same direction, that is, the angle of split is zero. Similarly we can say straight roll, straight stop shot, etc.

Straight triple A special kind of delayed triple peel in which the three peels are done as the striker's ball makes its last three hoops.

Striker The person in play or whose turn it is to play (4.c.).

Striker's ball The ball the striker elects to play during a particular turn (4.c.).

Take-off A croquet stroke played with a large angle of split, in which the accurate positioning of the striker's ball is of paramount importance.

Take position A single ball stroke played to get the striker's ball into a position from which it can run its hoop.

Three-ball break A break played using three balls.

Three-ball croquet A variation used for friendly games when three players wish to play together.

Thick take-off A take-off with an angle of split between sixty and eighty degrees.

Thin take-off A take-off in which the croqueted ball hardly moves.

Tice A ball sent a calculated distance away from an enemy ball or baulk (if the opponent is due to play a ball from baulk) to tempt the opponent to shoot at it and miss.

Time limit The time allowed for a game or match (reg. 13).

Time turn Name for a turn played or finished after time has been called, but before the scores are totalled (reg. 13.c.ii.).

Toe The end of the mallet head used to strike a ball in a particular stroke.

Touch The ability to monitor accurately and apply the correct amount of power required for a given stroke.

Trap The positioning of two balls in a leave which, if shot at and missed by the adversary, would give you the opportunity to construct a break

Treble (target) Three balls so positioned as effectively to treble the size of the target area when shot at.

Triangulating Positioning your ball at a roughly equal distance from two enemy balls which are themselves well separated.

Triple peel (TP) Break in which a ball is peeled through the last three hoops it requires and is pegged out. *Note*: quadruple, quintuple, sextuple, septuple and octuple describe more complicated finishes.

Triple peel on the opponent (TPO) A triple peel in which it is an enemy ball that is peeled and pegged out.

Turn The stroke or series of strokes that a striker plays or is entitled to play since the adversary's last stroke, or since having taken a bisque and before taking another bisque, or the adversary's next stroke (4.d.).

Two-ball break A break using two balls.

Two-ball Croquet A fun game, often used as part of coaching sessions.

Two-ball stroke A croquet stroke.

USCA United States Croquet Association.

US Nine-wicket Croquet A variation of croquet, mainly played in North American backyards, with a court setting of two pegs and nine hoops.

US Six-wicket Croquet The variation of croquet used in clubs and tournaments in North America, which utilises the Association Croquet one-peg, six-hoop setting.

Upright Name given to the stanchion of a hoop. (2.b.i.).

Vertical Spread A special lift leave in advanced play.

Wafer cannon A cannon in which the striker's ball and the third ball are only separated by a wafer-thin gap and the mallet is swung along the rush line.

Wicket Term for the hoop in US Croquet.

Windscreen wiper In handicap play, shooting back and forth at a ball in the middle of the court and missing it, thereby wasting bisques.

Wire The upright of a hoop.

Wiring lift A lift in certain circumstances when a ball does not have an open shot on any of the other balls on court (13).

WCF World Croquet Federation.

Yard-line An imaginary line one yard (90cm) inside the boundary of the court (1.d.).

Yard-line area The area between the boundary and the yard-line. (1.d.).

Yard-line ball A ball that is, or will be, positioned on the yard-line (12.a.ii.).

Yard-line cannon A cannon in which any one of the balls is a yard-line ball (16.d.ii. and 19.b.).

Bibliography

Books

Croquet Association, The, *The Laws of Association Croquet and Golf Croquet and The Regulations for Tournaments,* 4th edn, CA 1984

Miller, D.W. and Thorp, R.F. *Croquet and How to Play It,* Faber & Faber, 1966

Ormerod, Dr G.L. *Know the Game: Croquet,* 3rd edn, A & C Black (Publishers) Ltd, 1985

Osborn, J. and Kornbluth, J. *Winning Croquet,* Simon & Schuster, 1983

Prichard, D.M.C. *The History of Croquet,* Cassell Ltd, 1981

Solomon, J.W. *Croquet,* B.T.Batsford Ltd, 1966

United States Croquet Association, The, *The Official Rules of the United States Croquet Association American Six-wicket Game and American Nine-wicket game and Golf Croquet,* 3rd edn, USCA, 1984

Wylie, K.F. *Expert Croquet Tactics,* K.F.Wylie, 1985

Other Publications

Australian Croquet Gazette
Croquet, formerly *The Croquet Gazette*
Croquet (USA)
Irish Croquet (newsletter of CAI)
New Zealand Croquet Gazette
Scottish Croquet Association Bulletin
South African Croquet Gazette
US Croquet Gazette
US Croquet News

INDEX